North Carolina's Criminal Justice System

North Carolina's Criminal Justice System

Paul Knepper

Associate Professor

East Carolina University

Carolina Academic Press

Durham, North Carolina

ISBN 0-89089-826-X
LCCN 99-

Carolina Academic Press
700 Kent Street
Durham, North Carolina 27701
Telephone (919) 489-7486
Fax (919) 493-5668
E-mail: cap@cap-press.com
www.cap-press.com

Printed in the United States of America

Contents

Preface

Many students of criminal justice in North Carolina know that basketball great Michael Jordan grew up in Wilmington, that Pepsi Cola began at a drugstore in New Bern, that the Wright Brothers achieved the first flight at Kitty Hawk, and that evangelist Billy Graham attended church in Charlotte as a boy. North Carolina opened the first public university, the University of North Carolina at Chapel Hill, and boasts the largest private residence ever built in the United States, the Biltmore House and Garden near Asheville.

How many students of criminal justice in North Carolina know about North Carolina's criminal justice system? Until 1996, North Carolina was the only state in which the governor had no veto power over the legislature. It is the only state in which prosecutors set the criminal trial calendar, and it operates a unique system of judicial rotation. North Carolina has one of the most unified court systems and the most decentralized prison system. There are about a hundred individual prisons in North Carolina, more than any other state. The Declaration of Rights, written into the state constitution, grants more rights to citizens than the Bill of Rights in the federal constitution.

How many know the name of Henry Frye, who became the first African American on the North Carolina Supreme Court in 1983? Or Suzie Sharpe, the first woman? Or, James Edward O'Hara, who in 1868 became one of the first African Americans licensed to practice law in the state, or Margaret Hambrick, who became the first woman to administrate a federal prison when she became warden at the Federal Correctional Institution at Butner. Or what about Thomas Ruffin, whose reputation as a jurist saved the state supreme court, or James Iredell and Alfred Moore, two North Carolinians who served on the U.S. Supreme Court. Then there was David Marshall Williams, who invented the M-1 Carbine while serving time on a North Carolina prison farm and helped the Allies win World War II; and Joseph Hyde Pratt, whose "good roads and good men" campaign led to the state system of chain gang roadwork in North Carolina that employed more convicts for more years than any other state. And Z. Smith Reynolds, who was murdered in his home, and which would have led to the most sensational trial in state history.

In part, my aim in writing this book is to recognize some significant "firsts" in North Carolina's criminal justice history. But the main purpose is to explain how North Carolina's criminal justice system developed as it did, and how it resembles and diverges from the systems of other states. The first chapter covers crime in the state, followed by chapters in lawmaking, the state constitution, law enforcement, courts and adjudication, and corrections. The last four chapters cover juvenile justice, education and training, the federal presence, and victims and related social services. This book began as an effort to give my students concrete examples drawn from North Carolina's experience of the institutions and practices of criminal justice that are described in the introductory textbooks. Textbooks designed for a national audience overlook significant aspects of state systems because it is difficult to generalize about criminal justice in the United States.

Although commonly used today, few people used the term criminal justice system before 1960. Rather, people thought of prosecutors, police, jails, prisons, courts, and so on as separate agencies of government. The idea that all these agencies to-

gether made up a national system began with an American Bar
Foundation (ABF) study commissioned by U.S. Supreme Court
Justice Robert F. Jackson in 1953 (Remington 1990; Walker
1992). The ABF study provided a way to understand the flow
of cases from police arrest to release from prison; the relationship between courts, police departments, and corrections agencies; and the process of decision making by those who apply
criminal law. But the idea of a single national criminal justice
system also blurs the fact that criminal justice is a collection of
federal, state, and county systems. The system of ciminal justice
that developed in the world's premiere democracy is like no
other.

Understanding the criminal justice system requires more
than knowing the statistics, the flowcharts, and the legal terms.
The U.S. Constitution and the Bill of Rights—the founding
documents of the American democracy—are preserved in a
special vault in the National Archives for all to see. Thousands
of visitors to the nation's capital view them everyday. But these
documents do not mean much unless people understand how
the principles they contain are to be found in the places they
live and work. The ideas of liberty, freedom, equality, and justice that were written about in Philadelphia 200 years ago only
mean as much as the day-to-day activities of a deputy sheriff in
Buncombe County, a correctional officer at Central Prison in
Raleigh, an attorney assigned to represent a defendant in Halifax, or a juvenile court counselor in Lincoln County.

So in order to appreciate the significance of agencies that
make up North Carolina's criminal justice system, I have used
race relations as a benchmark. Each chapter includes a section
on the place of African Americans in the system. Crime rates,
as I explain in chapter 1, reflect demographic changes in age
structure and other features of society. Crime rates are not a re-
liable measure of the effectiveness of the system. Rather, crime
and criminal justice are both part of the larger society. They

both originate in the social, political, cultural and economic factors that have shaped the history of this state and that make the people of North Carolina what they are today. It is the administering of the system that provides the best measure of criminal justice. It is a standard as old as the law of Moses, "Ye shall have one manner of law, as well as for the stranger, as for one of your own country: for I am the Lord your God" (Lev. 24.22). Viewing North Carolina's criminal justice system with this standard in mind is a subtheme of this book.

My approach to African Americans in North Carolina's criminal justice system describes the process of institution-building, not the behavior of Whites toward Blacks. White people in North Carolina enacted slave codes and Jim Crow laws, designed prison farms and road gangs, and maintained separate colleges and courtrooms. But my aim is not so much to talk about what some White people did as to celebrate the achievements of Black North Carolinians who, despite the structures of exclusion, distinguished themselves in the legislature, judiciary, law enforcement, corrections, law, and juvenile justice system. My goal is to show something of the contribution that African Americans have made to North Carolina's criminal justice system.

The information in this book has been pulled together from a variety of federal, state, and local government publications, as well as from books, articles and directories. Lisa A. Marcus's *North Carolina Manual 1995/1996*, published by the Department of the Secretary of State, and Joan G. Brannon's *The Judicial System in North Carolina*, published by the Administrative Office of the Courts, provide excellent descriptions of key elements of North Carolina's criminal justice system (Brannon 1994; Marcus 1995). The publications of the Institute of Government at the University of North Carolina-Chapel Hill are an invaluable resource for anyone who wants to know about North Carolina's political institutions. I would like to acknowledge the expertise of the Institute faculty whose books and articles I have relied on throughout this book: Joan Brannon, Stevens Clarke, Anne Dellinger, James Drennan, Robert Farb, David Lawrence, John Orth, and Janet Mason. I also would like to thank those who gave me information, answered my questions, and helped me understand:

Mavis G. Williams, Consultant, Community-Based Alternatives, Greenville

Yolanda Burwell, Associate Professor of Social Work, East Carolina University

Charles Newton, Director, Stonewall Jackson School, Concord

W.H. Payne, Professional Standards/Inspections Sergeant, Raleigh Police Department

Thomas Haigwood, District Attorney, Pitt County

William A. Webb, Federal Public Defender, Eastern District, Raleigh

Janice Mckenzie Cole, U.S. Attorney, Eastern District, Raleigh

Malcolm J. Howard, Judge, U.S. District Court, Eastern District, Greenville

Daniel K. Martin, Chief U.S. Probation Officer, Eastern District, Raleigh

James M. Campbell, Associate Professor of Criminal Justice, East Carolina University

James B. French, Warden, Central Prison, Raleigh

Marjorie Shahravar, Public Information Assistant, Department of Correction, Raleigh

Glen Mills, Chief, Judicial Division One, Divison of Adult Probation/Parole, Greenville

Don Stacy, Librarian, Justice Academy, Salemburg

Patty McQuillan, Director of Public Information, Department of Correction, Raleigh

Earl Ijames, Archivist, Department of Archives, Raleigh

The generosity of these individuals made much of the information in this book possible. I bear sole responsibility for the analyses and interpretations expressed here, as well as for all errors and omissions. If you have information you would like to share about North Carolina's firsts in criminal justice, or any aspect of this book, please let me know. Thank you.

References

Brannon, Joan G. 1994. *The judicial system in North Carolina.* Raleigh: North Carolina Administrative Office of the Courts.

Marcus, Lisa A. 1995. *North Carolina manual 1995/1996.* Raleigh: North Carolina Secretary of State.

Remington, Frank J. 1990. Development of criminal justice as an academic field. *Journal of Criminal Justice Education* 1:9-20.

Walker, Samuel. 1992. Origins of the contemporary criminal justice paradigm: The American Bar Foundation survey, 1953-1969. *Justice Quarterly* 9:47-76.

North Carolina's
Criminal Justice System

Chapter 1

Crime

Crime in North Carolina, according to official statistics, is no worse and no better than the rest of the country. North Carolina's overall crime rate approximates the national average. Trends for various crimes during the past ten years in North Carolina have followed the national pattern. From a high in the 1970s, crime rates declined during the 1980s, only to begin climbing again in the 1990s. Delinquency rates also match those of the nation as a whole. Rates of delinquency in the past ten years, particularly violent crimes among juveniles, have increased in North Carolina as they have elsewhere in the nation.

For the crime of murder, however, North Carolina differs from the national pattern. North Carolina's murder rate fits with the southern pattern. Although in recent years the West has rivaled the South in murder rates, the South has had a higher murder rate than other regions of the country for a number of decades. In a recent book entitled *1001 Things Everyone Should Know About the South*, the authors refer to the phrase "below the Smith and Wesson line" as a means of defining the South. "Below the line" refers to the southern United States that has a homicide rate which has been "historically twice that of the other regions in the United States," and although the gap has narrowed since 1970, "this regrettable statistic can still be used to map the South" (Reed and Reed 1996, 4).[1]

---

1. Federal Bureau of Investigation (FBI) annual arrest statistics for murder between 1971 and 1995 do indicate a slight, but consistently higher offense rate for the South than for other regions. During the 1970s, the South had a

3

The South's murder rate has led to a perennial and provocative theory: the southern subculture of violence. While there are several versions of this theory, the basic idea has to do with southern race relations and historic patterns of violence in the South. Murder is more prevalent in the southern region, according to this theory, due to a southern attitude toward violence that encourages, or does not discourage, violent means of settling conflicts. North Carolina has had its share of celebrated murder cases (Rhyne 1988, 1990). The hanging of Tom Dula in Iredell County in 1868 for the murder of Laura Foster inspired a ballad in the North Carolina Mountains that led to a hit folk song for the Kingston Trio a hundred years later, "Hang Down Your Head, Tom Dooley" (West 1993). In recent years, murders in North Carolina have inspired books and films, including the trial of Dr. Jeffrey McDonald for the murder of his wife and two daughters at Fort Bragg (McGinnis 1993). The McDonald case became the basis for the best selling book *Fatal Vision* by Joe McGinnis and the film *The Fugitive* starring Harrison Ford.

Is there really a southern subculture of violence? Does it explain North Carolina's murder rate? These issues will be discussed in this chapter. But first, a look at the statistics for crime, delinquency, and murder in North Carolina.

---

double-digit murder rate while rates for the West, Midwest, and Northeast generally averaged less than 10. During the 1980s, the murder rate for the South declined along with rates for the rest of the nation, although the rate for the South was still higher than others. Since 1990, annual murder rates have tended to follow the 1970s pattern: the southern rate has climbed to double-digits while the western, midwestern and northern rates have not reached 10 (Sourcebook 1997, 397). John S. Reed also points out that the category of "romantic triangle" used in the FBI's Supplemental Homicide Reports as the motivation for a majority of homicides in the southern states is also a staple theme of country music (Reed 1993, 85-86).

Crime Rates and Trends

Crime rates are used to compare crime across cities and states of varying populations. The fact that more crimes are committed in Florida than in North Carolina comes as little surprise because more people live in Florida than in North Carolina. So, in order to compare the amount of crime within two or more jurisdictions of varying populations, the number of crimes is divided by the number of people, then multiplied by 100,000. The result is the *crime rate*—the number of crimes per 100,000 people.

Rates

To find the crime rate in North Carolina for 1995, for example, we need to know the number of crimes reported and the number of people living in the state that year. Then we divide the number of crimes (405,764) by the number of people (7,195,000), then multiply by 100,000. The result, 5,639.5 is North Carolina's crime rate. For example:

$$\frac{405,764 \times 100,000}{7,195,000} = 5,639.5$$

When Federal Bureau of Investigation statistics for index offenses are used, the result is the *index crime rate*, a statistic frequently quoted by newspapers and journalists. The index crimes are homicide, forcible rape, robbery, aggravated assault, burglary, larceny, theft, motor vehicle theft, and arson. The index crime rate appears in the *Uniform Crime Reports* (UCR), published by the FBI every year since 1930. FBI statisticians compile data from reports submitted by about 16,000 state and local law enforcement organizations across the country.

Compared to that of other states, North Carolina's crime rate is about average. About half the states have higher crime rates, half lower crime rates. In 1995, for example, North Carolina's index crime rate was 5,639.5 compared to 7,701.5 for Florida and 3,433.7 for Virginia. The index crime rate for the United States as a whole was 5,277.6 (State Bureau of Investigation 1997, 217). North Carolina's rates for property and violent crimes are also about average. There are a number of states with higher rates of property crime than North Carolina; these include Florida, Georgia, and Louisiana. North Carolina's property crime rate is 4,993.1, lower than the rate for the whole United States which is 4.593.0. There are a number of states with higher rates of violent crime than North Carolina; these include Florida, Louisiana and South Carolina. North Carolina's violent crime rate is 646.4, slightly lower than the national violent crime rate of 684.6 (State Bureau of Investigation 1997, 218). Rates can also be calculated for counties simply by using the number of index crimes reported for the county within a given year and the population for the county that year. Within the state of North Carolina, Cumberland, Durham, Mecklenburg, and New Hanover Counties have the highest index crime rates. For 1996, the index crime rate in Durham County was 10,254.5 compared to 1,704 in Gates County and 2,249.5 in Pamlico County (State Bureau of Investigation 1997, 70-71). Generally, higher crime rates are found in major urban areas of the state. The correlation between urban areas and crime is true across the country, as crime rates are higher in major cities across the country compared to rural areas.

Trends

North Carolina's UCR rates of robbery, aggravated assault, burglary and larceny have generally followed trends in national UCR rates. UCR crime rates for North Carolina have generally been lower than national rates (Clarke 1992, 36). From 1987 to 1996, North Carolina's index crime rate increased 19%. During this same ten year period in North Carolina the violent crime rate increased 22%; the murder rate increased 5%; the rape rate increased 8%; the robbery rate increased 75%; the aggravated assault rate increased 10%; the property crime rate increased 19%; the burglary rate *decreased* 1%; the larceny rate increased 27%; the motor vehicle theft rate increased 51%. Similar increases are found for these crimes for the United States as a whole during this time (State Bureau of Investigation 1997, 53-69).

Nationally, crime rates fell during the 1980s, then began to rise during the 1990s past the 1970s rates. Why did crime rates fall during the 1980s? Why did crime rates increase during the 1990s? Politicians like to attribute increases in crime to various social problems (that they will fix, if elected) and say that decreases in crime are due to government programs and policies (that they initiated while in office). Journalists tend to write about increases in crime because "crime waves" sell newspapers and raise TV ratings. Criminologists, on the other hand, offer less lively explanations, related to demographic and other factors. The most likely explanation has to do with the changing age structure of the population. Crime rates are extremely age sensitive, meaning that persons ages 16-24 commit much of the crime, and criminal activity decreases throughout a person's lifetime. Crime rates fluctuate with the relative number of persons in their "crime-prone" years. A large number of people were born in the late 1940s and early 1950s when many soldiers returned home to their families after World War II. When the children of the post-war baby boom entered their crime prone years in the late 1960s and early 1970s, the United States experienced a crime wave as crime rates reached record levels (Wilson 1985, 19-23).

Most likely, crime rates fell during the 1980s due to an "aging-out" of the U.S. population. During that period of time, the average age of Americans increased as the baby boomers grew older and left relatively fewer people in the crime-prone years. Fewer people between 16 and 24 years old in the 1980s left fewer people to commit crimes. Similarly, a mini-baby boom in the years after the Vietnam War produced a relatively high number of persons in their crime prone years by the 1990s and, not surprisingly, higher crime rates. In 1988, in fact, criminologists Darrell Steffensmeier and Miles D. Harer explained the decline in crime rates during the Reagan presidency (1980-1988) as a function of the aging-out of the baby boom population, and they predicted a rise in crime rates during the 1990s as a function of the mini-baby boom. And that is just about what happened (Steffensmeier and Harer 1991).

Delinquency Rates

The word *delinquency* means "juvenile crime." Offenses that would be crimes for persons 18 years and older are known as "delinquent acts" for persons under age 18. Actually, there are two categories of delinquency: *Public offenses* which are crimes, and *status offenses*, which are violations of the law that would not be violations for persons age 18 or older. Status offenses include curfew violations, truancy, and running away from home.

The juvenile violent crime index is calculated by adding arrest rates for crimes of murder, forcible rape, robbery and aggravated assault, and dividing that total by the population of juveniles between ages 10 and 17. At 424 per 100,000, North Carolina is among those states with relatively high violent juvenile crime index rates. New York had the highest juvenile violent crime index rate of 996, followed by Florida at 764. Other states with rates higher than North Carolina's are California, Missouri, Louisiana, Indiana, Maryland, Rhode Island, New Jersey, Connecticut, and Massachusetts. West Virginia and Vermont, with rates under 100 per 100,000, have the lowest rates (Office of Juvenile Justice and Delinquency Prevention 1997, 22).

Violent crime among juveniles has increased across the nation in the past decade or so. Violent crime rates for juveniles increased from 1985 to 1994, and declined in 1995, which may mean the trend in violent crime has ended. Between 1987 and 1994, the violent crime rate increased 70%. Then in 1995, the index crime rate decreased by 3%. Still, a greater portion of violent crimes were attributed to juveniles in 1994 and 1995 than in any of the past twenty years. In 1995, 19% of persons entering the justice system via arrest for an alleged violent crime were under age 18. The age of the first violent act among those arrested for violent crimes in the United States appears to be decreasing; violent criminals seem to be getting younger (Office of Juvenile Justice and Delinquency Prevention 1997, 18).

Murder of juveniles has increased sharply. More than 25,000 juveniles were murdered in the United States between 1985 and 1995, a 66% increase during that ten-year period. In 1995, one-third of the juvenile murder victims lived in ten counties with major cities: Los Angeles, Chicago, New York City, Detroit, Dallas, Houston, Phoenix, San Bernardino, Philadelphia, and St. Louis (Office of Juvenile Justice and Delinquency Prevention 1997, 2). Most victims were male (85%), about half were White and the other half Black, and about three in ten victims were under age 18 (Office of Juvenile Justice and Delinquency Prevention 1995, 12). The majority was killed with a firearm, in fact most of the increase in juvenile homicide in the past ten years has been related to firearms (Office of Juvenile Justice and Delinquency Prevention 1997, 1). The rate of murder by juveniles has also increased. In 1995, there were more than 2,300 juvenile murderers; 25% of these in five counties with the following cities: Los Angeles, Chicago, Houston, Detroit, and New York City (Office of Juvenile Justice and Delinquency Prevention 1997, 11).

North Carolina does not have a high juvenile murder rate compared to some states— Illinois, Maryland, Louisiana, California—the states with the highest rates (Office of Juvenile Justice and Delinquency Prevention 1997, 2). In 1991, however, murder became the leading cause of death for young, African-American men in North Carolina. Almost half the deaths of men between ages 15 and 24 in 1991 were murdered; the next most common means of death, motor vehicle crashes accounted for just 15%. Professor Stevens Clarke, at the Institute of Government, explains that this pattern is not unique to North Carolina, but is part of the national trend (Clarke 1995, 7). Murder in North Carolina, as elsewhere in the country, is likely related to the supply of firearms and it may also be explained by the drug trade (Clarke 1995, 11).

Professor Alfred Blumstein, at Carnegie-Mellon University, explains the increase in juvenile murder across the country with reference to the illegal drug market. Drug traffickers recruit juveniles, partly because punishment for juvenile offenders is less than that for adults, and arm them with guns. Juveniles are also more likely to be recruited because they are more willing to take risks than adults, and they will work for less money. Teenagers engaged in illegal drug trafficking likely carry guns for self-protection, and other teenagers not involved in drug trafficking, also carry guns for protection. As more guns appear, there is an incentive for more teenagers to arm themselves with guns (Clarke 1995, 13). Professor Clarke points out that Blumstein's explanation only partially explains juvenile murder in North Carolina, because murder rates increased among those older than 15 years of age who are not considered juveniles under state law (Clarke 1995, 13).

Murder Rates

Generally, North Carolina's murder rate has been higher than the national average and has followed the same pattern as the rest of the South. Both North Carolina's and the South's murder rates decreased during the 1980s, but North Carolina's rate decreased more than the South's. Both rates rose in the 1990s. North Carolina's murder rate increased from 11.1 in1970 to 12.6 by 1973, and decreased to 8.0 by 1988. Since then, it has surpassed the 1970 rate (Clarke 1995, 4-5).

As is true in other states, the number of murders in North Carolina varies considerably by county. During 1996, there were no murders in about one fourth of North Carolina's counties. A number of these counties were located in the northeast and southwest corners of the state. At the same time, there were 71 murders in Mecklenburg, 30 in Forsythe, 37 in Guilford, 41 in Durham, and 33 in Wake Counties (State Bureau of Investigation 1997, 33). This is a predictable pattern: counties with larger populations have a higher number of murders. When murder rates are examined by county, a more interesting pattern emerges.

Using data collected from the North Carolina medical examiner, Professor Stevens Clarke found that in two counties, Tyrell and Clay, there were no murders during a three-year period in the 1990s. During the same period, the murder rate was 34.1 in Hoke County, 31.2 in Anson County, 24.7 in Hyde County, and 23.0 in Robeson County—the counties with the highest rates. The average murder rate across the state was 13 per 100,000 people (Clarke 1995, 14). Curiously, the geographic distribution of murder for North Carolina does not match that of the rest of the nation. In North Carolina, murder rates were highest in several rural counties, while for the rest of the country, murder rates are highest in counties with large cities. Mecklenburg County ranked 5th in murder rates within the state, Guilford County 43rd, and Wake County 77th.

Why does murder occur more often, relatively speaking, in rural counties of North Carolina than in urban counties? Professor Clarke statistically correlated several other statistics to measure a variety of social and economic factors with murder rates. These included population density, percentage of the population between ages 15 and 24, percentage of African Americans, median family income, percentage of unemployed residents, percentage of teenage pregnancies, percentage of households on Aid to Families with Dependent Children (AFDC) or welfare, the percentage of children living in poverty, reports of child abuse and neglect, percentage of families with no husband present, and the percentage of children living without both parents. Of all these factors, he found five with the highest correlation to the murder rate: families with no husband present, children living without both parents, teenage pregnancies, AFDC rate, and the percentage of children living in poverty. These five factors explained about 54% of the statistical variance across counties (Clarke 1995,15).

These findings do not mean that receiving AFDC leads to murder, that family dissolution leads to murder, or even that poverty leads to murder. Just because two statistics are correlated does not mean that one causes the other. What the findings suggest is that statistically speaking, poverty and family dissolution are, relative to the other factors, good predictors of murder.

The Southern Subculture of Violence

Why does the South have a higher murder rate than the national average? One of the most enduring and controversial explanations is called the *southern subculture of violence*. According to this explanation, Southerners resort to violence as a means of settling conflict more often than Americans living outside the South. While fatal violence is unthinkable for most Americans, it becomes thinkable for Southerners as a class because it represents "part of the southern way of life." The southern subculture of violence is a perennial explanation for southern crime.[2]

The Subculture of Violence

Certainly one of the characteristics of the Southern subculture of violence thesis is an elastic definition of subculture. Exactly what aspect of southern culture—race relations, love of firearms, poverty, and so on—is responsible for the violence varies with the theorist and the application. But the story about how the southern penchant for violence came to be generally begins with the pattern of race relations in the South and its impact on Whites and Blacks. The southern subculture of violence melded together elements from the sense of honor among aristocrats within the Cavalier culture of southern planters, the experience of lynchings and institutionalized violence after the Civil War, and the impoverishment of families throughout the South resulting from the destruction of the Confederacy by the North. Although the social conditions that gave rise to the culture of violence no longer exist in the South, the subculture of violence still persists due to inter-generational transmission of culture. The subculture of violence continues because it is passed on from generation to generation, as fathers continue to

---

2. Recently, Thomas Petee, a sociologist at Auburn University, offered the southern subculture of violence as an explanation for shootings at an Arkansas school. According to Petee: "...people in rural areas in the South grow up to some degree with firearms around the house...they're familiar with them, they have accessibility to them, and kids are sometimes socialized into it." Gary Kleck, a criminologist at Florida State University argues that the cultural distinctiveness of the South has declined to insignificance. "Whatever cultural forces were driving violence, they don't differ by region to the extent they did before," Kleck holds, "the Southern subculture of violence is fading" (*Daily Reflector* 1998, B6).

teach their sons about firearms, about protecting the virtue of women, and so on (Vold, Bernard, and Snipes 1998,192).

The subculture of violence theory comes from a 1958 study of homicide in Philadelphia (Wolfgang 1958) and from a subsequent book by Marvin Wolfgang and Franco Ferracuti (1967). Wolfgang and Ferracuti rely on "psychological and sociological constructs to aid in the explanation of the concentration of violence in specific socioeconomic groups and ecological areas" (Wolfgang and Ferracuti 1967, 161). Their conclusion, that certain segments in society place a positive value on violence has become "one of the most cited, but one of the least tested, propositions in the sociological and criminological literature" (Cao, Adams, and Jensen 1997, 367). So far, most researchers have applied the subculture of violence theory to regional variations in crime rates. Specifically, researchers have compared rates of violent crime in the South to other regions of the country, along with patterns of firearms ownership and homicide rates among Black and White Americans.

The Black Subculture of Violence

The southern subculture of violence theory has been used to explain the disproportionate crime rates of African Americans. Although Black Americans comprise about 12% of the U.S. population, they constitute 46% of those arrested for violent index crimes. According to the Black subculture of violence theory, higher murder rates among African Americans can be attributed to their lower-class, southern heritage. This idea can be found in the work of Wolfgang and Ferracuti, who speculated that there was a distinct subculture of violence among Black Americans. "Our subculture-of-violence thesis," they wrote, "would, therefore, expect to find a large spread to the learning of, resort to, and criminal display of the violence value among minority groups such as Negroes" (Wolfgang and Ferracuti 1967, 264).

There are at least two versions of the Black subculture of violence. One version ties violence to social disorganization within the Black community brought about by slavery and the aftermath of the Civil War. The destruction of families during the period of slavery left generations of African American youth without role models. Emancipation created an impoverished class of former slaves who had little education and few marketable skills. Black southerners clung to traditional African cultural practices adapted to life in the rural South, which left them out-of-place in the industrialization of America. Unable to assimilate into American culture, Blacks formed ghettos in northern cities, turned to violence, and turned on each other. In the other version, the Black subculture of violence flows directly from the pattern of White violence in the South directed at Blacks. Slavery was an extremely violent institution; slave owners used slave codes and brutal bodily punishments to maintain slavery. After slavery, white supremacists turned to lynching and other means of violence to enforce racial segregation. The Black experience in this country has differed from other races, and this unique historical experience has led to a legacy of violence among African Americans (Hawkins 1986,112).

The Black subculture of violence becomes an explanation for higher murder rates in the South and for disproportionate rates of violent crime among African Americans in general. The murder rate for the South is explained by arguing that the murder rate for Black Americans is higher than for White Americans, and African-Americans comprise a larger percentage of the population of the South than elsewhere in the country (Hawkins 1986, 112). The Black subculture of violence is also used to explain higher murder rates in northern cities. African Americans in northern cities are primarily the descendants of the South, which has a higher murder rate than elsewhere. The fact that murder rates are highest in Northern cities is explained by the concentration of Black Americans, who migrated to northern cities following the Civil War. In their migration north, African Americans carried with them the values they had learned in the South and passed them on to their children. While the African Americans living in northern cities may not have been born in the South, Southern values of violence are carried with them by parents or grandparents of southern heritage (Staples 1986,139).

Southern Stereotypes and Southern Culture

Certainly another reason for the durability of the southern subculture of violence theory is that it draws on the South of popular imagination. As an explanation for regional variations in murder rates, the southern subculture of violence references powerful stereotypes of Southerners. The southern subculture of violence endures because it casts the South in stark images: gun-toting White trash and violent Blacks.

As it turns out, researchers have consistently found, contrary to the expectations of the Black subculture of violence thesis, that Black Americans are less likely to support the use of violence than are White Americans (Dixon and Lizotte 1987; Ellison 1991; Cao, Adams, and Jensen 1997). At the same time, Black southerners are not more violent than African Americans elsewhere in the United States. In fact, the murder rate among African Americans in the South is actually lower than in any other region of the country. Murder rates among Whites in the South are higher than elsewhere in the country. If there is a southern subculture of violence, it is a White, and not a Black, subculture (O'Carroll and Mercy 1989; Nelsen, Corzine, and Huff-Corzine 1994; Vold, Bernard, and Snipes 1997, 192). Yet even a subculture of violence among White Southerners lacks statistical support. Researchers have failed to find a meaningful statistical correlation between growing up in the South or currently residing in the South and support for the subculture of violence (Cao, Adams, and Jensen 1997, 373).

Most murder is *intra*racial, and not *inter*racial, as Wolfgang found in Philadelphia. White murderers kill other Whites and Black murderers kill other Blacks. To apply the southern subculture of violence theory to the reality of intraracial violence means arguing that violence connected to white supremacy has led to Black-on-Black crime; or in other words, that Blacks learned victimize other Blacks from White violence directed historically against Blacks. But this explanation would make more sense if Whites continued to kill Blacks as they have historically, and Blacks targeted Whites for murder in revenge. The White southern subculture of violence makes a good explanation for hate crimes, which typically involve White offenders and Black victims, but appears less saleable when used as an explanation for murder in general.[3] There is a simple explanation for intraracial murder.

Murder rates have at least as much to do with contemporary social and economic patterns as they do with cultural legacy. The explanation for why Black murderers choose Black victims and White murderers choose White victims can be easily explained by enduring patterns of social segregation in the North and the South, and the way murder typically occurs. Murder in North Carolina fits the pattern across the United States. A relatively small percentage of murders are committed during the course of another felony such as robbery. Rather, the majority involve an argument between relatives or acquaintances that

---

3. The FBI does collect statistics on hate crime, and hate groups do persist in the South (as they do elsewhere). Murders motivated by race hatred, however, account for only a fraction of murderers—11 out of 24,530 in 1993. FBI statistics show for the majority of murders in which the relationship between the victim and offenders is known to police, Black murderers choose Black victims, and White murderers choose White victims.

ends up in a killing. The majority occur in a residence-house, mobile home or dwelling place of the victim or another person's. The majority also involve a firearm—usually a handgun. In many murder situations, alcohol is involved (Clarke 1995). Blacks kill Blacks and Whites murder Whites because murders occur when arguments between people who interact day-to-day with each other escalate into deadly violence, and given that social life in American society remains segregated, social interaction is generally limited to family and friends of the same race.

In reality, the patterns of race relations on which the southern subculture of violence theory is based were never exclusively Southern. The South has never held a monopoly on racism. The infamous system of racial segregation in place in the South until the Civil rights movement actually originated in the North prior to the Civil War. "One of the strangest things about the career of Jim Crow," writes Yale University historian C. Vann Woodward, "was that the system was born in the North and reached an advanced age before moving South in force" (Woodward 1974, 17). The phrase "Jim Crow" refers to the system of state laws and local ordinances that required separate facilities for Whites and Blacks; a system that extended from neighborhoods, churches and schools to restaurants and public transportation. Further, President Lincoln resisted the raising of Black troops because he feared the North would not support a war to free slaves. Political support depended on the war remaining strictly a "white man's war" to save the union. When he authorized the first troops, White residents of New York City and other northern cities erupted in violent protest, just as President Lincoln feared (Oates 1977, 258; Quarles 1989, 235). Beginning with the Montgomery bus boycott, the civil rights movement enjoyed success in destroying Jim Crow in cities all across the South, despite the crowds of angry bigots who jeered the marchers. Only when Dr. Martin Luther King, Jr. took the marches to Chicago did the freedom movement stall (Oates 1994, 387-395, 405-416). Given the historical reality of racism in the North, it would not have been necessary for Blacks to import a violent subculture born of southern racism.

Similarly, race itself is more fluid and flexible than the statistical categories imply. To talk about a Black subculture assumes that racial groups are homogenous, when they are not. The category of "Black" in official crime statistics makes it appear as if there is a single Black race. In reality, there is no pure Black race (or pure white or red or yellow race, for that matter). The majority of those counted has Black in government statistics possess documentable multiracial genealogies. Between 75% and 90% of those who check the box labeled "Black" on government forms, for example, could check a box labeled "Multiracial" if it were available. In fact, contrary to the popular images of the segregation era, the problem of determining who exactly was Black and who was White generated considerable dilemmas for segregationists. The problem led to litigation across the South by Whites, who having been mistaken for Blacks, were required to ride in separate railroad cars (Bell 1980, 84).

The category "Black" in FBI crime statistics constitutes a diverse reality of Blacks of Carribbean, African, Central and South American origin; the mixture includes those who identify as Puerto Ricans, Cubans, Virgin Islanders, Jamaicans, Africans, Haitians, Dominicans and others. "Is it not possible," Professor Daniel Georges-Abeyie asks, "that social distance between Blacks and Whites might impact every phase of processing of Black ethnics? Is it not conceivable that different Black ethnic groups are more involved in extralegal and illegal activity than are others, and that certain Black ethnics dominate certain criminal activties (or are believed to) and are thus more threatening than are other Black ethnics....?" Crime statistics, divided into categories of "White" and "Black" simply do not allow for the kind of research required to explore accurate conceptions of Black, White, and southern culture (Knepper, 1996).

A Subculture of Violence in North Carolina?

North Carolina's murder rate has been higher than murder rates for the nation. In this respect, North Carolina's murder rate more closely resembles the rate for other states in the South. Several rural counties have high rates of murder, not those counties with the largest cities, and the murder rates for African Americans in the state is higher than that for White North Carolinians. Does the subculture of violence explain North Carolina's murder rate?

The subculture of violence contains simplistic notions of race relations in the South as well as of race itself, impoverished Black sharecroppers and southern colonels, of duels and family feuds, of lynchings and Klan. In myth, Blacks and Whites stood apart, socially and culturally. In truth, relations between Blacks and Whites in North Carolina, as in the rest of the South, have been much more complicated.

North Carolina's slave code was as brutal as any other. North Carolina enacted its first slave code in 1715, and another in 1741, which dealt primarily with runaways. The 1741 law provided for whippings, to be administered by the sheriff or constable, and for use of the iron collar, inscribed with the initials "P.G" for public gaol. Slaves accused of a crime could be executed and their owners compensated by the general assembly. Executions were particularly brutal. In 1780 the Johnson County court tried a slave named Jenny for poisoning her master; though she denied the accusations, she was burned at the stake. The Halifax County court found the slave Peter guilty of murdering his master and mistress; he was hanged, his head cut off, hung on a pole, and his body burned (Crow, Es-

cott, and Hatley 1992, 21). But enforcement of slave law was
never absolute. Judge Thomas Ruffin of the North Carolina
Supreme Court sustained the sentence of death in 1839 for a
North Carolina slaveholder convicted of murdering his female
slave (Yanuck 1955). In 1834, Ruffin let stand the decision in
State v. Will, which overturned the conviction of a slave whose
master had tried to shoot him for running away.[4]

Lynchings and "mob justice" were common across North
Carolina as well (Huber 1998). The lynching of William A.
Parker of Beaufort County in 1888 was one of many in North
Carolina. Parker had been arrested in 1880 for the murder of
Major General Bryan Grimes, a Confederate war hero from
Pitt County who was shot to death at a bridge over Bear
Creek. Although more than one person had a grievance against
General Grimes, a former Washington police officer who ap-
parently took it upon himself to investigate the murder
brought Parker to trial. At the trial, the judge heard testimony
about tracks leading in the direction of Parker's house. One
witness, who had been paid $100 from a prosecutor in the case,
claimed that he could "tell a white man from a colored man's
tracks" (Campbell 1983, 104). After one of the jurors became
ill, the judge declared a mistrial. At Parker's second trial in
Williamston, he was acquitted after six days of evidence that
the defense did not bother to refute. On a Saturday morning
seven years later, the bridge tender at the drawbridge in Washington found Parker's body hanging from a rope. Next to the
victim's head, a placard read "Justice at Last." One month earlier, a lynch mob had taken three Black men from the Ply-
mouth jail, tied them to trees, and shot them to death. A few

---

4. In retaliation, the master sold the slave, Will, and his wife down the
river to Mississippi. Will's wife later returned to North Carolina and reported that Will had been hung for killing another slave. As the woman re-
called "Will sho'ly had hard luck. He killed a white man in North Carolina
and got off, and then was hung for killing a nigger in Mississippi" (Genovese
1974, 36).

hours before his body was found, Parker had been jailed in Washington for public drunkenness. Not the sheriff, sheriff's deputy, nor anyone in authority could be found in at the jail when the mob came for Parker (Campell 1983).

North Carolina also had its share of white supremacy groups organized after the Civil War. A group of Confederate veterans organized the Ku Klux Klan in Pulaski, Tennessee, in 1866, and night riders terrorized the South for a number of years. The Klan in North Carolina had an elaborate "invisible empire" headed by Colonel William L. Saunders, a prominent resident of Chapel Hill. There were other groups similar to the Klan, including the Constitutional Union Guard and the White Brotherhood, who rode in red, as well as white robes, and often wore horns (Zuber 1996, 27). Such groups whipped, beat, and killed countless Black citizens and also influenced jury trials by serving on juries unrecognized and threatening those who disagreed. Klansmen stabbed to death John W. Stephens, a White Republican leader, in the Caswell County courthouse, and hung Wyatt Outlaw, a prominent Black Republican, on a tree outside the Alamance County courhouse (Crow, Escott, and Hatley 1992, 90). Klan violence had an underlying political motivation. Klan activities centered in just two counties, Alamance and Caswell, the two counties in which the Republican Party had gained the most strength in the elections of 1868 and the Klan had a chance of winning Democratic seats. They never operated successfully in counties with a majority African American population, those counties in which Black culture remained the strongest. It seems unlikely that Klan violence had much impact on Black culture and the way Black North Carolinians thought about themselves (Zuber 1996, 28).

Race relations in North Carolina have been ambiguous and contradictory. From the beginning, free Blacks have always been part of the North Carolina African American population. They created such a threat to the slave system in 1785 that the legislature required them to wear badges of cloth embroidered with the word "FREE." By 1860, there were 30,000 free blacks. While subject to restrictive rules from Whites who feared them, some acquired considerable wealth and property, including slaves (Crow, Escott, and Hatley 1994, 7, 52). There were Blacks in North Carolina who fought for the Confederacy during the Civil War. They fought not so much out of blind loyalty to masters, but out of a sense of duty to defend the places where they had made homes despite the efforts of Whites. They fought because masters promised freedom if the South won; and if the South lost, they knew they would be free anyhow (Young 1994). From the beginning, there was interracial marriage, despite the attempts to outlaw it. There were Blacks who passed as White, and Whites who hid Black ancestry. Shirlee Taylor Haizlip provides a fascinating but by no means unique family history. Her family, which extends from 1680 across North Carolina and other states, includes Black, White and Indian ancestry. Some members of the family remained Black, others passed into White society to later learn of Black ancestors (Haizlip 1994).

If the southern subculture of violence theory has any merit, the definition of southern culture must be large enough to include the complex historical reality of the South. The images of southern life in *Gone With the Wind* and *Uncle Tom's Cabin* make great literature, but an authentic view of southern culture includes a more confusing mixture of Whites who enslaved Blacks, Blacks who owned slaves themselves, poor Blacks and Whites, wealthy free Whites and Blacks, Blacks who fought for the Confederacy, Whites who joined white supremacist organizations and killed other Whites, Blacks who became Whites, Whites who looked Black, and countless Blacks and Whites who grew up in the South but never followed the southern way of life.

References

Bell, Derrick. 1980. *Race, racism and American law*. Boston: Little, Brown & Co.

Campbell, James M. 1983. The lynching of William Parker: The criminal justice system at work in nineteenth century North Carolina. *Southern Journal of Criminal Justice* 7:99- 109.

Cao, Liquin, Anthony Adams and Vickie Jensen. 1997. A test of the black subculture of violence thesis: A research note. *Criminology* 35:367-379.

Clarke, Stevens H. 1995. Murder in North Carolina. *Popular Government* 61:3-17.

Clarke, Stevens H. 1992. Crime: It's a serious problem, but is it really increasing? *Popular Government* 58:34-39.

Crow, Jeffery J., Paul Escott and Flora Hatley. 1994. *A history of African Americans in North Carolina*. Raleigh: North Carolina Division of Archives and History.

Daily Reflector. 1998. Expert rejects theory blaming southern culture. 29 March, B6.

Dixon, Jo and Alan Lizotte. 1987. Gun ownership and the southern subculture of violence. *American Journal of Sociology* 93: 383-405

Ellison, Christopher G. 1991. An eye for an eye? A note on the southern subculture of violence thesis. *Social Forces* 69:1223-1239.

Genovese, Eugene. 1974. *Roll, Jordan, roll: The world the slaves made*. New York: Vintage Books.

Haizlip, Shirlee T. 1994. *The sweeter the juice: A family memoir in black and white*. New York: Touchstone.

Hawkins, Darnell F. 1986. Black and white homicide differentials: Alternatives to an inadequate theory. In *Homicide among black Americans* (Darnell F. Hawkins, ed.). Lanham, Md.: University Press of America.

Huber, Patrick J. 1998. 'Caught up in the violent whirlwind of lynching': The 1885 quadruple lynching in Chatham County, North Carolina. *North Carolina Historical Review* 75:135-160.

Knepper, Paul. 1996. Race, racism and crime statistics. *Southern University Law Review* 24:71-112.

McGinnis, Joe. 1993. *Fatal vision*. New York: G.P. Putnam's Sons.

Nelsen, Candace, Jay Corzine and Lin Huff-Corzine. 1994. The violent west re-examined. *Criminology* 32:149-161.

Oates, Stephen B. 1977. *With malice toward none: The life of Abraham Lincoln*. New York: Mentor Books.

Oates, Stephen B. 1994. *Let the trumpet sound: A life of Martin Luther King, Jr.* New York: Harper Perenial.

O'Carroll, Patrick and James Mercy. 1989. Regional variation in homicide rates: Why the *west* is so violent. *Violence and Victims* 4:17-25.

Office of Juvenile Justice and Delinquency Prevention. 1997. *Juvenile offenders and victims: 1997 update on violence*. Washington, D.C.: Office of Juvenile Justice and Deliquency Prevention.

Potter, Jerry A and Fred Bost. 1995. *Fatal justice: reinvestigating the McDonald murders*. New York: W.W. Norton.

Reed, John S. and Dale V. Reed. 1996. *1001 things everyone should know about the South*. New York: Double Day.

Reed, John S. *My tears spoiled my aim and other reflections of southern culture*. Columbia: University of Missouri Press, 1993.

Rhyne, Nancy. 1988. *Murder in the Carolinas*. Winston-Salem: John F. Blair Publisher.

Rhyne, Nancy. 1990. *More Murder in the Carolinas*. Winston-Salem: John F. Blair Publisher.

Staples, Robert. 1986 The masculine way of violence. In *Homicide among black Americans* (Darnell F. Hawkins, ed.). Lanham, Md.: University Press of America.

Steffensmeier, Darrell and Miles D. Harer. 1991. Did crime rates rise or fall during the Reagan presidency? The effects of an 'aging' U.S. population on the nation's crime rate. *Journal of Research in Crime and Delinquency* 28:330-359.

State Bureau of Investigation. 1997. *State of North Carolina: Uniform crime report.* Raleigh: North Carolina State Bureau of Investigation.

West, John F. 1993. *Lift up your head Tom Dooley.* Asheboro: Down Home Press.

Wilson, James Q. 1985. *Thinking about crime.* New York: Basic Books.

Wolfgang, Marvin E. 1958. *Patterns of criminal homicide.* Philadelphia: University of Pennsylvania Press.

Wolfgang, Marvin and Franco Ferracuti. 1967. *The subculture of violence.* London: Social Science Paperbacks.

Woodward, C. Vann. 1974. *The strange career of Jim Crow.* New York: Oxford University Press.

Vold, George, Thomas Bernard, and Jeffrey Snipes. 1998. *Theoretical criminology.* New York: Oxford University Press.

Yanuck, Julius. 1955. Thomas Ruffin and the North Carolina slave law. *North Carolina Historical Review* 21:456-475.

Young, Rudolph. 1994. Black confederates in Lincoln County, North Carolina. In *Black Southerners in gray: Essays on Afro-Americans in confederate armies* (Richard Rollins, ed.). Redondo Beach, Calif.: Rank and File Publications.

Zuber, Richard L. 1996. *North Carolina during reconstruction.* Raleigh: North Carolina Division of Archives and History.

Chapter 2

The Constitution

The North Carolina Constitution is the state's fundamental law. It is, within the American democratic form of government, formally supreme in every field where it is not limited by the powers of the U.S. Constitution. The North Carolina Constitution contains a Bill of Rights that draws the line between the power of state authority and the power of the individual. The North Carolina Constitution also contains principles for separation of power among the three branches of government—legislative, judicial, and executive—and specifies the bureaucracy designed to implement those principles. North Carolina has had three constitutions and each one has shaped the state's criminal justice system.

Constitutional law is important to criminal justice not only for what the document says about the rights of defendants, but also for what it says about the administration of justice. Every agency within the public criminal justice system must have *legal authority*. For some agencies, this legal authority may be found in the state constitution. Some have statutory authority granted by the general assembly. Others derive their legal authority from the authority granted to local governments such as cities by the general assembly. Legal authority is important because it is an agency's *raison d'etre*—its "reason for existence." As a practical matter, legal authority establishes the agency's mission, its jurisdiction, its organizational structure, and its means of financial support. As a matter of governance, legal authority is the

Figure 1. Chowan County Courthouse, Edenton, 1939. Built in 1767 it is the oldest courthouse in continuous use in North Carolina. James Iredell practiced law here.

difference between a public execution and a lynching, between a police officer and a vigilante, between vengeance and justice.

Three Constitutions and Criminal Justice

North Carolina has had three constitutions. Each constitution contained significant changes for criminal justice in the state and provide a convenient way to understand the history of the state's criminal justice system.

1776 Constitution

On May 20, 1775, Mecklenburg County residents met in Charlotte to draw up a declaration of independence from England. Within a year, the American Revolution would come to North Carolina, where patriots defeated loyalists at the battle of Moore's Creek Bridge. Independence left the colony without legal authority to govern and delegates to the provincial congress met at Halifax in the winter of 1775 to draft a constitution for the state. The first, the Independence Constitution of 1776, created a republic of free white males with full participation reserved for property owners (Orth 1993, 1).[1]

Working from copies of the constitutions adopted in other states, and English documents including the English Bill of Rights of 1689 and the Magna Carta of 1215, the framers of North Carolina's constitution drafted an extensive declaration of rights. The declaration forms "an effective blend of revolutionary theory and practical politics" (Orth 1993, 3). It contains prohibitions against excessive bail, cruel and unusual punishment, ex post facto laws, coerced confessions, and imprisonment for debt. It prescribed requirements for issuing of warrants, the process of indictment, and service of process. It also established principles for fairness in judicial proceedings equivalent to contemporary concepts of due process and equal protection, such as "law of the land" (Orth 1993, 56-58).

---

1. The constitution did not make race a requirement per se, although a statute enacted in 1715 did. The 1715 statute, in additional to the criteria below, specifically excluded Blacks, mulattoes, Indians and foreign-born males who had not become naturalized citizens. The 1776 constitution required that adult males possess a fifty-acre freehold and a year's residency to vote, and to have paid public taxes. The constitution also prohibited Catholics, Jewish persons and atheists from holding any elective or appointive office in state government (Price 1991:5,8).

The Independence Constitution of 1776 left undisturbed the colonial criminal justice system. The colony relied upon the county for administration of justice, specifically, justices of the peace. The justices of the peace, who were appointed by the governor, collectively formed a court known as the Court of Pleas and Quarter Sessions. This court had dual judicial and administrative responsibilities. The court had jurisdiction in criminal cases in which the punishment did not extend to life, limb, or member. In addition, the court appointed the county sheriff, the coroner, and constables (Marcus 1995, 942-943).

The Independence Constitution of 1776 also left undisturbed a system of slavery which made possible an agricultural economy based on tobacco, rice, and naval stores. North Carolina's black population grew after 1663, when Charles II granted eight Lords Proprietors a tract of territory south of Virginia. They recognized that a slave colony held the greatest commercial profit and in Carolina's Fundamental Constitutions (1669) granted to slave holders "absolute power and authority" over slaves. The large plantations envisioned by the Lords Proprietors developed in South Carolina due to North Carolina's treacherous coast and lack of harbors. Yet by the American Revolution, slavery was firmly rooted in North Carolina. The legislature enacted its first slave code in 1715, followed by major revision in 1741 (Crow, Escott, and Hatley 1994, 1-7).

1868 Constitution

For North Carolina, the Civil War ended on April 26, 1865, when General Joseph E. Johnston surrendered to General William T. Sherman at Bennett House, near Durham. The armies of Johnston and Sherman had fought the last major battle of the Civil War at Bentonville (west of Goldsboro), North Carolina, in late March of 1865. Johnston realized further mil-

Figure 2. State Capitol, Raleigh. The capitol housed all of state government until about 1888. Today, the building contains offices of the governor, lieutenant governor, and secretary of state.

itary resistance was pointless after Sherman marched into the state capital at Raleigh three weeks later. Governor Zebulon B. Vance fled to Statesville, where he was arrested and taken to prison in Washington, D.C. The war claimed the lives of more than 40,000 North Carolinians and freed about 350,000 North Carolinians of African descent. When it ended, Whites and Blacks together faced an uncertain future as the banking system failed, farms had been damaged, and state and local governments had collapsed (Zuber 1996, 1).

When Sherman left the state in April he placed General John Schofield in charge, and North Carolina was under military rule until July 1868. Concerned about the welfare of the state's Black citizens, Schofield issued a statement that slavery no longer existed, and in an effort to maintain law and order, he arranged for each county to have a police force (Zuber 1996, 2). The Freedman's Bureau, a federal relief agency that operated in North Carolina from July 1865 until the end of 1868, set up courts and tried Blacks accused of crimes rather than allowing them to be tried in county courts. The North Carolina legislature, in response to General Schofield and the Freedmen's Bureau, passed the "Black Code" in 1866 which prescribed harsher penalties for Blacks accused of victimizing whites, and prohibited Blacks from testifying in court (Browning 1930; Zuber 1996, 6).

Early in 1868, legislators met to draw up a new constitution for the state, necessitated by defeat in the war and the end of slavery. The Constitution of 1868 made changes in all three branches of government, but particularly in the judicial branch. The new organic law transferred the lawmaking power formerly held by county courts to boards of elected county commissioners. Judges could no longer keep their positions for life, but had to run for reelection every eight years. Other officers, including sheriffs and clerks, would no longer be appointed by the courts, but would be elected by the people as well (St. Clair 1953; Zuber 1996,17).

The legislature took further measures to reform the criminal justice system a year later. The assembly abolished whipping for crimes and took steps to establish a state prison. North Carolina numbered among only three states in the Union that did not have a state prison prior to the Civil War. And, in an effort to limit the activities of the Ku Klux Klan, the legislature made it a crime to wear a mask or disguise on a public highway for the purpose of frightening a citizen (Zuber 1996, 22).

1971 Constitution

By 1970, North Carolina had the largest population of any southern state, except for Florida, and emerged as the South's leading state in manufacturing. Textiles, tobacco, and chemicals had become the major products. Charlotte, Durham, Raleigh, Greensboro, and Winston-Salem made the state a symbol of the "New South" in which industry replaced agriculture as the chief commercial activity. The state's African American population declined to 22.2% in 1970, as Black citizens migrated to cities in the north and west. North Carolina retained, however, its distinction as the state with the largest rural population; half of its residents in 1970 lived outside urban areas. The state was both industrial and rural because many of the state's industrial plants had located in small towns.

The constitution had been amended so many times since 1868 that the North Carolina State Bar and North Carolina Bar Association formed the North Carolina State Constitution Study Commission. The commission's work resulted in the state's third constitution, effective July 1, 1971, although the changes made do not compare with the magnitude of changes made in 1868 (Orth 1993, 2). The document did, however, lead to a reorganization of the executive branch of state government, which led to changes in state law enforcement and corrections.

When voters adopted the 1971 Constitution, they also approved a measure adding sections (ART. 3, SEC. 5, ss. 10; ART. 3, SEC. 11) empowering the governor to implement administrative reorganization. The changes gave the general assembly four years within which to reorganize the administration into no more than twenty-five departments. Although the general assembly prescribes the functions, powers, and duties of administrative departments, the governor may make changes in the allocation of offices and agencies necessary for efficient administration (Orth 1993, 95).

The Executive Organization Acts of 1971 and 1973 reorganized agencies within the executive branch. This reorganization created in the Department of Crime Control and Public Safety. The department provides law enforcement and emergency services, serves as the state's chief coordinating agency to control crime, and assists local law enforcement agencies. The department is comprised of four commissions (Governor's Crime Commission, Governor's Commission on Military Affairs, the State Emergency Response Commission, and the Crime Victims Compensation Commission) and nine divisions: Alcohol Law Enforcement, Butner Public Safety, Civil Air Patrol, Crime Prevention, Emergency Management, N.C. National Guard, Governor's Crime Commission, State Highway Patrol and Victim and Justice Services. The department is administered by a secretary appointed by the governor (Marcus 1995, 344-353).

Declaration of Rights

The North Carolina Declaration of Rights grants a longer list to citizens than the federal Bill of Rights. This is significant because many provisions of the U.S. Bill of Rights apply only to the federal government, and not to the states. Professor John V. Orth of the University of North Carolina at Chapel Hill, provides excellent commentary on the major criminal justice rights included in the state constitution:

> *Suspending laws* (ART. 1, SEC. 7). This safeguard ensures that the government's lawmaking power resides in the legislature and limits the power of the governor to suspend a law by refusing to enforce it. The governor does have the power of clemency (ART. 3, SEC. 5, ss. 6); however, and may reduce or eliminate the punishment imposed on a lawbreaker. District attorneys may also choose not to charge defendants despite evidence of lawbreaking. So long as the decisions are made on a case-by-case basis, they do not amount to an unconstitutional suspension of the laws (Orth 1993, 44-45).

Ex post facto laws (ART. 1, SEC. 16). The government cannot punish persons for acts committed before the existence of laws prohibiting such an act; nor can persons be more severely punished than the punishment written into law at the time of the act. If the punishment specified at the time of the offense was life in prison, no judge or jury may impose a death sentence. A law that changes, but does not increase, the punishment is constitutional. When the common law punishment for larcency—whipping and imprisonment—changed to imprisonment alone, there was no constitutional violation (Orth 1993, 52).

Courts shall be open (ART. 1, SEC. 18). Although originally intended to ensure that the courts were available to persons who desired to file civil suits, this section has been interpreted by the North Carolina Supreme Court to guarantee that criminal trials are public and speedy. These guarantees exist within certain limitations, however. Trial courts may be closed to the public; for example, during testimony of child sexual abuse victims. Trial judges may also restrict access by spectators who distract juries (Orth 1993, 55).

Law of the land; equal protection of the laws (ART. 1, SEC. 19). "Law of the land" is an archaic legal phrase that has come to have significant meaning for individual rights. For example, the idea that a person is "innocent until proven guilty" cannot not be found in the constitution, but courts have determined that "law of the land" reflects this concept (Orth 1993, 59). "Equal protection of the laws" prohibits discrimination by state government on the basis of race, color, religion, or national origin. Not only must a law be fair on its face; it must be fairly applied (Orth 1993, 59-60).

General warrants (ART. 1, SEC. 20). The government may
search for evidence of crime or arrest those suspected
of crime but may not do so arbitrarily. This section
specifically prohibits "general warrants"; warrants to
search for evidence of crime and warrants to arrest
persons suspected of crime must be specific. An unlawful search does not become lawful by discoveries
made during the search. Evidence produced by means
of an unlawful search may not be admitted in a criminal trial, not because it is unreliable, but because the
legal process must be free of the taint of unfair procedure. While the emphasis in this provision is on justi-
fying the search and seizure in advance; the courts
have recognized the constitutionality of warrantless
searches conducted with a valid waiver, seizure of evidence in plain view, and search and seizure of evidence
in exigent circumstances (in cases involving autos, for
example, where the evidence may be destroyed or removed) (Orth 1993, 60-61).

Inquiries into restraints on liberty (ART. 1, SEC. 21). This provision restricts government abuse of imprisonment. The
remedy is authority to inquire into the lawfulness of
the restraint and to be freed from restraint if unlawful.
North Carolina courts have interpreted this provision
narrowly. A writ of habeas corpus may be filed by a
prisoner in the state prison; for example, challenging
the authority that imposed the restraint, but not the
fairness of the restraint (Orth 1993, 62).

Modes of prosecution (ART. 1, SEC. 22). This provision identifies the formal legal documents required to initiate a
criminal action in felony cases: indictment, presentment, and impeachment. Indictment and presentment
involve the grand jury, a body at common law comprised of no more than twenty-three persons; in North

Carolina, eighteen persons. Impeachment has to do with the removal of a public official from office for malfeasance. Grand jury proceedings are not required for district court proceedings in misdemeanor cases (Orth 1993, 62–63).

Rights of accused (ART. 1, SEC. 23). Defendants in criminal proceedings possess several specific rights:

1. To be informed of the accusation. Usually, the indictment contains all the necessary information. To be informed of the specific charge enables the defense to prepare, and gives meaning to the prohibition in Section 19 against double jeopardy (Orth 1993, 63).

2. To confront accusers. The defendant in a criminal trial has the right to respond to the charges. This entails the right of the defense counsel to question witnesses for the government through cross-examination. Courts have determined that this clause generally requires the presence of witnesses and accusers, although there are exceptions such as statements made by a dying person whose death prevents return to trial (Orth 1993, 64).

3. To defense counsel. At a minimum, this means the right to retain a lawyer to conduct a legal defense. This right exists not solely at trial, but at every critical stage leading to trial. The North Carolina Supreme Court determined that this right requires the trial court judge to appoint a lawyer for any defendant unable to afford one (Orth 1993, 64–65).

4. Not to be compelled to self-incriminating evidence. Defendants have the right to remain silent, and this silence cannot be taken as an admission of guilt. This protection includes testimony and other personal documents, for example, which contain

"self-incriminating evidence." This provision does not extend to "objective characteristics" of defendants, such as handwriting samples, blood samples, fingerprints, and other identifying physical characteristics (Orth 1993, 65). Voluntary confessions are admissable.

5. Not to be compelled to pay costs...unless found guilty. Defendants are protected from paying to prove their innocence (Orth 1993, 66).

Right of jury trial in criminal cases (ART. 1, SEC. 24). Although the number of jurors is not specified, the North Carolina Supreme Court has ruled that the number required under common law is necessary—twelve. The jury's decision or verdict to convict must be unanimous and must be made in open court, not in secret. In North Carolina, jury trial is available to misdemeanants who appeal. When appealed, the charge must be proved in a second trial *de novo* "anew" without regard to the earlier trial. The general assembly has the power to define misdemeanors as used in this section (Orth 1993, 66–67).

Bails, fines, and punishments (ART. 1, SEC. 27). Bail, security received from the defendant to ensure a later court appearance at trial, and fines and punishments, which are imposed after the trial, may not be excessive. What constitutes "excessive" is difficult to define, but an amount based on precedent serves as a guide to what is constitutionally permissable (Orth 1993, 70).

Legal Authority

Every agency within the public criminal justice system must have legal authority. For some, this enabling authority may be found in the state constitution. Some have statutory authority granted by the general assembly. Still others derive their legal authority from the authority granted to local governments, such as cities, by the general assembly. Some criminal justice agencies could be eliminated after a local election; to eliminate others would require a constitutional amendment and a statewide referendum. It is all a matter of legal authority.

City-county consolidation provides a good example of the difference the source of legal authority makes. While voters have rejected consolidation plans so far, there has been interest in city-county consolidation in North Carolina since 1927. Consolidation plans have come before voters four times in Wilmington and New Hanover County, twice in Durham and Durham County, and once each in Charlotte and Mecklenburg County and Asheville and Buncome County (Whitaker 1993, 205). If the voters within a county approved a consolidation plan, a city police department could be abolished altogether or dramatically reconstituted because it derives its legal authority to exist from statutory authority given to the city council. The sheriff's department, on the other hand, would be much more difficult to abolish because the office of sheriff is enabled by the state constitution. To abolish a sheriff's office in a single county would require a constitutional amendment and approval of voters statewide in a public referendum.

State Agencies

Enabling authority for some agencies of criminal justice may be found in the state constitution. The sheriff is a state office that dates to the 1776 constitution. ART. 7, SEC. 2 reads, "In each county a Sheriff shall be elected ... and shall hold his office for a period of four years, subject to removal for cause as provided by law" (Orth 1993, 141). The North Carolina Supreme Court determined in *Gowens v. Alamance County* (1939) that as an official directly elected by the people, the sheriff has inherent power to appoint deputy sheriffs. The general assembly has established the "law" necessary for removal: an unfit sheriff may be removed by the resident superior court judge for the county (N.C. Gen. Stat, § 128-16).

The supreme court itself is not mentioned, however, in the state's first constitution. The high court does have constitutional status; the 1868 Constitution stated that the supreme court, which had existed as a court of three members since 1818, should have five members. Constitutional amendment in 1876 returned the number to three, and another amendment in 1888 raised the number to five. The court's present size was fixed by a 1937 statute authorized by constitutional amendment two years earlier. Today, the court is comprised of a chief justice and six associate justices. Some of the administrative duties of the chief justice are inherent in the office of a presiding judge, some are found directly in the constitution, and others are found in statute (Orth 1993, 106).

The Court of Appeals is a statutory court. The court of appeals was authorized by constitutional amendment in 1965 and created by statute effective January 1, 1967. The court's structure, organization, composition and jurisdiction are all created by statute (Orth 1993,107). Both the North Carolina District Court Division and North Carolina Superior Court Division are statutory courts as well.

Other state agencies, such as the North Carolina Department of Correction and the Department of Crime Control and Public Safety, are executive offices within the executive branch. These are directed by secretaries, who are appointed by the governor, and serve as a cabinet at the governor's pleasure. The State Bureau of Investigation came into being in 1937, when Governor Clyde R. Hoey received legislation needed to create a State Bureau of Identification and Investigation "at his discretion" (N.C. Gen. Stat. § 114-12; Brown 1987, 20). Two years later, the Bureau became part of North Carolina's new Department of Justice, under the direction of the state attorney general (Brown 1987, 24).

Local Government Authority

For other criminal justice agencies, such as the City of Greenville Police Department, enabling authority is somewhat more complex. By the authority of state statute, cities may create police departments. Art. 7, Sec. 1 establishes that municipalities resemble business corporations that draw their authority to govern from charters. Each unit of local government is essentially an agency of state government, and its powers are derived from statutory enabling legislation.

The city is a *municipal corporation*. The municipal corporation is not unlike a corporation organized for private business except that while business corporations are organized for the purpose of returning a profit to their investors, the city is organized to provide public services and regulate activities within a particular community. Cities in North Carolina owe their existence to the general assembly; the legislature can abolish them, and grant or remove their powers. The general assembly authorizes cities to act through a general law, which applies statewide to all cities of, for example, a population of five thousand or more; or through a local act, which applies to one city or a few cities. There is no right of self government or "home rule" in North Carolina which allows cities to write their own charters as in other states (Lawrence 1996, 33).

The general assembly has determined that a city's governing board, which may be called the council, the board of commissioners, or board of aldermen—holds ultimate authority to act for the city. Board members are elected, typically in a nonpartisan election. There is no typical structure for a city's governing board; each board's structure is set out in the city's charter. The board determines what services the city provides. The number of board members and terms of office vary across the state (Lawrence 1996, 25-26).

The majority of the largest cities in the United States has what political scientists call a strong-mayor form of government. The strong-mayor form makes the mayor the chief executive with authority to hire and fire department heads, prepare and administer the budget, and veto acts of the city council. (Wicker 1996, 23). North Carolina's mayors, however, enjoy few formal powers as there are no strong-mayor cities in the state (Lawrence 1996, 36; Wicker 1996, 23). The general assembly has authorized cities to adopt one of two forms of governance: the council-manager form and the mayor-council form.

    Council-Manager Form. Many North Carolina cities operate according to the council-manager form of governance in which the board appoints a professional manager, who is the city's chief administrator. The mayor, usually elected separately, presides over the council but has few independent powers. The manager prepares and administers the budget, supervises all city departments, and hires and fires employees, including the police chief. (In a few council-manager cities, such as New Bern, the charter requires that the council appoint the chief of police) (Wicker 1996, 68). All but one (Mint Hill) of North Carolina's cities with a population over 10,000 have a council-manager form of governance (as does the majority of those with a population between 2,500 and 10,000) (Wicker 1996, 23).

    Mayor-Council Form. The mayor-council form of governance has an elected city council and separately elected mayor. The city council establishes policy, and the mayor has some overall administrative responsibility, but little authority. Department heads, including the police chief, are typically appointed by the city council. The mayor-council form is one of the most widely used forms of governance in small cities in North Carolina (Wicker 1996:23). A number of small cities without a manager have a mayor who in fact carries out the functions and responsibilities similar to those vested in the mayor within the strong-mayor form (Wicker 1996:23).

The county in North Carolina resembles the city in several ways. It is a legal entity much like a corporation. Each county has a board of commissioners, and all but one appoints a county manager. Boards of county commissioners vary in size, term of office, method of election, and administrative structure. Unlike the city, however, which is formed at the request of people within its jurisdiction to serve the needs of its residents, the chief purpose of the county is a division of state government created to serve state functions in a given geographic area. Counties exist as part of the general administration of state policy (Marcus 1995, 945). One of the principal aspects of state policy for the county is the judicial system and law enforcement. Within each county there is a court, courthouse, sheriff, jail, clerk, and court records. The court is not a county court; the judge, district attorney, and sheriff are not county officials who administer county law, but state officials who administer state law (Marcus 1995, 946).

Financing Criminal Justice

Art. 5 of the constitution specifies the means of financing state and local government. The general assembly approves a budget for the state each year. Financing North Carolina's criminal justice system involves public budgeting. State law requires that each city and county adopt an annual budget, including planned expenditures and revenue for the coming year.

Financing State Criminal Justice

The Budget Process. The budget process for the Judicial Department begins when the director of the Administrative Office of the Courts submits a detailed proposed budget to the state Budget Office. The budget request is divided into three categories (Brannon 1994, 27):

1. *Base budget.* Requests funds needed to continue the operation of the department at the level of existing support.

2. *Expansion budget.* Requests for additional funds to provide for salary increases, increases in case loads, and new programs.

3. *Capital improvements budget.* Requests for additional funds for new buildings.

After the state Budget Office has reviewed the proposed budget, the governor and an advisory budget committee decide the amount of funds the governor will request from the general assembly (Brannon 1994, 27).

Appropriate committees within the state house and senate consider the governor's request. The general assembly may rely on the governor's proposed budget, or may draft its own budget through appropriations committees within the legislature. The general assembly has its own Fiscal Research Division which provides technical assistance to legislators (Brannon 1994, 28).

Generally, the appropriations committees spend twelve to fifteen weeks reviewing the entire state government budget. The director of the Administrative Office of the Courts (AOC) may appear at the committee hearings and request funds in addition to those recommended by the governor and the Advisory Budget Commission. Also, the committees consider other bills carrying appropriations requests. If the judiciary committee has approved a bill creating new judgeships or increasing the number of assistant district attorneys, these bills will also be considered by the appropriations committees. The appropriations committees submit to the full legislature a revised budget bill containing the changes made from the bills submitted. The bills may be amended on the floor of the state house and senate. When, as often happens, the house and senate adopt budget bills that differ, the differences are resolved by a joint conference committee of members from both houses (Brannon 1994, 28).

Citizens believe that the court system does less and costs more than it actually does. A study undertaken by the Commission on the Future of Justice and the Courts in North Carolina found that none of the citizens who participated in focus groups could correctly identify the number of case filings per year. Citizens guessed that state courts deal with about 250,000 cases a year; the actual number is more than 2.5 million. Citizens believed that state courts consume 18% to 20% of the state budget; in reality the proportion in less than 3% (Crowell 1996, 31).

Financing Local Criminal Justice

The Budget Process. The budget process in medium and large North Carolina cities (council-manager cities) is described below (Whitaker 1993:95-111):

1. Each city department (police, fire/rescue, recreation and parks, and so on) prepares an estimated budget based on the projected costs of maintaining service. Department heads meet with the city manager to discuss the estimate.

2. The city manager compares estimated revenues and expenditures. The manager prepares the budget for the governing board. If revenues are higher than estimates, the manager likely proposes additional programs, tax cuts, or both. If proposed expenditures are higher than revenues, then the proposal will likely involve cuts in services, tax increases, or both.

3. The governing board for the city reviews the proposed budget. Before the board adopts a budget, the board must hold a public hearing. In adopting the budget, the board formally appropriates the expenditures (Whitaker 1993, 97-100).

Capital projects may be financed through borrowed money. Capital projects involve the purchase of land or construction of buildings. Local governments borrow money through bonds. There are two types of bonds: general obligation bonds and revenue bonds. General obligation bonds pledge the "full faith and credit" of the government, that is, the government will raise taxes to repay the bonds if necessary. These bonds are used to finance nonrevenue producing projects, such as jails. They require a public referendum; they can be issued only if a majority of the voters approve. Revenue bonds are repaid from the project itself. Revenue bonds are used to finance revenue-producing projects, such as parking garages and public golf courses (Whitaker 1993, 100-101).

Sources of Revenue. Local governments gather revenue from a variety of sources. The largest single source is the property tax. Property tax is based on a combination of real property (land and buildings) and personal property (cars, business equipment, etc.). The sum of all property a city or county can tax is known as that city's or county's tax base. The rate is set by the governing board.

State collected taxes provide a substantial source of revenue. These include taxes on gasoline, retail sales, food and beverage, and cable television. Under state statute, each county may levy a tax of $.02 cents on each dollar of sales in the county (the state levies an additional $.04 cents, which makes North Carolina's sales tax rate $.06 or 6%). The state collects tax receipts from businesses and returns the appropriate portion to local governments.

Other sources of revenue include user fees and intergovernmental grants. Local governments may charge customers for services including business licenses, garbage collection, building permits, and inspection fees. Additionally, cities and counties with water, sewer or electrical power charge customers. Intergovernmental assistance, in the form of state and federal grants, provides revenue for local services as well (Whitaker 1993, 102-110).

References

Brannon, Joan G. 1994. *The judicial system in North Carolina.* Raleigh: North Carolina Administrative Office of the Courts.

Brown, Dick. 1987. The formative years: SBI. *Popular Government* 52:19-27.

Browning, James B. 1930. North Carolina's black code. *Journal of Negro History* Oct. 461-473.

Crowell, Michael. 1996. What do North Carolinians think of their court system? *Popular Government* 61:31-33.

Ferrell, Joseph S. 1990. *The general assembly of North Carolina: A handbook for legislators.* Chapel Hill: Institute of Government.

Howard, Lucille. 1990. *North Carolina: Our state government.* Charlotte: League of Women Voters of North Carolina Educational Fund.

Lawrence, David M. 1995. Appendix: County government in North Carolina. In *Municipal government in North Carolina*

(David M. Lawrence and Warren J. Wicker, Eds.). Chapel Hill: Institute of Government.

Marcus, Lisa A. 1996. *North Carolina manual 1995/1996.* Raleigh: Secretary of State.

Orth, John V. 1993. *The North Carolina constitution with history and commentary.* Chapel Hill: University of North Carolina Press.

Price, William S. 1991. *The bill of rights and North Carolina.* Raleigh: North Carolina Division of Archives and History.

St. Clair, Kenneth E. 1953. Judicial machinery in North Carolina in 1865, *North Carolina Historical Review* 30:415–439

Whitaker, Gordon P. 1993. *Local government in North Carolina.* Raleigh: North Carolina City and County Managers Association.

Wicker, Warren J. 1996. Introduction to city government in North Carolina. In *Municipal government in North Carolina* (David M. Lawrence and Warren J. Wicker, Eds.). Chapel Hill: Institute of Government.

Zuber, Richard L. 1996. *North Carolina during reconstruction.* Raleigh: North Carolina Division of Archives and History.

Chapter 3

Lawmaking

The U.S. Constitution created the Congress to make laws for the nation. The U.S. Congress, comprised of the House of Representatives and the Senate, writes federal law, including federal criminal law. The U.S. Congress creates the *United States Code*, the federal law specifying what acts are to be considered criminal and what the punishments are for violations of the code. Each state has a legislature as well. The North Carolina General Assembly is comprised of a House of Representatives and a Senate like the U.S. Congress. The North Carolina General Assembly writes the *North Carolina General Statutes*, which specifies what acts are criminal in North Carolina, and specifies the punishment for each violation of the code. In addition to the federal and state legislatures, the governing boards of cities and counties have legislative authority. The boards of county commissioners and boards of city commissioners across North Carolina make laws that comprise the ordinance book of that county or city.

The North Carolina General Assembly has been regarded historically as the most powerful of all state legislatures. Yet even North Carolina's legislature does not retain ultimate lawmaking authority. The North Carolina Supreme Court has a lawmaking or policy making role as well. Although the North Carolina constitution does not give the state supreme court this authority, the court has this authority due to the doctrine of judicial review. The doctrine of judicial review gives to the state supreme court the final say in interpreting the state consti-

49

tution. The U.S. Supreme Court derives its lawmaking authority from this same principle expressed in the landmark case of *Marbury v. Madison* (1803). North Carolina's Supreme Court's power of judicial review extends from the case of *Bayard v. Singleton* (1787), a case cited, in fact, by Chief Justice John Marshall in the famous *Marbury* case.

There is a source of lawmaking authority even greater than either the general assembly and supreme court. It is known as the common law and extends from historical roots in medieval England. Common law draws its authority however, from an even higher source. The source to which Thomas Jefferson referred to when he wrote "All men are endowed by their Creator with certain inalienable rights." Practically speaking, it is the common law that fixes the absolute authority of lawmakers. In other words, it is the legislature that has the power to decide what citizens can and cannot do; it is the common law that has the power to decide what laws lawmakers can and cannot make.

The Common Law

Common law refers to a system of lawmaking that originated in England and found its way to the United States during the colonial period. It refers to the unwritten laws of England, or more specifically, to the broad principles of reason and common sense that guided the decisions of judges in specific cases. Common law differs from statutory law, which is written by legislatures to deal with specific issues, and organized into codes by topic (Hogue 1985).

Henry II, King of England, sent his judges out from London to ride the circuit, settle cases, and do justice among the people. These judges would listen to the facts, determine the issues involved in disputes, listen to the arguments of the lawyers, and arrive at decisions. Often, they reserved judgements on novel cases until after they had returned to London and discussed them with other judges. Over the years, decisions in cases began to reflect not local customs and traditions, but principles common to all English people. The common law or judge-made law emerged as judges began to follow decisions by other judges in similar cases. "It is an established rule," William Blackstone explained, "to abide by former precedents where the same points come again in litigation; as well as to keep the scale of justice even and steady, and not liable to waver with every new judge's decision" (Coates 1976, 256).

The common law took root in North Carolina through lawyers who had received their legal education at the Inns of Court in London. This rule obligated judges to follow precedent unless "the precedent is flatly absurd or unjust" (Coates 1976, 257). While much of substantive criminal law has been codified, the common law of England continues to guide the law of North Carolina. In *State v. Crocker* (1954), the North Carolina Supreme Court referred to common law prohibition of double-jeopardy even when the principle could not be found in the constitution of the state. "It is a fundamental and sacred principle of the common law...," wrote the court, "that no person can be twice put in jeopardy of life or limb for the same offense" (Orth 1993, 59).

The State Supreme Court

The primary function of appellate courts is to decide questions of law that have arisen in trial courts and before regulatory agencies. Appellate courts selectively review cases and issue written opinions to guide application of the law. In this role, the courts do not merely serve as interpreters of the law, but as policy makers. The decisions of both federal and state courts affect criminal procedure, corrections policy, and other criminal justice activities in the state. Appellate courts have a role in public law, that is, to make decisions that are not limited to deciding outcomes in individual cases but that affect the public. These decisions are in the area of criminal procedure and the administration of justice as a whole.

In the landmark case of *Marbury v. Madison* (1803), Chief Justice John Marshall first introduced judicial review. The doctrine of *judicial review* means essentially that the U.S. Supreme Court is the sole or final interpreter of the U.S. Constitution. The U.S. Supreme Court may overturn an act of Congress, or the act of a state legislature, if the Court determines that the law is unconstitutional. The subordination of state laws to the federal constitution is what constitutes, legally speaking, the "united" in the United States. Similarly, state supreme courts review state legislation. The state supreme court is the final interpreter of the state constitution, sovereign in all matters that do not conflict with the federal constitution. Application of state criminal laws and constitutional rights, in fact, constitutes the largest category of judicial review cases among state supreme courts (Glick 1993, 408).

The North Carolina Supreme Court established power of judicial review in North Carolina more than a decade before *Marbury v. Madison* (1803) established it at the federal level (Orth 1993, 7). The case of *Bayard v. Singleton* (1787), cited by Chief Justice John Marshall in *Marbury v. Madison*, had to do with legal procedure in establishing title to property confiscated during the American Revolution. The suit was brought by Elizabeth Bayard of New York against Spyers Singleton of New Bern. Bayard, who was the daughter of Samuel Cornell, the wealthiest person in North Carolina prior to the Revolution, she had a document signed by her father, conveying to her all his property which included warehouses, a residence, and furnishings. Cornell, a loyalist, had signed the document in

Figure 3. Justice Building, Raleigh. The courtroom, conference room and chambers of the justices of the N.C. Supreme Court are located on the third floor.

1777 during a brief stay in New Bern before he fled to New York. Under the terms of the State Confiscation Act (1785), Singleton had purchased Cornell's holdings in New Bern. Singleton's attorneys argued that the suit should should be dismissed based on the 1785 law. Bayard's attorneys countered with a provision in the state constitution which provided for jury trial "in all controversies at law respecting property" (Price 1991, 12).[1]

The case created a dilemma: Should the court follow the legislation enacted by the general assembly, or the provision in the state constitution? In its decision, the state supreme court followed the constitutional provision and established the principle that the judiciary, and not the general assembly, had the final say in interpretation of state law. Curiously, the North Carolina Supreme Court was not itself a constitutional court at that time. In other words, the state supreme court has decided it was the final interpreter of the constitution, although it did not at the time have constitutional authority to exist, and existed only by legislation passed by the general assembly. North Carolina's 1776 Constitution did not establish a supreme court. At first, the supreme court operated as a matter of practical necessity and, later, operated under statutory authority authorized by the

---

1. Bayard secured a "dream team" of attorneys in colonial North Carolina to argue her case: Samuel Johnston, who had served in the continental congress and as governor from 1878 to 1789; William R. Davie, who would later become governor and a U.S. District Court Judge; and James Iredell, who would be appointed by President George Washington to serve on the U.S. Supreme Court in 1790. Singleton countered with a "dream team" of his own: Abner Nash, who had been governor from 1780-1881 and Alfred Moore, who would replace Iredell on the U.S. Supreme Court in 1799. In striking down the 1785 law, however, the North Carolina Supreme Court ruled that Samuel Cornell was a British subject and could not convey property in North Carolina. In the end, Bayard took nothing in her suit and Singleton retained the property (Price 1991, 12).

general assembly until the constitution of 1868 revised the judicial article. The Constitution of 1868 made the supreme court a constitutional court owing its existence to the fundamental law of the state rather than legislative enactment (Marcus 1995, 698).

North Carolina's 1776 Constitution authorized the general assembly to appoint "Judges of the Supreme Courts of Law and Equity" and "Judges of Admiralty." Until 1799, the state had no appellate court. In that year, two superior court judges met in Raleigh to dispose of appeals. This meeting developed into a twice-yearly meeting with a short docket that came to be known as the "Court of Conference." In 1805, the general assembly renamed the Court of Conference the North Carolina Supreme Court, and in 1810, made the state supreme court a court of record: the judges were ordered to produce written decisions and deliver them in open court. The judges of the court elected John Louis Taylor to be chief justice. It was not until 1818, however, that the general assembly created an appellate court to be known as the supreme court. The legislators elected John Louis Taylor chief justice, and elected John Hall and Leonard Henderson judges (Marcus 1995, 695).

From the beginning, the state supreme court came under criticism. Politicians criticized the judges' salaries, which at $2,500 per year were higher than the governor's ($2,000 a year). Superior judges objected to a court with the power to reverse one of their decisions on appeal. Legislation in 1832 reduced the salaries of the judges to that of the governor, but more than anything else, it was the appointment of Thomas Ruffin and William Gaston to the court that made the state supreme court saleable. Ruffin, a former superior court judge and state bank president, was later ranked by Harvard Law School Dean Roscoe Pound as one of the ten greatest jurists in American history. Gaston, who had sponsored the 1818 supreme court bill while serving in the legislature, ascended to the high court in 1833. According to legal lore, the judges elected Ruffin as chief justice that year over Gaston by a coin toss (Marcus 1995, 696–697).

The chief purpose of the state supreme court is to decide questions of law that have arisen in the lower courts and before state administrative agencies. The supreme court meets in Raleigh on the third floor of the Justice Building. The justices spend most of their time outside the courtroom considering numerous petitions in which a appellate seeks to bring a case before the court and deciding cases before the court. They read records and briefs prepared by litigants and then write opinions containing the reasoning on which decisions are based. The concurrence of four justices is required for a decision; each of the seven justices on the court participate in every case except in those rare situations when a justice must recuse himself or herself (Marcus 1995, 670).

Using the doctrine of judicial review and the authority of an appellate court, the state supreme court acts as judicial policy maker. For example:

> *State v. Collins* (1874). The North Carolina Supreme Court recognized a duty of a trial court to appoint a lawyer for indigent defendants.

> *State v. Rogers* (1913). The number of persons constituting a jury in this state must be a body of twelve; so integral is this number to jury proceedings that a defendant cannot consent to a jury composed of fewer (Orth 1993, 67).

> *State v. Hall* (1965). An unlawful search does not become lawful by any discoveries made during the search.

> *State v. Dawson* (1968). Citizens have the right to possess a firearm in order to exercise the "common law right of self-defense"; this right is, however, subject to reasonable regulation (Orth 1993, 73).

Figure 4. Legislative Building, Raleigh. Chambers for the Senate and House of Representatives, N.C. General Assembly, occupy the east and west wings of the second floor.

The General Assembly

The charter from the Crown in 1663 granted to the Lords Proprietor of the Colony of Carolina "full and absolute power...to [make] any laws whatsoever." The Concessions of 1665 vested this authority in the general assembly. As a colony, Carolina remained part of the British empire and subject to its jurisdiction. Until 1776, any law passed by the general assembly was subject to veto by British authorities in London (Coates 1976, 263). However, the general assembly in 1711 determined that the "Laws of England are the Laws of this Government, so far as they are compatible with our way of living and Trade..." (Coates 1776, 255). It was just that sort of thinking that fueled the American Revolution.

A "legislative assembly of free holders" met for the first time around 1666. Until 1697, the legislature remained unicameral;

it did not become a bicameral legislature until 1776. North Carolina's Independence Constitution of 1776 conferred legislative authority on a general assembly composed of "two distinct branches"; a *Senate* and a *House of Commons*. The Constitution of 1868 changed the name of the House of Commons to the House of Representatives, and eliminated the "property qualification" for holding office. Tryon Palace in New Bern served as the state's first capitol building, but it was abandoned during the Revolutionary War due to the risk of enemy attack. The seat of government moved from town to town with each new general assembly until 1792 when Raleigh became the permanent capital. A two-story brick building, completed in 1796, served as the capitol building until 1831 when it was razed by fire. A new capitol went up in 1840 and served as the state house until 1963 when the general assembly convened in the present building for the first time (Marcus 1995, 436-438). Presently, the North Carolina General Assembly meets in the North Carolina Legislative Building in Raleigh; the senate and house chambers occupy the east and west wings of the second floor.

Like the U.S. Congress, the North Carolina legislature is comprised of two houses: the Senate and the House of Representatives. There are 50 senators and 120 House members in the general assembly. Members of the house and senate are elected for two-year terms. They are elected from districts which are supposed to be equally divided. Senators are elected from thirty-five districts and House members from seventy-two districts (Howard, 1990, 15). North Carolina has historically been the most powerful of state legislatures. Until 1996, when a veto amendment to the state constitution passed by popular referendum, North Carolina was the only state in which the governor did not have the power to veto legislation.

The laws enacted by the general assembly may be divided into five categories (Howard 1990, 19):

(1) laws regulating individual conduct;

(2) laws providing for services of the state;

(3) laws empowering or directing local governments to act;

(4) laws determining how much money should be raised by the state and how it should be spent; and

(5) amendments to the state constitution (Howard 1990, 19).

The General Assembly at Work

The North Carolina General Assembly convenes in odd-year biennial sessions on the first Wednesday after the second Monday in January. The session is divided into segments with the time set by the general assembly. The governor may call special sessions. Since 1975, the general assembly has met during even numbered years for a shorter session devoted to the budget. Traditionally, the senate and the house meet in their respective chambers on Monday evenings, early afternoons on Tuesday through Thursday, and Friday mornings during the legislative session. Committee meetings are held in the mornings and late afternoons.

The elected members of the general assembly are supported by a staff that is housed under the Legislative Services Commission (LSC). LSC staff conduct legal and financial research, draft bills, and write reports as directed by the general assembly.

Legislative Committees

Deciding what a new law should say is not decided on the floor of the assembly. Writing laws takes place in committees

comprised of members of both houses. Every legislator is appointed to work on several committees.

Standing committees are established in the rules adopted for
each body for a session. Select or one-issue committees are also
convened as needed. Some study committees function between
legislative sessions to complete research and necessary business.
When house and senate drafts of legislation differ, senate and
house leaders meet in conference committees to work out a
compromise (Howard 1990, 20).

The power within the general assembly rests with house and
senate leaders who appoint committee members and assign proposed legislation to particular committees. Appropriation committees are considered to be most "important" because they decide where the state's money will be spent. Other committees,
such as those that regulate large industries, including banking
and insurance, are "important" as well (Howard 1990, 21).

Budget appropriation committees report on the money
needed to continue state programs. Appropriate expansion
budget committees decide how much money can be spent for
existing programs and for new, proposed programs. Finance
committees deal with bond issues, tax collection, and other
matters related to the taxing power of the state or local government. In the senate, the Ways and Means Committee retains
the authority of final review over bills assigned to other money
committees before bills are considered on the senate floor
(Howard 1990, 21).

Most laws dealing with trial procedure and substantive criminal law must pass through the judiciary committees of the
house and senate. The senate has three judiciary committees.
The house has a Judiciary Committee with sub-committees on
Civil and Criminal Justice, Courts and Administrative Hearings, Corrections, Law Enforcement and Public Safety, and
Elections and Constitutional Amendments. The House Appropriations Committee also has a sub-committee for Justice and

Public Safety (Ferrell 1990, 72-74). The house also has a Courts and Justice Committee, which handles matters concerning the administration of the courts, including bills adding judges or magistrates, providing for additional assistant district attorneys, and setting up public defender systems. Usually, before acting on any bill related to administration of the court system, the Courts and Justice Committee or judiciary committees consult with the director of the Administrative Office of the Courts. If these committees decide favorably on a bill requiring expenditure of public funds, the bill is referred to an appropriations committee, which must approve it before it comes to the floor of the legislature for a vote (Brannon 1994, 27).

How A Bill Becomes a Law

The process of lawmaking begins when a legislator (or more than one) sponsors a bill. The bills are drafted by a specialist who writes the bill into the required form. The state attorney general's office, which has authority to draft legislation for state agencies and departments, may also be used to to prepare bills (Howard 1990, 23).

Once the language of the bill has been written, the bill is "pre-filed" by the sponsor by giving a copy to the principal clerk on the day preceding the introduction of the bill. When the time arrives on the calendar for the introduction of bills, the reading clerk reads the bill's title and its number and assigns it to a committee (Howard 1990, 23).

Bills may be introduced in either the house or senate, but the language of the bill must be approved by both houses before the bill can become law. Since only legislators may sponsor legislation, the governor and heads of state agencies must find a

Major Steps in the Legislative Process[1]

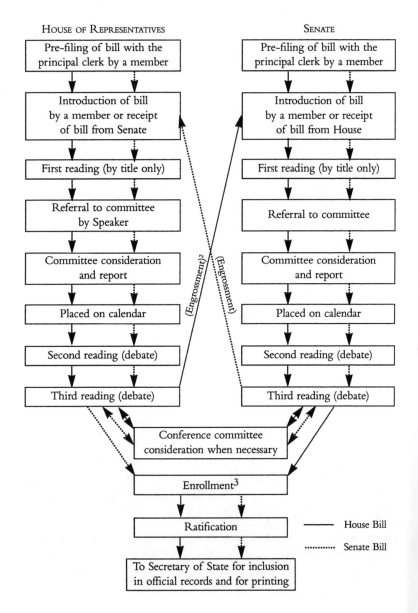

HOUSE OF REPRESENTATIVES

Pre-filing of bill with the
principal clerk by a member

Introduction of bill
by a member or receipt
of bill from Senate

First reading (by title only)

Referral to committee
by Speaker

Committee consideration
and report

Placed on calendar

Second reading (debate)

Third reading (debate)

SENATE

Pre-filing of bill with the
principal clerk by a member

Introduction of bill
by a member or receipt
of bill from House

First reading (by title only)

Referral to committee

Committee consideration
and report

Placed on calendar

Second reading (debate)

Third reading (debate)

(Engrossment)[2]

(Engrossment)

Conference committee
consideration when necessary

Enrollment[3]

Ratification

To Secretary of State for inclusion
in official records and for printing

——— House Bill

············ Senate Bill

willing legislator sponsor to introduce their proposals (Howard 1990, 23).

The appropriate committees review each bill and may schedule public hearings before returning the bill to either the house or senate in which it originated. The committee reports on each bill by giving it one or more of the following recommendations (Howard 1990, 23):

(1) Favorable;

(2) Report without prejudice (house option only);

(3) Postponed indefinitely;

(4) Unfavorable; and

(5) Unfavorable as to the bill but favorable as to a committee substitute prepared by the committee (Howard 1990, 23).

Committees may report a bill without prejudice or a minority report may accompany an unfavorable recommendation. If the minority report is signed by at least three committee members in the senate, or by one-fourth of the committee members in the house present and voting when the bill was considered in committee, a vote may be taken on the floor. If the bill is passed by a majority of those present, the bill is placed on the favorable calendar for consideration (Howard 1990, 23).

If the bill is passed with a favorable recommendation from the committee, then it is considered on the floor of the house

---

Footnotes for **Major Steps in the Legislative Process**

[1] Adapted from a chart by Michael Crowell and Milton S. Heath, Jr., *The General Assembly of North Carolina, A Handbook for Legislators* (Chapel Hill: Institute of Government), fourth edition, 1981, p. 56.

[2] Engrossment is the process of incorporating amendments into the original text of a bill.

[3] Enrollment is the process of retyping a bill in its final form before it is submitted to the presiding officers for their signature.

in which it was introduced. The North Carolina Constitution requires that bills are read three times in each house and are voted on at each reading. The introduction of the bill constitutes the first reading. The second and third readings occur after the bill has been reported favorably out of committee (Howard 1990, 24).

Principal debate on the bill and consideration of proposed amendments to the bill occurs on the second reading, and sometimes on the third reading as well. When the debate ends, the legislators vote on the bill as amended, either by voice or electronic means. The presiding officer declares the bill to have passed or failed on the basis of the required number of votes. An approved bill is sent to the other house for consideration. Bills must be *engrossed* (written into final form) before going to the other house (Howard 1990, 24).

The bill must be passed in identical form by the other house, or a form approved by a joint-committee of conferees from the house and senate. If the conference committee cannot agree, or if either house rejects the conference committee's version, the bill dies. Final passage of the bill is called *ratification*. In this procedure, enrolled bills are signed by the appropriate leaders of both houses. The bill then becomes state law and is delivered to the secretary of state.

Lobbyists and Interest Groups

A lobbyist is a person who attempts to influence specific legislation through personal appeals to legislators. Any citizen may lobby his or her own representative to express personal concerns, and volunteers may lobby on behalf of their own organizations and associations. If a lobbyist is paid to perform these services, however, he or she is required to register, pay a fee, and report to the secretary of state the amount of money spent for lobbying. Although public officials are exempt from registration and reporting requirements, the governor and heads of state agencies are required to file and report to the secretary of state (Howard 1990, 25).

Many organizations and associations hire lobbyists who lobby in full-time, paid positions or lobby to fulfill job description. There are many organizations and associations within criminal justice that take positions of interest to the group and lobby for or against specific bills in the general assembly. Two of those private organizations are: North Carolina Academy of Trial Lawyers and the North Carolina Association of Defense Attorneys (Brannon 1994, 30-31).

Local Law Making

From 1663 to 1776, the colonial assembly created counties and subdivisions of counties as local units of government and authorized these units to make laws applying to people within the prescribed territorial limits. The 1776 Constitution continued this practice. Cities and counties, specifically the boards of commissioners, have lawmaking power delegated to them by the general assembly to make laws extending to the limits of cities and counties. While there are differences between cities and counties, as well as variation among cities and among counties, the process of local lawmaking in North Carolina follows a basic pattern (Ferrell 1990, 15-16).

The governing boards of cities and counties may take several forms of action including ordinances. An *ordinance* is a rule of conduct imposed by a local government upon its residents; it is a legislative act of a local governing board analogous to an act of the general assembly. Ordinances cover matters ranging from zoning, animal control, noise, use of parking lots, loitering, and curfew (Lawrence 1996, 39). For example, a curfew ordinance enacted by the city of Charlotte in 1995 places persons up to age 15 under curfew from 11PM to 6AM on weekday nights and from midnight to 6 AM on weekend nights (Maguire and Pastore 1997, 102).

Ordinances may not be passed in secret. The state's open meetings law requires that all office meetings of public bodies are open to the public. Local governing boards may hold closed sessions only after meeting in an open session to vote on holding a closed session, and then only for particular reasons provided for under statute. Also, an ordinance may be passed at any meeting in which a quorum is present. A *quorum* is a majority of the members of a governing board. In, for example, a city governed by a five-member board of commissioners plus the mayor, four of the six are needed for a quorum. Some ordinances, such as bond ordinances and zoning ordinances, can only be passed after a public hearing

Once an ordinance is adopted, it must be filed in an *ordinance book*. All ordinances are placed in the ordinance book when adopted, and if there is no code, they remain there permanently. The law requires that cities with populations over five thousand codify their ordinances. A *city code* is a compilation of the city's ordinances arranged systematically by subject into chapters or articles; it is the local equivalent of the North Carolina General Statutes. The law prohibits the courts from enforcing any ordinance not found in the ordinance book or code (Lawrence 1996, 43-44).

The Governor's Crime Commission

Although the Governor's Crime Commission does not have lawmaking authority under the state constitution or statute, it does exert a major influence over criminal justice policy within North Carolina. The Governor's Crime Commission is comprised of forty members from all parts of the criminal justice system, local government, the legislature, and citizens. The commission serves by statute as the chief advisory board to the governor and the secretary of the Department of Crime Control and Public Safety. Besides advising the governor, the commission awards federal and state grant money to local criminal justice agencies, and develops a legislative agenda for improving the system. The Governor's Crime Commission Division serves as staff to the commission. The Crime Commission Division researches issues under review by the commission and writes reports for the governor.

The Governor's Crime Commission grew out of the Law and Order Committee, created in 1968 within the Department of Natural and Economic Resources. The Governor's Committee on Law and Order had been established under the federal Omnibus Crime Control and Safe Streets Act of 1968 as a means for allocating federal funds within the state's criminal justice system. In 1977, the Law and Order Committee was transferred to the newly-created Department of Crime Control and Public Safety. The commission has provided a leadership role in criminal justice planning, issue analysis, and program development and coordination. The commission has initiated a number of statewide programs including driving while intoxicated (DWI) legislation, community service restitution, crime prevention/community watch, rape victim assistance, victim compensation, and sentencing reform. The commission also oversees federal grant programs to the state including the Juvenile Justice and Delinquency Prevention Program, the Victims of Crime Act Program, the Justice Assistance Program, and the Drug Enforcement Program (Marcus 1995, 348).

African Americans in the General Assembly

Beginning in 1868 African-American men gained election to the North Carolina General Assembly for the first time. The Republican Party, the party of Abraham Lincoln and Frederick Douglass, included many Black Tar Heels. When the constitutional convention assembled that year, the Republican Party of Black and White legislators, won 107 of 120 seats in the convention; 15 seats were won by Black people (Crow, Escott, and Hatley 1992). Among the lawmakers elected to the 1868 North Carolina General Assembly were twenty Black men, three senators and seventeen representatives. All of them came from eastern counties where the majority of the population was African American (Crow, Escott and Hatley 1992, 85).[2]

One of the most prominent African-American legislators of the Reconstruction Era was James H. Harris. Most likely a freeman of mixed ancestry, Harris had been apprenticed to an upholsterer in Warren County and opened his own business when his employer went bankrupt. Before the Civil War, he traveled throughout the United States, Canada, and West

---

2. Much of the contemporary structure of North Carolina's criminal justice system can be traced to the Republican legislature. The "Negro-Carpetbagger" legislature of 1867 abolished whipping for crimes and provided for establishment of a state penitentiary. There had been no state prison before the war. The legislature ratified the Fourteenth Amendment to the U.S. Constitution which provided for due process and equal protection of the laws for both black and white citizens. With Republicans in the legislature, and in a variety of state and local offices, Black citizens could expect judges and constables to treat them with reasonable fairness and dignity, and not side with former slaveholders and Klan members. The legislature also delivered the initial blow to the Klan in 1869 by making it a crime to wear a mask or disguise on a public highway for the purpose of intimidating a citizen. Following federal legislation in 1871, federal troops and U.S. marshals poured into North Carolina. There were hundreds of arrests and fourteen hundred indictments. Some were tried in the federal courthouse in Raleigh in September 1871 and 1872; about thirty were sentenced to federal prison at Albany, New York (Zuber 1996, 47).

Africa. During the Civil War, he accepted a commission in Indiana to raise the Twenty-eighth Regiment of Colored Troops. After the war, he returned to North Carolina to work for the Freedmen's Bureau and the Union League, a republican organization (Crow, Escott, and Hatley 1992, 85).

Annie Brown Kennedy became the first African-American woman elected to the legislature. In 1971, Governor Robert W. Scott appointed Alfreda Johnson Webb to the state general assembly. Webb, a Guilford County biology teacher, was the first African American woman veterinarian. She was appointed to the North Carolina House of Representatives after the close of the session and lost her bid for reelection to the next term. In 1979, Governor James B. Hunt, Jr. appointed Annie Brown Kennedy, a Forsythe County attorney, and she became the first African American woman to serve in the general assembly. She skipped the 1981-1982 term, won election to the 1983-1984 term, and continued to hold her seat until 1994 (Hammerstein 1995, 108-109).[3]

In the years between 1877 and 1890, Edgecombe County sent eleven different Black men to the state legislature to serve fifteen terms. New Hanover County during the same period elected six Black men to twelve terms. Between 1877 and

---

3. The first woman elected to the N.C. General Assembly was Lillian Exum Clement. Clement, the choice of the Democratic Party in Buncombe County, won election to the House of Representatives in 1921 by a margin of 10,368 to 41. She had lived in Black Mountain, North Carolina, before moving to Asheville where her father worked on George Vanderbilt's famous house. After completing high school and study at Asheville Business College, Clement took a job as a sheriff's deputy and studied law at night with the help of private tutors. She had one of the highest scores on the bar exam out of seventy students and established a law practice—the first woman in North Carolina to do so without men for law partners. When elected to the legislature, she also became the first woman to serve in any state legislature in the South. Rather than seek another term, she directed the State Hospital at Morganton and founded the Asheville Business and Professional Women's Club before her death at age 31 (Hammerstein 1995, 101).

1890, 43 African Americans became state representatives and eleven became state senators. By 1890 when the Era of Jim Crow began, Black lawmakers faced increasing hostility and declining numbers. During the Civil Rights movement of the 1960s, Blacks had to reclaim ground lost during the years so that when Henry Frye gained election in 1969, he was the sole African American in the general assembly. In 1971, Joy J. Johnson joined Frye in the general assembly, and by 1977, there was a total of six African Americans (Jordan 1989, 41). Ten years later, Black legislators had enough clout to rewrite the election laws for superior court judges (they are elected statewide), and added new judgeships, making it possible for African American superior court judges to increase from two to ten in 1988. Representative H.M. "Mickey" Michaux became the longest serving Black legislator, and in 1989, Representative Milton Fitch became the first African-American in this century to preside in the North Carolina House of Representatives (Jordan 1989). In 1978, President Jimmy Carter appointed Mickey Michaux to serve as U.S. attorney for the middle district of North Carolina, the first Black federal prosecutor in the state. In 1983, Henry Frye became the first African-American to sit on the North Carolina Supreme Court.[4]

References

Brannon, Joan G. 1994. *The judicial system in North Carolina.* Raleigh: North Carolina Administrative Office of the Courts.

---

4. The second congressional district, the famous "Black Second," sent to U.S. Congres James E. O'Hara of New Bern from 1883 to 1887 and Henry Plummer Cheatham of Vance County from 1889 to 1893. George H. White of New Bern, who served from 1897 to 1901, proved to be the last African American Congressional member from the South until after the Civil Rights movement in the 1960s (Crow, Escott, and Hatley 1994, 109).

Coates, Albert R. 1976. *Bridging the gap between the law on the books and the law in action.* Chapel Hill: Institute of Government.

Ferrell, Joseph S. 1990. *The general assembly of North Carolina: A handbook for legislators.* Chapel Hill: Institute of Government.

Glick, Henry R. 1993. *Courts, politics and justice.* New York: McGraw Hill.

Hammerstein, Carol. 1995. *Women of the North Carolina General Assembly.* Raleigh: North Carolina Division of Archives and History.

Hogue, Arthur R. 1985. *Origins of the common law.* Indianapolis: Liberty Fund.

Howard, Lucille. 1990. *North Carolina: Our state government.* Charlotte: League of Women Voters of North Carolina Educational Fund.

Jordan, Milton. 1989. Black legislators: From political novelty to political force. *North Carolina Insight* 12:40-58.

Lawrence, David M. 1995. Appendix: County government in North Carolina. In *Municipal government in North Carolina.* (David M. Lawrence and Warren Jake Wicker, eds). Chapel Hill: Institute of Government.

Maguire, Kathleen and Ann L. Pastore. 1997. *Sourcebook of criminal justice statistics 1996.* Washington, D.C.: U.S. Department of Justice, Office of Justice Programs.

Marcus, Lisa A. 1995. *North Carolina manual 1995/1996.* Raleigh: Secretary of State

Orth, John V. 1993. *The North Carolina constitution with history and commentary.* Chapel Hill:University of North Carolina Press.

Price, William S. 1991. *The bill of rights and North Carolina.* Raleigh: North Carolina Division of Archives and History.

Zuber, Richard L. 1996. *North Carolina during reconstruction.* Raleigh: North Carolina Division of Archives and History.

Chapter 4

Law Enforcement

All police officers are law enforcement officials but not all law enforcement officials are police officers. This is true because *police officer* generally refers to the most common law enforcement official, a city employee with a blue uniform, holstered firearm, and a badge, while *law enforcement official* includes employees at all levels of government with powers of arrest or investigation ranging from deputy sheriff to alcoholic beverage control officer. State statutes give "peace officer" status to a variety of government officials not popularly recognized as police officers.

According to the Bureau of Justice Statistics, there are more than 17,000 state and local law enforcement agencies nationwide, which makes the law enforcement in the United States one of the most decentralized in the world. (Other countries in Europe, Latin American, and Asia have national police forces.) Counting 751 constable offices gives Texas the most agencies (about 1,700 altogether); not counting constable offices makes Pennsylvania the state with the highest number of agencies at over 1,100. New York City has the largest police department with more than 35,000 officers although the typical city police department across the county has ten officers or fewer. There are about 450 state and local law enforcement agencies in North Carolina. Charlotte has the largest police department with 900 or so officers (Maguire and Pastore 1997, 37, 46).

Figure 5. Raleigh Police Department, Raleigh. 1895. The Raleigh police department issued hats to officers in 1882; officers provided their own trousers and coats. (Courtesy of the N.C. Division of Archives and History.)

Law enforcement in North Carolina may be divided into three areas: state, county, and city. There are a number of "special forces" that do not fall in any of these three categories, but state, county, and city account for the bulk of law enforcement officials within the state. Special district police include airport police, harbor police, and railroad police (Gray 1998). There are police departments at Asheville Regional, Charlotte/Douglas International, New Hanover International, Piedmont Triad International, Raleigh-Durham, and Smith Reynolds Airports. Harbor police are located at the Port of Wilmington and the U.S. Coast Guard Group at Fort Macon. The Winston-Salem Southbound Railway is one of several railroads in the state with law enforcement agencies. There are also more than seventy-five campus police departments, located at colleges, community colleges, and universities throughout the state.[1]

---

1. Duke University's campus police began in the 1920s (the university

State Agencies

While there are early examples of state law enforcement, state police agencies are relatively recent. The Texas Rangers, established in 1835 (before Texas was a state), possessed some characteristics of state law enforcement organization, although they were a unique and irregular military force more closely resembling a militia or vigilante group (Mirandé 1987, 68). Almost by definition though, state police departments are inventions of the twentieth century, organized in response to the development of automobile traffic, labor violence, and narcotic drugs. The Pennsylvania State Constabulary, established in 1905, is considered to be the first modern state police organization (Walker 1992, 48).[2]

---

was known as Trinity College then). In 1939, the force had four officers and had primary responsibility for traffic control of about three hundred cars on the campus. By 1961, the force had expanded to ten officers and had one patrol car. After 1965, when state law gave campus police the option to cease being special deputies and to acquire full police power to arrest and carry firearms, Duke expanded from Traffic and Security to Public Safety. The Public Safety Department was divided into Police Operations and the Safety and Traffic Divisions. A detective unit was organized in 1972. The department continued to expand, and by 1994, ranked twenty-fifth in size within North Carolina. The Duke police division had sixty-nine police officers, fifty-nine security officers and ten vehicles (King 1997, 168-169).

2. North Carolina had a state police organization founded by Governor William W. Holden during the Reconstruction years after the Civil War. The state general sssembly enacted legislation in 1869 authorizing the governor to "employ a detective force as he may deem sufficient, to pursue and apprehend any felon who is a fugitive from justice" (Massengill 1985, 1869). The force employed twenty-four detectives, about half had been served in either of the Confederate or Union armies, to combat criminal violence of the Ku Klux Klan. (One of them, Stephen A. Douglas Jr. was the son of the U.S. senator from Illinois who debated Abraham Lincoln in the Lincoln-Douglas debates.) Operation of the detective force belonged to Adjutant General Abial W. Fisher, a former Union officer. Fisher instructed the detectives to secretly collect evidence of criminal activities, to take out warrants on suspects, and to make arrests, but only if local law enforcement refused. The

Generally speaking, there are three major categories of state law enforcement. *State police agencies*, which have general jurisdiction statewide for criminal investigation and traffic enforcement; *highway patrols*, which have jurisdiction limited to enforcement of the state's motor vehicle code and traffic cases; and *investigative branches* of agencies, which regulate alcoholic beverages, fish and wildlife, and transportation (Walker 1992, 48). In some states, "state police" refers to a single general service law enforcement organization; in others, there are separate state agencies for criminal investigation and traffic enforcement. North Carolina has the North Carolina Highway Patrol and the North Carolina Bureau of Investigation, along with other regulatory agencies.

State Highway Patrol

The dramatic increase in the number of automobiles led to creation of the North Carolina State Highway Patrol. In 1921, the state general assembly passed the Highway Act which authorized creation of a "unified state highway system" and gave North Carolina national prominence in road construction. In a special session that same year, the general assembly authorized the secretary of state to appoint two or more automobile inspectors to enforce the motor vehicle code and deal with the problem of stolen vehicles, which could be registered in other states with ease. By 1928, there were more autos registered in North Carolina (473,623) than had been registered in the en-

---

detective force lasted until 1870, when Governor Holden authorized use of military force in Alamance and Caswell Counties and denied requests for release under habeas corpus requests for those arrested. Holden's political opponents in the legislature repealed the law that had created Holden's detective force in 1870, and impeached Holden a year later (Massengill 1985).

tire United States in 1910, and the rise of traffic fatalities and property damage motivated the legislature to pass the Highway Patrol Act. The act established the North Carolina Highway Patrol as a division within the State Highway Commission (Ireland 1990, 86).

The State Highway Commission appointed a captain as commanding officer and nine lieutenants. These ten were dispatched to Harrisburg, Pennsylvania, to attend a two-week training school for police (Marcus 1995, 349). Captain Charles D. Farmer, who had been chief of the Raleigh Fire Department, became the first commander. The commission created a headquarters at Raleigh within the State Highway Building and nine patrol districts throughout the state. Each patrol officer re-

Figure 6. N.C. State Highway Patrol Officer assists Governor Luther H. Hodges with auto registration, c. 1955. (Courtesy of the N.C. Division of Archives and History.)

ceived a 61-cubic-inch Harley Davidson motorcycle, and each lieutenant received a Model A Ford coupe. The commander drove a Buick. Each patrol officer received one pair of wool trousers, one blouse, six shirts, leggings, and a cap. Officers wore their own shoes. The uniforms were of gray whipcord with the red insignia of the Highway Patrol on the shoulders; the same insignia was displayed on olive-colored motorcycles and coupes. Patrol officers received individual vehicles, equipped with radios, in 1937 (State Highway Patrol 1979, 169-170, 177).

On July 1, 1929, the original thirty-seven members of the North Carolina Highway Patrol were sworn in at the House Chamber of the Capitol Building by Judge Henry A. Grady of Clinton (State Highway Patrol 1979, 171). State Highway Commissioner R.A. Doughton emphasized that the primary function of the patrol would be aiding motorists highway safety; officers would "as a last resort" arrest citizens. The State Highway Commissioner warned, however, that the patrol would stop overloaded vehicles from tearing up roads and that "drunken drivers who menace the safety of others will be handled with a firm hand" (State Highway Patrol 1979, 171).

The primary responsibility of the Highway Patrol remains that of safeguarding life and property on state highways (Marcus 1995, 349). The Highway Patrol enforces laws and regulations regarding travel on state highways, enforces the state motor vehicle code, and assists the motoring public. In addition, the Highway Patrol is fully authorized to perform other peace officer duties as the governor may direct. The Highway Patrol has statewide jurisdiction; patrol officers have authority to make arrests for any crime committed in their presence or on any state highway (Lynch 1995, 622). Major activities of the Highway Patrol include DWI and drug enforcement. In 1996, Highway Patrol officers made more than 44,000 DWI arrests;

about 3,500 each month. Between 1986 and 1997, the Highway Patrol seized about 1.4 million grams of cocaine, 10,800 pounds of marijuana, and $5.8 million in currency (State Highway Patrol 1997).[3]

The Highway Patrol was transferred from the State Highway Commission to the State Revenue Department in 1933. The Highway Patrol was then transferred to the Department of Motor Vehicles, then the Department of Transportation, before arriving at its present location in the Department of Crime Control and Public Safety in 1977 (Marcus 1995, 349). The Highway Patrol is administratively organized into a headquarters at Raleigh and nine troop locations throughout the state. Headquarters is divided into administrative services, communication/logistics, inspection/internal investigation, training section, zone 1 operations, zone 2 operations, and research and planning.

The State Bureau of Investigation

The State Bureau of Investigation (SBI), North Carolina's version of the FBI and its G-men of national fame, began in 1937 when Governor Clyde R. Hoey received legislative support for a State Bureau of Identification and Investigation (SBI&I). Governor Hoey had made creation of the bureau one of his campaign planks with the promise that the force would be free of political taint and provide scientific and investigative assistance to local law enforcement as needed. The legislation authorizing the SBI financed the agency with half of the proceeds from a special $1 court fee (Brown 1987, 21).[4]

---

3. For a contemporary account of one trooper's experience, see Marie Bartlett, *Trooper Down! Life and Death on the Highway Patrol* (Chapel Hill: Algonquin Books, 1988).

4. Perhaps the greatest manhunt ever conducted in North Carolina began in February of that same year, John Washington "Wash" Turner and William "Bill" Payne escaped with the use of a smuggled gun from Caledonia Prison

Hoey appointed Frederick C. Handy as the first director of the SBI. Handy, who had worked as a government secret service agent during World War I, received desk space on the first floor of the State Highway Building. After employing a secretary and its first agent, the bureau moved into three rented rooms in the annex of the Carolina Hotel. Handy did not hire graduates of the FBI training school as he had hoped, but he did find two former county sheriffs and an ex-police officer for his first three agents. Oscar F. Adkins, senior investigator, had been McDowell County sheriff and an inspector for the North Carolina Prison Department. The agents were to work out of the Raleigh office on request of the governor. From the beginning, Handy emphasized that "the chief concern of the Bureau should be to offer local units an independent agency for the enforcement of the laws and to furnish the work necessary to ensure arrests and convictions." The "physical work of searching and making arrests" should be left to the Highway Patrol, and the "Bureau should not interest itself in liquor control" (Brown 1987, 22).

Farm. The two men, who had been convicted of bank robbery, took along five other prisoners and two hostages: Captain I.D. Hinton, the superintendent, and Steward W.L. Roberts. After looting the prison arsenal and changing into new denims, they left in a laundry truck. The state offered a $100 reward for information leading to their capture and 200 police officers began the search. Within nine hours, all five of the convicts had been captured, excect for Turner and Payne. They released their hostages near Vass, North Carolina, then disappeared in a stolen model A Ford. Turner and Payne were spotted everywhere, but the pair of fugitives eluded capture throughout the Spring. The convicts racked up several more bank robberies and kidnappings despite the entrance of the FBI into the case. In August of 1937, Turner and Payne murdered highway patrolman George Penn near Asheville. Finally, four carloads of FBI agents surrounded the convicts' car outside the Wilrik Hotel in downtown Sanford. Three weeks later, they were tried and sentenced in Buncombe County for the murder of George Penn. Turner and Payne died in the gas chamber at Central Prison in Raleigh on the morning of July 1, 1938 (Cooke 1988, 109-128).

Since 1939, when the bureau joined the new Department of Justice, it has been under direction of the state attorney general. State statutes define the SBI's mission as "securing a more effective administration of the criminal laws of the state" by investigating crimes, identifying and apprehending criminals, and preparing evidence for use in criminal courts; scientifically analyzing evidence; exercising original jurisdiction in certain matters; receiving and collecting criminal justice information for statewide and national distribution; and conducting surveys and studies relating to criminal conspiracy, crime trends, and prevention. The bureau has original jurisdiction in cases of drug offenses, mob violence, election fraud, violations of social security and gaming laws, arson, and theft of state-owned property. The bureau may, on request, assist local law enforcement in identifying and apprehending suspects involving any crime in the state, and in scientific analysis and presentation of evidence to court (Lynch 1995, 623).

Today, the Bureau operates out of a central headquarters in Raleigh. The SBI is divided into three major areas of operation: the Division of Criminal Information, the Crime Laboratory, and Field Investigations.

Division of Criminal Information. The original 1937 act establishing the bureau gave it responsibility for compiling criminal statistics. Later the bureau was relieved of the responsibility, only to have it returned. In 1968, the Governor's Law and Order Committee conducted an extensive survey concerning the need for a central computer network of criminal justice information. The general assembly enacted legislation a year later creating the Police Information Network (PIN) within the Department of Justice. When responsibility for PIN was transferred by order of the attorney general to the SBI in 1985, the Division of Criminal Information (DCI) was created to maintain criminal history information (State Bureau of Investigation 1997, 3).

In addition to maintaining the state's criminal record information, DCI operates a 24-hours-a-day telecommunications center. Local law enforcement has access through DCI to communication networks of other state agencies, the Administrative Office of the Courts (AOC) data processing and State Information Processing System (SIPS) for access to the Division of Motor Vehicles (DMV), and to national networks, such as the National Crime Information Center (NCIC), maintained by the FBI in Washington, DC. NCIC is a nationwide computer network that serves federal, state and local agencies; NCIC contains information to identify wanted and missing persons, and to identify stolen or recovered property across the country (State Bureau of Investigation 1997, 3).

Crime Laboratory. Across the nation, about half of state police agencies operate crime laboratories. The FBI's crime lab, located in Washington, D.C., is the world's largest forensic laboratory, performing more than 1 million examinations every year. The first crime lab in the United States is that of the Los Angeles Police Department (LAPD). The LAPD crime lab was founded in 1923 by August Vollmer, chief of police, from Berkeley, California (Saferstein 1987, 6).

The SBI operates a crime laboratory in Raleigh and a regional facility in Asheville. The lab receives requests for analyses from local law enforcement agencies throughout the state. The SBI crime laboratory is one of the most comprehensive crime laboratories in the nation. Major sections of the laboratory include drug chemistry and toxicology, firearms and toolmarks, latent evidence, questioned documents, serology (including DNA), and trace evidence. The lab has received national recognition for exemplary forensic examinations, analyses, and expert courtroom testimony (McArthur 1996, 39). There is also the Charlotte-Mecklenburg Crime Laboratory in Charlotte, but the SBI maintains the only statewide forensic laboratory service in North Carolina.

Field Division. The field division is composed of SBI agents who conduct criminal investigations. Special agent duties include conducting interviews and interrogations, collecting evidence, testifying in court, and conducting surveillance and uncover investigations. Special agents assist local, federal, and state law enforcement organizations and work with judges and district attorneys. Field agents are assigned to one of eight geographic districts or one of many specialized units within the SBI.

Other Law Enforcement and Regulatory Agencies

In addition to the State Highway Patrol and SBI there are other state law enforcement organizations. A number of these have jurisdiction limited to particular geographic areas, such as the Butner Public Safety Division of the Department of Crime Control and Public Safety and the State Capitol Police, a division of the Department of Administration. The Butner Public Safety Division provides police and fire protection for state facilities at Butner. The State Capitol Police, with police powers throughout Raleigh, provides security and protection for state facilities in Raleigh and investigates crimes committed on state property.

Others are organized to provide law enforcement throughout the state; these include the Division of Alcohol Law Enforcement (ALE) and the Division of Motor Vehicles (DMV). The ALE enforces the alcoholic beverage control laws of the state and was created in 1977 when the Enforcement Division of the State Board of Alcoholic Beverage Control (ABC) was transferred from the Department of Commerce to the newly-formed Department of Crime Control and Public Safety. The Alcoholic Beverage Commission, and over 150 municipal and county boards, are responsible for regulating all aspects of the sale and distribution of alcoholic beverages through about 390 ABC stores throughout the state. No other state has the same system; in each case a vote of the people was required to initiate the system. ABC boards provide licensed outlets with infor-

Table 1: Selected North Carolina Agencies with Regulatory, Protective or Investigatory Functions

Regulatory Agency	Enforcement Activity
Department of the State Auditor	conducts special investigations related to possible embezzlements or misuse of state property
Secretary of State, Securities Division	administers state securities laws that provide for significant investigatory powers in civil and criminal actions
Department of Labor, Occupational Safety and Health Division	investigates complaints by workers and work-related accidents and deaths; conducts general inspections of randomly-picked firms
Department of Insurance, Regulatory/Public Services Group, Special Services Division	licenses and regulates insurance premium finance companies, professional bail bondsmen and runners, and collection agencies and clubs, and investigates all complaints involving these organizations
Department of Health, Environment and Natural Resources; Wildlife Resources Commission	manages and protects wildlife in the state; responsible for boater safety and boat registration; patrols state waters; and issues permits to hunt and fish on state lands and waters
Department of Health and Human Resources, Division of Social Services	enforces laws relating to financial support from absent parents and operates protective services for children at risk of abuse or neglect
Department of Revenue, Field Operations	collects delinquent taxes, examines tax records, and prosecutes for tax fraud
Office of Administrative Hearings, Civil Rights Division	investigates and negotiates resolution to allegations of discrimination against state employees or applicants for state employment

mation about ABC regulations, inspect premises and examine books. ALE agents prepare criminal and regulatory cases, present evidence to court, conduct permit investigations, and conduct undercover investigations. Agents are sworn peace officers and possess authority to arrest and make any investigatory or law enforcement activities for any criminal offense (Marcus 1995, 331, 345).

The DMV regulates ownership and operation of motor vehicles registered in the state and enforces laws applying to drivers and vehicles, including licensing drivers, registering vehicles, and administering safety inspections (Howard 1990, 52). The general assembly created the DMV in 1941 to consolidate services previously delivered by the secretary of state and the Department of Revenue. In 1971, the DMV became part of the Department of Transportation. The DMV is comprised of six major sections including the Enforcement Section. The DMV Enforcement Section patrols highways and rest areas, combats fuel tax evasion, and has a computer system that tracks vehicle theft reports. The Collision Reports Section is the official repository for all vehicle accident reports; all law enforcement agencies in the state file reports with the DMV Collision Reports Section (Marcus 1995, 412).

In addition to these law enforcement organizations, there are a number of other state agencies with regulatory, licensing, and protective functions that conduct investigations and enforce specific provisions of state statutes. A few of these are listed in Table 1.

County Agencies

While county police departments do exist in a few of North Carolina's counties (Gaston), the primary county law enforcement agency is the sheriff. Other county law enforcement officials include the coroner or office of the state medical examiner.

There are one hundred counties in North Carolina and one hundred offices of sheriff, although in Gaston County, the sheriff's duties have been divided. The sheriff retains all the usual sheriff's duties, except for law enforcement, which has been placed with a county police agency under control of the board of county commissioners. Mecklenburg County also had a county police force until 1993, when it merged with the Charlotte Police Department to form a county-wide department under control of the city commissioners (Lawrence 1995, 765).

Sheriff's Departments

The sheriff is oldest law enforcement institution in North Carolina. In 1729, the Lords Proprietors who had obtained the original charter to the Carolina colony from King Charles, sold their interest to the crown and the territory became a royal colony. The colony's royal status led to reform of the courts and law enforcement. In 1738 the assembly replaced the office of provost marshal and his deputies with a sheriff, and created the county sheriff (Spindel 1989, 21).[5]

The colonial sheriffs had many responsibilities for which they received a fee. They executed writs, maintained public accounts, arrested suspects, subpoenaed witnesses, kept prisoners,

---

5. As Professor James M. Campbell of East Carolina University points out, the provost marshal performed some of duties inherited by the county sheriff, but the title has "a distinctly military flavor." The provost marshal, who likely had responsibility for organizing the colonial militia, was not popular with colonists. The preamble to the enabling legislation for sheriffs reads; "Whereas the Office of Provost Marshall hath been found to be very inconvenient in the extended Province, the Deputy Marshall not only neglecting, but frequently refusing to do their duty, to the great delay of Justice, which hath occasioned great Murmurs and Discontents among the Inhabitants of this Province..." (Campbell 1986, 6-7).

carried out sentences, attended county court, summoned juries (and if necessary, filled them out with bystanders), broke up fights and suppressed riots (Spindel 1989, 35). The colonial sheriff was a mans of means and influence. In order to obtain the office of sheriff, the man had to post a bond of at least £500. If suspects tried to flee, the sheriff had authority kill them (Watson 1976; Spindel 1989, 35).

As an elected official, the *sheriff* remains the principal law enforcement officer in the county and a powerful political figure. The state constitution requires that each county elect a sheriff, but does not specify the duties of the office. The sheriff's department continues to carry the responsibilities that existed under common law: serving civil process, investigating crimes, arresting persons, transporting prisoners and the mentally ill, and maintaining the jail. In North Carolina, as in other states, sheriff's duties vary county to county. The sheriff's duties include (Palmiotto 1997, 45):

1. Providing police service in unincorporated areas of the county. This may include road patrol, juvenile services, traffic enforcement, crime investigation, and radio dispatch.

2. Maintaining the county jail and its prisoners, including the jail and work release programs.

3. Executing both criminal and civil processes, including warrants and writs of execution.

4. Serving as court bailiff; providing courtroom security, transporting prisoners, and executing commands of the courts.

5. Attending meetings of the board of county commissioners to maintain order and serving notice and subpoenas.

6. Investigating public offenses. This may include crime laboratory services and crime scene analysis.

7. Serving as a tax collector for the county.

Many sheriff's departments in North Carolina function like municipal police departments, performing basic police tasks and conducting criminal investigations. Although the sheriff's department retains jurisdiction throughout the county, as a practical matter, sheriff's deputies confine their jurisdiction to areas outside the boundaries of municipalities.

The Sheriff's Standards Division, established by the general assembly in 1983, administers programs of the North Carolina Sheriffs' Education and Training Standards Commission. The commission promulgates and oversees standards for employment, training and retention of sheriff's deputies and jailers. The division implements procedures for certification of deputy sheriffs and jailers, and accredits schools that deliver commission-directed training. Also, the division maintains the Sheriffs' Supplemental Pension Fund, which has paid benefits to retired sheriffs since its creation in 1985 (Marcus 1995, 274). There is also the North Carolina State Sheriff's Association, which provides a forum for sheriffs to share common information.

Medical Examiners

Several North Carolina counties still have a *coroner*, an elected official who determines whether a death occurred due to a criminal act (Dellinger, Farb, and Smith 1989, 499). Most counties have a *medical examiner*, a local physician appointed to investigate any death which occurred "under an suspicious, unusual or unnatural circumstance" (Dellinger, Farb, and Smith 1989, 499). Coroners and medical examiners, in counties where there are both, typically coordinate their services.

The office of the coroner existed under the common law. The English coroner was a county official who performed judicial and administrative duties. The coroner's primary judicial duty was to make inquiry into the causes and circumstances surrounding any death within the county that occurred through violence and under suspicious circumstances. The inquiry, called the "coroner's inquest," was held with a jury of persons upon viewing the dead body. Another of the English coroner's judicial duties was to inquire into shipwrecks. The coroner had to certify whether it was a wreck or not; who was in possession of the goods; and if there was a treasure trove on board, who knew about the treasure and where they might have hidden it (Black 1968, 408).

When the office of coroner passed into the American criminal justice system, the coroner became an elected official chiefly concerned with determining the cause of suspicious deaths (Black 1968, 408). In about half of the states, the coroner is an elected official; in the majority of these, the office of coroner is mentioned in the state constitution. Coroners do not necessarily possess a medical degree or credentials of a certified pathologist. The U.S. Department of Justice estimates that there are about 1,600 coroners or medical examiners in the United States (Walker 1992, 47). In 1939, Maryland became the first state in the country to establish a state-wide medical examiner system. The medical examiner—who is a medical doctor—has replaced the coroner in about sixteen states, including North Carolina.

North Carolina's state-controlled medical examiner system began in 1955. In that year, the general assembly enacted legislation allowing counties to appoint local officials as medical examiners, however; few counties accepted the invitation. In 1967 the general assembly mandated that counties participate in the state program. The present system came into being a year later when it received funding (Dellinger, Farb, and Smith 1989, 499). The chief medical examiner (CME) is employed by the Division of Health Services, Department of Health and Human Resources, and is appointed by the secretary. Presently the CME has a staff of twenty-five including five pathologists. The CME appoints at least one medical examiner for each county (currently there are about six hundred medical examiners in the state) who serves for a three-year term. By statute, the CME must select the nominee of the county medical society, or if there is none, any county physician who will accept the appointment. The CME supervises medical examiners from an office in Chapel Hill, near pathology services at the University of North Carolina-Chapel Hill School of Medicine (Dellinger, Farb, and Smith 1989, 500).

The county medical examiner must be notified of deaths occurring under suspicious circumstances; such as deaths resulting from violence, poisoning, accident, suicide, and homicide and deaths occurring suddenly while under care of a physician, or occurring in a jail or other correctional facility. The obligation to report typically falls to doctors, nurses, and police officers. Anyone who discovers any part of a human body must also report. The medical examiner has subpoena power, and can order an autopsy and inspect the deceased's medical records. The medical examiner closes the inquiry by completing a death certificate stating the cause of death and giving an opinion on whether it resulted from an accident, suicide, homicide or undetermined cause. About 15% of deaths in the state are investigated by the medical examiner each year (Dellinger, Farb, and Smith 1989, 501).

Municipal Police

History of Municipal Police

While the sheriff in colonial North Carolina occupied the primary law enforcement role in the county, the routine, ordinary tasks of law enforcement in the towns fell to the *constable*. Unlike the sheriff and other prominent officials, such as justices of the peace and clergy, the constable represented the humbler elements of colonial society. Appointed by the county court, the constable posted no bond but merely had to be "discreet" (Spindel 1989, 36). English common law required that persons appointed for the office meet three basic qualifications: integrity, knowledge, and ability. The constable in colonial North Carolina had to meet a fourth: literacy. Constables were drawn from farmers, ferry keepers, tavern keepers, and artisans (Watson 1991, 10).

The Fundamental Constitutions of 1669 created the office of constable and directed appointment of six constables, one for each of the precincts into which the colony was divided. Subsequent legislation allowed county magistrates to appoint as many constables each year as needed. Constabulary fees paled in comparison to the sheriff's fees, but constables did receive additional financial reward in the form of relief from paying county taxes, any taxes assessed for road work, and so on (Watson 1991, 8). During their one-year term, constables executed warrants and took suspects into custody (keeping them in their own home, if necessary). They assisted with juries, broke up fights, disarmed dangerous persons, suppressed riots, and generally dealt with all manner of "rogues, vagabonds and idle persons" (Spindel 1989, 36). "Taverns, exceedingly popular and numerous in North Carolina," Professor Alan Watson, a historian at University of North Carolina–Wilmington, explains "were often scenes of roisterous behavior that occasioned calls for constables" (Watson 1991, 10).

In addition, the constable had the responsibility for organizing the night watch. While on watch duty, citizen patrollers protected residents and property from lawbreakers, and also sounded early warning of fires, a constant threat to homes and stores in early North Carolina towns. The laws of 1822 authorized the commissioners of New Bern "to class the free white males, inhabitant of said town, over the age of eighteen years, into companies of five or more for the purpose of watching said town at night." As cities and towns grew, the night watch developed into municipal police departments. Although as late as 1970, Charlotte retained authorization to call citizens into night watch service either alphabetically or by lot (Coates 1976, 293).

In Raleigh, seven commissioners appointed by the general assembly selected the intendant of police (the title changed to mayor in 1857). The intendant of police employed and paid patrollers or organized citizens to take turns on the night watch. The court appointed city constables, who served as the daytime police, and brought lawbreakers before the intendant of police. The intendant tried and sentenced lawbreakers. The commissioners alternated between paid patrollers and the citizen watch until after the Civil War, when the citizen watch was abolished and a full-time paid police force established. According to city tradition, John Haywood, the state treasurer from 1787 to 1827 and one of Raleigh's first seven commissioners, served as the first intendant. Constable James H. Murray, known as "fearless and incorruptible," survived having his head split open by a rock-wielding defendant during trial to become one of the city's most legendary law enforcement officials (Raleigh Police Department n.d.).

Raleigh organized a department of paid police officers after the Civil War. In 1875, the city employed ten police officers for night service and six for daytime hours. The sixteen men were divided into three sections, each serving eight hours duty and sixteen hours off duty. Until 1899, when the city employed a sanitary inspector, law enforcement responsibilities included enforcement of sanitary ordinances and regular inspection of privies. Police officers received hats in 1882, but did not wear the badges and uniforms needed to be "readily recognized by the public as peace officers" until 1913. About 1910, the city installed an electric call-box system, the same year the governor participated in a demonstration of the "wireless" at the state capitol (Coates 1976, 139). In 1926, the department had two patrol cars, and officers had to use their personal automobiles. One-way radios arrived in 1934, followed by Maude Barnes, the first policewoman one year later. Two-way radios arrived in the 1940s, and the department began a records section in 1950.

Prior to that, officers kept their own written records in pockets and desk drawers (Raleigh Police Department n.d.).

Organization of the Municipal Police

State statutes confer law enforcement powers to cities. The law allows a city "to appoint a chief of police and to employ other police officers" (N.C. Gen Stat. §160a-281). The law further allows the city to employ non-sworn personnel but who must complete the same training as sworn officers and who answer to the chief of police (Lynch 1995, 621). A police officer within the city's corporate limits possesses all the powers vested in peace officers by statute and common law. Police officers have the power to serve criminal and civil process, and to enforce city ordinances and the laws of the state. Jurisdiction extends to the city's corporate limits, within one mile of the city limits, and on any property owned or leased by the city (Lynch 1995, 621).

The Raleigh Police Department is one of the largest in the state. The department was organized in 1795 when seven city commissioners were appointed by the general assembly "to make laws for the government of the city and also choose an intendant of police charged with the execution of the laws" (Raleigh Police Department n.d.). When first established in 1795, the city encompassed only a few hundred acres and had a population of less than six hundred. Currently, Raleigh has a population of 260,000 and covers over more than 105 square miles. The police department has more than 720 positions; about 600 sworn personnel and 100 non-sworn personnel. The department is administratively organized into four divisions and the office of the chief (Raleigh Police Department 1997):

Office of the Chief. The chief of police coordinates all activities, including operations, personnel, policy making, and fiscal management. The chief's office also includes the police attorney and internal affairs unit.

Field Operations. Field operations conducts the 24-hour patrol component and responds to calls concerning crimes, service, and emergencies. There are five platoons within this division; each platoon is comprised of a captain, a lieutenant, five sergeants, and about forty officers.

Special Operations. Special Operations includes specialized units, organized for community policing and tactical response, of sworn and non-sworn personnel. This division includes the Selective Enforcement Unit (which responds to hostage situations, conducts high-risk searches, etc.), Drug Enforcement Units, Community Police Assistance Stations (located in public housing areas), Park Police, the K-9 Unit, and other units.

Investigative Division. Investigators within this division conduct follow-up investigations and initial investigation involving drugs, organized crime and other criminal activity. The division has three lieutenants who oversee squads of five to nine investigators. A few of these squads are Drugs and Vice, Robbery Squad, Assault Squad, Auto Crimes, Residential Burglaries, Juvenile Squad, and Youth Violence Intervention Unit.

Administrative Division. This division, staffed by a major, captain, lieutenant, management analyst, and secretary who are responsible for the management of information systems, coordination of planning and budgetary functions, compliance with professional standards, and training. Some of the positions within this Division are: central records, accreditation, research and planning, crime analysis, evidence control, and court liaison.

The offices of the chief and all divisions are located at headquarters. Satellite stations are located in various parts of the city, along with several substations and community policing stations.[6]

---

6. For an overview of community policing in North Carolina, and descriptions of efforts in Lumberton and Cumberland County, see Champion (1998).

The Raleigh Police Department is exceptional in the variety of initiatives, the complexity of its organizational structure, and its sheer size. There about five hundred cities in North Carolina; about 325 of these have police departments. While the most visible departments are those in the state's largest cities, these are the exception: only thirteen cities have departments of 100 officers or more. The majority of municipal departments in the state (about 60%) employ ten or fewer sworn officers (Lynch 1995, 621).

More than 450 cities in North Carolina have populations of 10,000 or less; 220 of these cities have populations under 1,000. A number of these have no police department. Small cities may contract with the county or with other cities, for law enforcement. In agreements with other cities law enforcement officers have the same authority to make arrests in the requesting city as would law enforcement officers of that city (Lynch 1995, 621).

African Americans and Law Enforcement

"The slave patrol," writes historian Marvin Dulaney (1996, 2) "was the first distinctively American police system, and it set the pattern of policing that Americans of African descent would experience throughout their history in America." By the middle of the eighteenth century, every southern colony had a slave patrol. The patrols were authorized to stop, beat, and even kill African slaves caught off plantations without a pass, engaged in illegal activities, or attempting to escape. Although the slave patrol was primarily a rural enterprise, patrollers policed specific geographical areas called "beats." Paramilitary in nature, the patrols often cooperated with militias in southern colonies to suppress slave insurrections. North Carolina's general assembly authorized slave patrols to search slave quarters for weapons at least four times a year. As elsewhere in the South, state courts granted wide discretion to patrollers, instructing juries not to inquire too closely into the force used (Crow, Escott, and Hartley, 1992,6; Michael Kay and Cary 1986).

Following the Civil War, the entire nation had to adjust to the change in status of African Americans from slaves to free persons. The status of free Blacks improved in Southern cities. In almost every case, Black officers were appointed by Republican administrations to protect Black Americans from terrorism and mob violence of the Reconstruction Era (Dulaney 1996, 13). One of Governor William W. Holden's detectives in 1869, Alexander Bryant, was "mulatto"; he was a laborer from Wilmington (Massengill 1985, 454). By the 1870s, African Americans served as police officers in cities across the South, and in Raleigh, an African American was even appointed assistant chief. The 1868 board of city commissioners included two Black Americans, James H. Harris and Handy Lockart. The board named Major William H. Martin as chief, and Bryan Lunn, an African American, as his assistant. Another African American, B.H. Dunston, succeeded Lunn. Under Chief William H. Martin, the paid night watch consisted of three White officers and three Black officers: Wesley Hunter, Simon Craven, and Robert Clawson (Raleigh Police Department n.d.).

During the era of Jim Crow, few African Americans served on police forces in southern cities. In 1895, coalition politics between African Americans and Populists allowed a few Blacks to reclaim police jobs in Wilmington and New Bern, North Carolina. However, the arrest powers of Black police were restricted: Black police could not arrest Whites, and they patrolled only in areas inhabited by Blacks (Dulaney 1996, 15). By the early twentieth century, Blacks had to "integrate" police forces all over again. The first Post-Reconstruction African-American police officers were hired in Charlotte in 1941, Raleigh in 1942, and Durham in 1944 (Dulaney 1996, 118).

By the 1940s, however, police chiefs throughout the South praised the performance of Black police officers and their impact on crime in African American communities. In Greensboro, six of the first African Americans hired in 1944 and 1945 attended college. The city manager and police chief selected the "best men" for the job with the assistance of Greensboro's Black community leaders. Similar procedures were used in Charlotte (Dulaney 1996, 54). Greensboro city officials had hired the first two African American police officers in 1944 and were so pleased with the "Negro police experiment" that the city council authorized hiring an additional two a year later (Dulaney 1996, 53). By 1959, Greensboro had eight Black police officers (Dulaney 1996, 119). It was the era of "separate and unequal" and Black officers were assigned to the "Black beat" and "Black watch."

Equality within police departments was a slow and uncertain process. In 1953, the Negro Law Enforcement Association was organized in North Carolina, eighteen years after the first such organization, the Texas Negro Peace Officer's Association was organized in Houston. In 1956, Charlotte appointed its first African American police sergeant (Dulaney 1996, 120). Curtis Douglas, who had been a police officer with the city of Salisbury, became one of the first Black special agents of the State Bureau of Investigation in 1971. A graduate of Livingstone College, Douglas worked undercover drug investigation, arson investigation and with the DARE program while at the SBI (Douglas 1997). By the 1990s, African Americans had reached the hightest positions in law enforcement. In 1994, Mitchell W. Brown became chief of the Raleigh Police Department. Under Brown's leadership, the department carried out a major reorganization in order to accomodate growth in the number of specialized units within the department's community policing initiative. In 1993, Thurman B. Hampton, a graduate of N.C. A&T State University, was appointed Secretary of Crime Control and Public Safety.

References

Black, Henry C. 1968. *Black's law dictionary.* St. Paul, Minn.: West Publishing.

Brown, Dick. 1987. The formative years: SBI. *Popular Government* 52:19–27.

Campbell, James M. 1986. Is there historical evidence of respect for the police in North Carolina? *N.C. Criminal Justice Letter & Review* [North Carolina Justice Academy] 4:6–10.

Coates, Albert R. 1976. *Bridging the gap between the law on the books and the law in action.* Chapel Hill: Institute of Government.

Cooke, W. Alfred. 1988. *Caledonia: From antebellum plantation to state prison farm 1713–1988.* Raleigh: Sparks Press.

Champion, Darl H. 1998. "The police are the public": Community policing in North Carolina. *Popular Government* 63:18–28.

Crow, Jeffrey J., Paul D. Escott, and Flora J. Hartley. 1992. *A history of African Americans in North Carolina.* Raleigh: North Carolina Division of Archives and History.

Dellinger, Anne M., Robert L. Farb, and Michael R. Smith. 1989. The criminal justice system. In *County government in North Carolina* (A Fleming Bell, II). Chapel Hill: Institute of Government

Douglas, Curtis. 1997. *The overcoming: The life story of an African-American pioneer in North Carolina law enforcement.* n.p.: Parker-Thomas Press.

Dulaney, W. Marvin. 1996. *Black police in America.* Bloomington, Ind.: Indiana University Press.

Ennis, Alan M. 1996. Should a law enforcement agency seek national accreditation? *Popular Government* 61:14–20.

Gray, Jeffrey P. 1998. Company police in North Carolina: Much more than "rent-a-cops," *Popular Government* 62:25–37.

Howard, Lucille. 1990. *North Carolina: Our state government.* Raleigh: League of Women Voters of North Carolina Education Fund.

Ireland, Robert E. 1990. *Entering the auto age: The early automobile in North Carolina, 1900-1930.* Raleigh: North Carolina Division of Archives and History.

King, William E. 1997. *If gargoyles could talk: Sketches of Duke University.* Durham:Carolina Academic Press.

Lawrence, David M. 1995. Appendix: County government in North Carolina. In *Municipal Government in North Carolina.* (David M. Lawrence and Warren Jake Wicker, eds.) Chapel Hill: Institute of Government.

Lynch, Ronald G. 1995. Law Enforcement, In *Municipal government in North Carolina* (David M. Lawrence and Warren Jake Wicker, eds). Chapel Hill: Institute of Government

Maguire, Kathleen and Ann L. Pastore. 1997. *Sourcebook of Criminal Justice Statistics 1996.* Annapolis Junction, Md.: U.S. Department of Justice, Office of Justice Programs.

Marcus, Lisa A. 1995. *North Carolina manual 1995-1996.* Raleigh: Secretary of State.

Massengill, Stephen E. 1985. The detectives of William W. Holden, 1869-1870. *North Carolina Historical Review* 62:449-487.

McArthur, John R. 1996. The office of the attorney general and the North Carolina Department of Justice. *Popular Government* 62:37-40.

Michael Kay, Marvin L. and Lorin Lee Cary. 1986. Slave runaways in colonial North Carolina, 1748-1775. *North Carolina Historical Review* 63:1-39.

Mirandé, Alfredo. 1987. *Gringo justice.* Notre Dame, Ind.: University of Notre Dame Press.

Palmiotto, Michael. 1997. *Policing: Concepts, strategies and current issues in American police forces.* Durham: Carolina Academic Press.

Raleigh Police Department. 1997. *Employee Orientation Book.* Raleigh: City of Raleigh.

Raleigh Police Department. n.d. History of the Raleigh police department. Raleigh: City of Raleigh.

Saferstein, Richard. 1987. *Criminalistics: An introduction to forensic science.* Englewood Cliffs, N.J.: Prentice-Hall.

Spindel, Donna J. 1989. *Crime and society in North Carolina, 1663-1776.* Baton Rouge: Louisiana State University Press.

State Bureau of Investigation. 1997. *State of North Carolina uniform crime report 1996.* Raleigh: North Carolina State Bureau of Investigation.

State Highway Patrol. 1997. Patrol activities. *North Carolina Trooper* 10(1).

State Highway Patrol. 1979. *State highway patrol: Fiftieth anniversary 1929-1979.* Raleigh: North Carolina Department of Crime Control and Public Safety.

Walker, Samuel. 1992. *The police in America.* New York: McGraw Hill.

Watson, Alan D. 1991. The constable in colonial North Carolina. *North Carolina Historical Review* 68:1-16.

Watson, Alan D. 1976. The appointment of sheriffs in colonial North Carolina: A reexamination. *North Carolina Historical Review* 53:385-398.

Chapter 5

Prosecution and Defense

Prosecuting and defense attorneys are required positions for the adversarial process. The prosecutor, who represents the government in criminal cases, uses police arrest reports to prepare formal documents charging suspects with crimes. Prosecutors initiate the court process by filing these papers with the clerk, an event known as a *case filing*. The defense attorney, who represents the defendant, may be paid by the defendant or by the government. Government-paid attorneys, known as *public defenders*, or panel attorneys, represent indigent defendants. *Indigents* are those defendants too poor to pay for an attorney and are entitled to legal counsel at public expense.

North Carolina's system for prosecution is similar to that of other states. In North Carolina the state attorney general has authority to prosecute criminal cases, but most prosecutions are conducted by local elected officials. North Carolina's local prosecutors are called *district attorneys*. They have responsibility for bringing cases in both misdemeanor and felony courts within the state. District attorneys in North Carolina do, however, control the criminal trial calendar, a responsibility that local prosecutors in no other state possess. Court calendaring refers to the system of scheduling cases in trial court. In most states, trial judges set the criminal calendar.

North Carolina's public defender system resembles those of other states as well. While the majority of criminal defendants in North Carolina receive legal counsel at public expense, public defenders actually exist in only a handful of counties. This is true because "public defender" technically refers to a program or organization typical in larger, urban counties, while the majority of defenders in rural counties receive counsel from local attorneys in private law practice who are assigned by the court. While there are more than ten thousand active, resident attorneys in North Carolina, there are fewer licensed attorneys relative to the state's population, than in most other states. In fact, North Carolina had, at the beginning of this decade, the lowest concentration of attorneys of any state in the United States. The ratio of residents to lawyers in North Carolina was 658:1—one attorney for every 658 people. By comparison, this ratio was 189:1 in New York, 299:1 in California, and 389:1 in Florida. South Carolina, Arkansas, West Virginia, and South Dakota also have low numbers of lawyers relative to their populations (American Bar Association 1992, 16).

The Office of the Attorney General

In a few states—Alaska, Connecticut, Delaware, New Jersey, and Rhode Island— prosecutors are not locally elected officials. Rather, chief prosecutors are either appointed by, or are members of, the state attorney general's office (Neubauer 1996, 81). In North Carolina, the primary responsibility for prosecuting crimes in the state's trial courts resides with the district attorney, but the attorney general retains the power of prosecution. The attorney general of North Carolina is the elected head of the Department of Justice.

Attorney general is an office of government with roots extending to medieval England. English kings appointed legal agents to represent the interests of the Crown in legal proceedings. The office found its way to the English colonies, and prior to 1767, North Carolina shared with South Carolina a single attorney general who served as a representative of the attorney general of England. After the Revolution, the newly formed states retained the office of attorney general with much the same power granted at common law but as a representative of the people, not a king. The attorney general of North Carolina retains the common law powers of the English attorney general. North Carolina is among the states to have incorporated the common law powers of attorney general into its state constitution (Marcus 1995, 268-269).

The attorney general's chief responsibility is to represent the state in all actions in the appellate courts in which the state has an interest or is a legal party. When requested by the governor, secretary of state, treasurer, or other state official, the attorney general prosecutes or defends all lawsuits related to their departments. The attorney general represents state institutions, such as the Department of Correction and the Department of Crime Control and Public Safety, when requested to do so by the official head of the department (Marcus 1995, 268). The Correction Section within the Criminal Division of the attorney general's office, for example, represents the Department of Correction by providing legal counsel and representation on matters involving prison regulations, personnel actions, and statutory interpretations (Marcus 1995, 266).

Similarly, the attorney general consults with and advises judges, district attorneys, magistrates, and municipal and county attorneys when requested. The opinions of the attorney general, when formally written down, have the force of law. The opinion of the attorney general has the force of law whenever an interpretation is requested or on those matters not covered by statute, opinion, or regulatory law. The attorney general may intervene in proceedings before any courts, regulatory officers, agencies, or bodies, either state or federal, on behalf of the public interest (Marcus 1995, 269).

The attorney general also has the authority to initiate proceedings before courts, officers, agencies, or bodies on behalf of the state, its agencies, or citizens in all matters of the public interest. The Special Prosecutions Section, located within the Criminal Division, prosecutes or assists in the prosecution of criminal cases upon request of district attorneys or upon the approval of the attorney general (Marcus 1995, 270).

Organizationally, the Office of the Attorney General is divided into two major areas: The Legal Services Area and the Law Enforcement Area. Legal Services is subdivided into five divisions: Criminal, Civil Trade and Commerce, Administrative, and Special Litigation. The law enforcement area consists of the SBI, the Training and Standards Division, and the Law Enforcement Liason Section (Marcus 1995, 269-270).

The District Attorney

History and Present Organization

Across the country, the local prosecutor is known as county attorney, state's attorney, prosecuting attorney, or some combination of these titles (Neubauer 1996, 81). In North Carolina, prosecutors are known as *district attorneys*. The North Carolina Constitution (ART. IV, SEC. 18, subsection 1) authorizes the general assembly to divide the state into prosecutorial districts and to provide for the election of district attorneys in each district.

With one exception, these districts coincide with the districts established for district court. There is great variation across these districts in both geography and population. District 26, Mecklenburg County, has the largest population; it has one district attorney and twenty-three full-time assistant district attorneys. District 2, on the other hand, encompasses five counties (Martin, Beaufort, Tyrell, Hyde and Washington); it has one

Figure 7. Second-floor courtroom, Sampson County Courthouse, Clinton. Originally constructed in 1904, the courthouse was given a colonial design during a 1939 renovation.

district attorney and four assistant district attorneys (Brannon 1994, 34,37). Prosecutorial districts, like district court districts, have changed often with legislative action and growth in the state population.

In 1963, when the general assembly created the North Carolina Courts Commission to revise the state's judicial system, there were two local prosecutors. The Office of Solicitor prosecuted crimes in superior court and the Office of District Court Prosecutor prosecuted crimes in district court. In its review of this system of prosecution, the Courts Commission recommended an overhaul.

The Courts Commission found that prosecution of crimes in superior and district court was out-of-date and inefficient. Solicitors were part-time officials. While all received the same salary, some devoted time to their own law practice in addition to their public duties. There were fewer solicitor districts, which frequently overlapped two or more judicial districts, and led to confusion and time conflicts in scheduling cases. The commission recommended that a number of prosecutorial districts be added to equal the number of judicial districts. Solicitors were made full-time state employees and districts with high caseloads received assistant solicitor positions. The Office of District Court Prosecutor was merged into the District Attorney's Office, and the office became responsible for prosecuting all crimes in all trial courts within the state. Solicitors were renamed district attorneys in 1974 (Hinsdale 1981, 47).

District attorneys in North Carolina possess great discretionary authority. They have full control over deciding which cases to prosecute, which cases to accept guilty pleas for lesser offenses than those for which defendants are indicted, and over the scheduling of cases. Even if the prosecution decides to take a case, there is still a great deal of discretion in whether to accept a case for prosecution, in the selection of charges to file, negotiating pleas with defense counsel, in the level of case preparation, and in making recommendations to the judge about bail and sentencing.

Duties of the District Attorney

The primary duty of each district attorney is to prosecute all criminal cases filed in the trial courts (both superior and district) in the prosecutorial district. The district attorney's other duties include performing duties related to the appellate division as required by the attorney general, advising law enforcement officers, representing the state in juvenile delinquency cases, and preparing the criminal trial docket.

Case Screening. Not all persons arrested on felony charges are prosecuted. In many cases, the decision to prosecute is automatic, such as, cases in which the evidence is strong, or involve serious charges. The decision to prosecute is based on a combination of the seriousness of the offense and the strength of the evidence (if there are credible witnesses).

The criteria used in case screening, however, is seldom written policy. Few prosecutors have written guidelines (Galloway 1985, 30). When asked to explain the rationale for decisions, prosecutors indicate that case screening, like medical diagnosis, involves both "science and craft." Experienced prosecutors know how to mix legal requirements with good sense (Forst 1983, 2). Prosecution also reflects the district attorney's personal philosophy, the community standards, and organizational resources.

In North Carolina, as elsewhere, the majority of cases are settled by pleas rather than trial.[1] The defendant pleads guilty to an offense for which the punishment is less than the maximum for the offense or offenses as charged. Both prosecution and defense agree to the guilty plea rather than face the uncertainty, time and expense of adjudication. The extent to which trials are used varies across districts (Galloway 1985, 29).

Calendaring. North Carolina is the only state in which prosecutors control the criminal court calendar. This practice dates to 1949 when the general assembly enacted legislation for a uniform system of criminal trial calendaring. Prior to this, there was no uniform system; each county court maintained its own system. Between 1915 and 1937, the general assembly enacted separate local calendar statutes for twenty-one counties. Most of these statutes empowered the clerk of superior court

---

1. Plea bargaining is not a new practice; plea bargaining was common in colonial North Carolina. Court records from the era indicate that men and women claiming innocence were less likely to seek a bench trial than to plead guilty and "humbly move the Court for mercy." When a felony defendant approached the bar, the indictment was read and the defendant was asked for a plea. If the defendant confessed, the clerk recorded the admission and the words "and no more done till Judgment." When the defendant and accuser reached an agreement before pleading, the defendant pleaded guilty and paid "a small Fine" (Spindel 1989, 39-40).

to set the trial calendar and notify the prosecutor and defense of the order of cases. The 1949 legislation followed the recommendations of a commission for the improvement of justice in North Carolina chaired by Sam Ervin, a justice of the state supreme court. In assigning the calendar to prosecutors, Ervin's commission sought to reduce the inconvenience of witnesses awaiting trial (Hammer 1994, 2-3).

In recent years, this practice has generated considerable controversy. State statutes (N.C. Gen. Stat. § 7A-61, § 7A-49.3, and § 15A-931) empower district attorneys in North Carolina to prepare the calendar of criminal cases to be tried at each session of court; decide the order in which cases on the calendar are set for trial; and dismiss pending cases, whether set for trial or not, to a later time (Hammer 1994, 2-3). Stanley Hammer, an assistant public defender in High Point, argues that "the concentration of these powers in one party's hands has strained the values that are fundamental to a fair adversarial criminal process" (Hammer 1994, 3). By setting a case for trial during one week of court rather than another, prosecutors may place the case before a judge more likely to rule in their favor. Prosecutors may place the case on the calendar and not call it for trial, and coerce a defendant into a plea bargain. The practice makes it too easy to abuse; by denying a criminal defendant the right to a speedy trial, undermining the defendant's due process rights, and compromising the powers of the judiciary. Hammer argues that calendar control should be vested in the court, either in judges or trial court administrators (Hammer 1994, 5, 8).

Thomas J. Keith, Forsythe County District Attorney (District 21), argues that calendar control allows the state court system to deal with the number of cases. "North Carolina prosecutors handle double the cases with half the resources of other states because of the efficiency resulting from this authority [district attorney's authority to calendar cases for trial,]" (Keith

1995, 2). North Carolina spends less for criminal prosecutions than most other states, and prosecutorial control over the court calender enables prosecutors to handle a much higher caseload than their counterparts in other states. Keith contends that shifting calendaring authority to judges would interfere with judicial rotation, and the control over calendars by judges and trial court administrators in civil cases has not led to a comparable difference in reducing delay (Keith 1995, 13-14).

There is no consensus among district attorneys on the issue of calendar control. The largest number support calendar control by prosecutors; district attorneys are concerned that transferring control to judges will increase the problems associated with coordinating lay and law enforcement witnesses. Some district attorneys advocate developing a system of "shared control" and a smaller number are willing to let anyone have control who is "foolish" enough to want it. The Victims Rights Amendment, passed by popular referendum in 1996, also creates notification and information-gathering requirements for district attorneys that complicate efforts to share or transfer calendar control (Gore 1998, 16).

The District Attorney's Office

The district attorney is elected in a partisan election by the voters within the prosecutorial district for a four-year term. Although knowledge of the law was always a necessity, legal training for district attorneys did not become a requirement until 1983. The law license became a formal requirement for district attorneys in North Carolina in 1980 (Orth 1993, 116).

In single county districts, the district attorney's office is located in one place. In these counties, the district attorney's office is located in the courthouse. In some of these counties, the district attorneys share office space with judges or clerks due to lack of space. In others, county commissioners have secured other space. In multicounty districts, the district attorney's office is located in one county and prosecutors "ride circuit" to the others. In others, the district attorney may maintian multiple offices, a central office and satellite offices (Galloway 1985, 31).

Each district has two or more *assistant district attorneys* (depending on the caseload), who serve at the pleasure of the district attorney. Each district is authorized to have an administrative assistant, who may or may not be a licensed attorney, to aid in office administration and calendaring of cases, and a victim-witness assistant. Each district also has a staff investigator.

The number of staff positions (assistant district attorney, administrative assistant, investigator) is assigned by the state general assembly. The number of secretarial positions is assigned by the Administrative Office of the Courts. There are no state-mandated job descriptions for these positions, however, so district attorneys exercise great flexibility in assignment of duties. In larger districts, administrative assistants function as office managers and develop the trial calendar. In others, they function as legal assistants. In still others, they function as a secretary in a satellite office (Galloway 1985, 29).

Assistant district attorneys follow the same flexibility. District attorneys may assign assistant district attorneys solely to district or superior court. Other district attorneys assign new assistants to district court, and "move them up" to superior court. Some district attorneys use *vertical prosecution* in which an assistant receives a case in district court and remains with it until it is disposed of in superior court. In other districts, assistant district attorneys rotate every two or three weeks through superior and district court assignments (Galloway 1985, 32). In some larger districts, assistant district attorneys may specialize in particular kinds of cases, such as juvenile court. Most district attorneys give their assistants full authority within a general framework to negotiate guilty pleas (Galloway 1985, 33).

Relations with Other Agencies

The district attorney's office must work productively with other agencies of criminal justice, particularly law enforcement. Law enforcement officials rely on prosecutors to file charges against suspects they identify and to set the criminal calendar. District attorneys must rely on the information contained in arrest reports, and on the evidence gathered through police investigation, to prepare charging documents and bring judicial proceedings.

In single-county districts, the district attorney works with a few law enforcement organizations. In multicounty districts, district attorneys must work with many more law enforcement organizations. In one prosecutorial district, there are twenty one separate law enforcement organizations. Some district attorneys convene meetings, others send memos to communicate policies and procedures. Some district attorneys assign prosecutors, on a rotating basis, to meet with arresting officers at the point of intake and to discuss the case with officers as they come off duty. Many prosecutors have designed their own police report forms to help ensure that material is developed and presented in a uniform manner (Galloway 1985, 34).

In Pitt County (District 3A), District Attorney Thomas Haigwood sends out the "Pitt County DA Notebook" twice a year to inform other agencies of services, to circulate news and announcements, and "reminders" concerning procedure. The office has developed the Report to the District Attorney's Office, or "96 hour report" because the report is due within 96 hours of the time the warrant is drawn, to facilitate uniform case presentation. District Attorney Thomas Haigwood's policy is that these reports must be filled out completely. Supplemental reports prepared by law enforcement are attached in addition to this report (Haigwood 1996, 3-4). The Pitt County District Attorney's Office also maintains a "telephone stand-by" service.

If an officer or witness is subpoenaed to court, he or she may request to be placed on telephone stand-by. The officer leaves a phone number or pager number, and the district attorneys office will contact the officer when needed for court (Haigwood 1996, 3).

Public Defenders and the Defense Bar

The North Carolina Constitution guarantees (ART. 1, SEC. 23) that "every person charged with crime has the right...to have counsel for defense." The North Carolina Supreme Court recognized the duty of the trial court to provide attorneys for defendants who could not afford to secure private legal counsel. *Indigent defendants* are entitled to counsel at every critical stage of legal proceedings and to effective representation. Defendants may waive the right to counsel and conduct their own defense. There is an old saying among lawyers that "anyone who acts as his or her own lawyer has a fool for client" (Orth 1993, 65).

North Carolina provides public defense in two ways: about a dozen of the state's thirty-five judicial districts are served by a public defender program; in the others, the court assigns private attorneys to represent indigent defendants (Brannon 1994, 34–37). North Carolina's current system of public defense dates to 1963 when the U.S. Supreme Court expanded indigents' right to legal counsel in the landmark case *Gideon v. Wainwright* (372 U.S. 335). The Court essentially mandated the development of systems for defense of indigents, but left the methods of financing and delivery to states and counties. In some states, state government is responsible for providing indigent defense. In others, local governments are responsible. In about half the states, indigent defense is organized on a county level (Neubauer 1996, 109).

The North Carolina Courts Commission recommended that the general assembly enact a comprehensive statute specifying the situations in which legal counsel ought to be provided at public expense, the procedures for assigning counsel from the private defense bar to represent indigents, and recommended establishing pilot public defender systems in two judicial districts (Hinsdale 1981, 51).

The Office of Public Defender

North Carolina's public defender system began in 1970, when the first Offices of Public Defender were established in Guilford County (District 18) and Cumberland and Hoke Counties (District 12). Since then, the *public defender system* has expanded to the other another ten or so districts, primarily, those counties with the largest populations.

With one exception, public defenders are selected by the governor from a list of two or three names nominated by written ballot of licensed attorneys in the district. The ballot procedure occurs according to guidelines established by the North Carolina Administrative Office of the Courts. Public defenders are appointed for four-year terms (Lind 1983; Brown 1989).

Most defendants in districts with public defenders are represented by the public defender's office. Occasionally, there is a conflict of interest and the judge appoints a private attorney to represent the defendant from a list of attorneys who have expressed an interest in public defense work. A conflict of interest arises, for example, when there are two defendants identified in a criminal action; it would be unethical for the same attorney to represent both (Lind 1983, 6-7).

Public defenders primarily handle criminal cases—traffic, assault, larceny, robbery, rape, and murder. The organization of public defenders' officers varies with the public defender and district. Public defenders typically organize defense *vertically*, meaning that one attorney stays with a felony case, for example, from district court until disposition in superior court. In single-county districts, such as Mecklenburg County (District 26), the office of public defender is centrally located. The North Carolina Association of Public Defenders is a private organization of public defenders that meets annually to discuss common issues.

In 1980, the Office of Appellate Defender was established. This office operates statewide and specializes in appeals filed by indigents. Several attorneys within this office specialize in appeals before the North Carolina Court of Appeals (Lind 1983, 7).

Assigned Counsel

In those districts without an office of public defender, the court assigns private attorneys to represent indigent clients in what is called an *assigned-counsel* system. Assigned-counsel systems involve appointment of attorneys from a list or panel of available private attorneys. The list is comprised of all attorneys who volunteer or, in smaller counties with few licensed attorneys, all licensed attorneys in the jurisdiction. Assigned counsel systems are common in counties with fewer than 50,000 residents, where there are too few cases to warrant setting up an office of public defender (Neubauer 1996, 110).

Assignment of lawyers to cases is done by the senior regular resident superior court judge. When the lawyer has completed defense work, the judge assigns a fee, paid from a contigency fund within the Administrative Office of the Courts.

Judges appoint counsel in either district or superior court. Prior to assignment of counsel (or referral to the public defender's office), the defendant fills out an affadavit of indigency the courts use to assess the defendant's financial need. Using this information, along with questions from the bench, the judge makes a finding that the defendant is indigent and assigns counsel, or finds that the defendant can afford private legal counsel. If appointed counsel is denied, the judge allows a continuance (delay in proceedings) to allow the defendant time to secure a lawyer (Lind 1983, 6).

The North Carolina Academy of Trial Lawyers is a private association of attorneys who represent plaintiffs in civil actions and defendants in criminal actions. The academy regularly offers continuing legal education programs in the areas of criminal and civil litigation and has a representative who lobbies the general assembly for or against bills of interest to the academy. (Brannon 1994, 31). The five standing committees of the organization deal with education, legislation, legal affairs, membership, and public information. The academy has a president, president-elect, five vice presidents, and a forty-member board of governors.

Race Relations in the Legal Profession

On Friday, December 13, 1997, the North Carolina Bar Association and the North Carolina Association of Black Lawyers met at the North Carolina Bar Center in Cary to discuss race relations in the legal profession. This was first time that these two organizations convened together for a joint initiative, and likely, the first time in more than three centuries of law practice in North Carolina that so many Black lawyers and White lawyers ever convened together.[2]

It was during the period of Reconstruction after the Civil War that African Americans first entered the practice of law in North Carolina. The second African American to practice law in North Carolina was John Sinclair Leary. Leary graduated

---

2. For an introduction to southern legal history, see Finkelman (1985) and Bynum (1998).

from Howard University School of Law in 1873. Leary represented Cumberland County in the legislature from 1968 until 1872, the year he was admitted to the state bar. In 1888, Shaw University created a law department and appointed Leary as its first dean; he served on the law faculty at Shaw until 1914, when the university announced the law school would be closed (Smith 1993, 202).

The first African American to practice law in North Carolina was either George L. Mabson or James Edward O'Hara, depending on the source. In *Emancipation: The Making of the Black Lawyer 1844-1944*, Howard University law professor J. Clay Smith, Jr. writes that Mabson was admitted to the North Carolina Bar at Raleigh in 1871 and became, in the words of the *New National Era* of June 29, 1871, "the first colored man...ever permitted to be a lawyer in North Carolina." Mabson had received a position as a police officer at the U.S. Capitol in Washington, D.C., with the help of a U.S. senator on the condition that he study law. He enrolled in the Howard University Law School from which he graduated in 1871. Days after Mabson was admitted to the bar, he successfully defended a man accused of murder in Edgecombe County. He earned a reputation as a skillful trial lawyer after winning an acquittal for a Raleigh man accused of murder shortly thereafter (Smith 1993, 201-202). According to an article entitled "The African American Lawyer in North Carolina," by Irving L. Joyner, associate dean of the law school at North Carolina Central University, James Edward O'Hara became the first African American admitted to the North Carolina State Bar in 1868 (Joyner 1992, 12). O'Hara, who attended Howard University School of Law in Washington, DC, began his law practice in Enfield, Halifax County. He became one of four African American Congressional members to serve from North Carolina. In 1882, O'Hara won election to Congress and was elected to a second term during which he took an aggressive role in legislation related to civil rights for Blacks. After his congressional term ended, O'Hara returned to North Carolina and eventually settled in New Bern, where he joined the law firm of Raphael O'Hara, his son (Boyd 1995, 29).[3]

When John H. Collins won election as solicitor in 1878, he became the first Black prosecutor. The second African American prosecutor in North Carolina was George H. White. White was elected to the North Carolina Senate in 1886, two years before he defeated John H. Collins. White served as solicitor in the second judicial district (Edgecombe County) for eight years (Smith 1993:204). He also served in the U.S. Congress; during his four years there, he was the only Black person in congress. White also became the last African American to be elected until 1985 when Governor James Hunt appointed Carl Fox as district attorney for District 15B (Joyner 1992, 14). Of thirty-nine judicial districts in 1996, only two had African American district attorneys. Of eleven judicial districts with public defender offices, three are headed by Black Americans (Commission on Race Relations in the Legal Profession 1996, 71). Angus Thompson, appointed public defender for district 16B in 1989, may have been the first African American to serve as public defender in North Carolina.

Other early Black lawyers included Edward A. Johnson, the first graduate of the law department at Shaw University, and James Y. Eaton, who practiced in Henderson. By 1890, there were fourteen African Americans admitted to the bar (Joyner 1992, 12). That number continued to increase as Shaw graduated more students. Another Shaw graduate, Roger D. O'Kelly completed the law course in 1909 and was admitted to the bar by examination one year prior to graduation. O'Kelly also applied to Yale University's law school. He was accepted in 1910 and graduated two years later. He opened a law office in Raleigh in 1921. O'Kelly was also a deaf-mute, one of the first

---

3. Smith (1993, 202) writes: "James Edward O'Hara, admitted to the North Carolina bar in 1873, was that state's third black lawyer."

deaf mutes of any race to practice law in the United States (Smith 1993, 206).[4]

The onset of legal discrimination and segregation slowed progress in integration of the legal profession. In 1940, there were still only forty-six Black lawyers in the entire state (Crow, Escott, and Hatley 1994, 120). Today, the percentage of African American lawyers in North Carolina is somewhat higher than in other states, although the state's comparably larger African American population continues to be underserved and under-represented by the legal profession (Commission on Race Relations in the Legal Profession 1996, 6). The Commission on Race Relations in the Legal Profession, chaired by Charlotte attorney James E. Ferguson, organized itself to develop "ways to eliminate, root and branch, any and all forms of racial discrimination, racial equity, racial impropriety or unfair distinctions that exist within the legal profession" (Commission on Race Relations in the Legal Profession 1996, 1). Commission members worked for three years to study the impact of race on the practice of law and the legal profession in the state. The commission concluded that "Today, there is both a perception and a reality of continued racial discrimination. In North Carolina and nationally, the legal profession remains largely segregated in practice" (Commission on Race Relations in the Legal Profession 1996, 1). The commission concluded that it makes no difference "where reality ends and perception begins," both the perception and reality of racial discrimination must be eliminated (Commission on Race Relations in the Legal Profession 1996, 5).

---

4. By 1926, O'Kelly had built "a lucrative business among his own race and [had] business connections with prominent white lawyers and men of affairs." He was corporate counsel for Eagle Insurance Company and the Progressive Real Estate Company, two prominent white firms. "My pad and pencil," O'Kelly said of his disability, "they carried me through Shaw and Yale and they have carried me through many important business deals" (Smith 1993, 207).

References

American Bar Association. 1992. *Legal education and professional development—An educational continuum.* Chicago, Ill.: American Bar Association, Section of Legal Education and Admissions to the Bar.

Boyd, Raphael O'Hara. 1995. Legacy: Portrait of James Edward O'Hara. *North Carolina State Bar Quarterly* 42:28-30.

Brannon, Joan G. 1994. *The judicial system in North Carolina.* Raleigh: North Carolina Administrative Office of the Courts.

Brown, Richard A. 1989. A need for reform: North Carolina's indigent defense system. *North Carolina State Bar Quarterly* 36:6-13.

Bynum, Victoria E. 1998. 'White negroes' in segregated Mississippi: Miscegenation, racial identity, and the law. *Journal of Southern Legal History* 64:247-276.

Commission on Race Relations in the Legal Profession. 1996. *Final report and recommendations.* Cary: North Carolina Bar Association and North Carolina Association of Black Lawyers.

Crow, Jeffrey J., Paul D. Escott, and Flora J. Hatley. 1994. *A history of African Americans in North Carolina.* Raleigh: North Carolina Division of Archives and History.

Finkelman, Paul. 1985. Exploring southern legal history. *North Carolina Law Review* 64:77-116.

Forst, Brian. 1983. Managing prosecution. *Popular Government* 48:1-10.

Galloway, Patton. 1985. Management: A new role for district attorneys. *Popular Government* 50:29-34.

Gore, Rex. 1998. Hot button issues for North Carolina prosecutors. *North Carolina State Bar Journal* 3:14-16.

Haigwood, Thomas. 1996. *Pitt County DA Notebook.* Greenville: Pitt County District Attorney's Office.

Hammer, Stanley. 1994. Should prosecutors control the criminal trial calendar? *Popular Government* 59:2-10.

Hinsdale, C.E. 1981. Changes in the North Carolina court system. *Popular Government* 46:47-52.

Joyner, Irving. 1992. The African American lawyer in North Carolina. *North Carolina State Bar Quarterly* 39:12-19.

Keith, Thomas J. 1995. A prosecutor's view of criminal trial calendaring. *Popular Government* 60:2-17.

Lind, Frederick G. 1983. The public defender program in North Carolina. *Popular Government* 48:5-10.

Marcus, Lisa A. 1995. *North Carolina manual 1995/1996.* Raleigh: Secretary of State.

Neubauer, David W. 1996. *America's courts and the criminal justice system.* Belmont, Calif.: Wadsworth Publishing.

Orth, John V. 1993. *North Carolina constitution with history and commentary.* Chapel Hill: University of North Carolina Press.

Smith, J. Clay. 1993. *Emancipation: The making of the Black lawyer 1844-1944.* Philadelphia: University of Pennsylvania Press.

Spindel, Donna J. 1989. *Crime and society in North Carolina, 1663-1776.* Baton Rouge: Louisiana State University Press.

Chapter 6

Courts and Adjudication

In every court case, there are two sides. The *plaintiff*, the party filing the lawsuit, and the *defendant*, the party named in the lawsuit. In a criminal case, the plaintiff is the state of North Carolina. The government's attorney, the district attorney, files the case against the defendant, the suspect identified by law enforcement. The defendant is accused of breaking the laws of North Carolina as written in the *North Carolina General Statutes*. The decision about whether the defendant did in fact break the law and if so, what should be done to the defendant, are matters for the court to decide.

There are two kinds of courts: *trial* and *appellate*. Trial courts are courts of original jurisdiction, the place where papers are filed charging the defendant with a crime. Prosecution and defense introduce witnesses, consider evidence, and make arguments, and a judge or jury renders the verdict based on the facts. This is the process of adjudication, of deciding guilt or innocence. Because the outcome may result in a restriction of liberty, the process involves a series of steps including arrest, probable cause hearing, grand jury indictment, trial, and sentencing. In appellate courts, there are no witnesses, no considering of evidence. Appellate courts review the decision to determine if the trial court made an error in its application of the adjudication process. The court considers an appeal, filed by the defendant, to decide if the trial court's decision should stay or be reversed.

North Carolina has two levels of trial courts, district and superior, and two levels of appellate courts, the court of appeals and the state supreme court. The court systems of other states are organized similarly, although North Carolina has reorganized its courts several times to create one of the most centralized systems of any state. In 1995, the Commission on the Future of Justice and the Courts in North Carolina conducted a study to find out what North Carolinians think of their court system. The Futures Commission found that citizens possess little knowledge of state courts. None of the participants in ten focus groups could identify the number of cases filed in courts each year. Citizens guessed that there are about 250,000 case filings per year; in reality, there are about 2.5 million case filings per year, and roughly the same number are resolved. Only 40% of those in a telephone poll answered correctly that justices of the North Carolina Supreme Court are elected, not appointed. Nearly three-fourths of those polled believed that courts worked better for the wealthy (Crowell 1996, 31). The majority of those polled (about 60%) thought that magistrates were elected, when the law provides for appointment. Focus group members believed the court to consume 18 to 20 percent of the state budget when it requires only about 3% (Crowell 1996, 31).

Court Unification

North Carolina has, since 1970, operated one of the most centralized court systems of any state (Fleer 1994, 133). This centralization resulted from a new judicial article in 1967 which consolidated the state's courts into three divisions: appellate, superior, and district. The District Court Division replaced a confusing array of trial courts including justice of the peace

Figure 8. Court of Appeals Building, Raleigh. Created by constitutional amendment in 1965, the N.C. Court of Appeals reviews cases from the state's trial courts.

courts, city and county recorders courts, domestic relations courts, and juvenile courts (McCain 1954).[1]

---

1. The charter from the Crown in 1663 produced the first court in North Carolina. Four levels of state courts appeared after the colony was divided into counties: superior court, the highest trial court with circuit-riding judges to hear major crimes; the justice of the peace, which heard petty crimes; county courts, which heard intermediate criminal cases; and the supreme court, established in 1819 as the state's appellate court. The Constitution of 1868 abolished the county courts and divided the caseload between superior courts and the justices of the peace. A constitutional amendment in 1875 gave the general assembly power to create special courts, and a confusing array of mayor's courts, city courts, county courts, and city-county courts appeared. By 1957, there were about 940 justices of the peace in the state. Some had an office and worked fulltime, others decided cases part-time on a front porch, over the counter in a butcher shop, or at a fairground ticket booth (Coates 1976, 296). For additional history of North Carolina's courts, see McCain (1954) and St. Clair (1953).

Court unification has been a major theme of judicial reformers since 1900. Organizations such as the American Judicature Society and the American Bar Association have advo-
cated a consolidated court structure to deal with the problems
that the variety of local courts suffer from, such as inadequate
financing, lax court procedures, inadequate facilities, and unbal-
anced caseloads. *Court unification* involves a simplified court
structure, centralized administration and rule making, and
statewide financing (Neubauer 1996, 54). In 1939 U.S. Congress passed the Administrative Office Act, which established
the Administrative Office of U.S. Courts. Most states did not
follow the federal example until New Jersey passed a new state
constitution in 1947 which provided that the chief justice
could appoint an administrative director. When North Carolina
created the position of administrative assistant to the chief justice in 1951, the state became a leader in the movement for
unification. Within five years, fourteen other states followed
suit with similar measures (Peak 1995, 62).

North Carolina's court unification initiative began in November 1955 with the Bell Committee. At the direction of the
North Carolina Bar Association and with financial support
from several private foundations, the Bell Committee (named
for its chair, Senator J. Spencer Bell of Charlotte) began a study
of the state's court system. The committee found that with
nearly two hundred city and county courts across the state, no
two counties had the same courts. Most were conducted by
part-time officials, and some judges did not have law degrees.
A few counties had juvenile courts, in others, juvenile matters
were handled by the clerk of court. Hundreds of justices of the
peace competed with each other to determine guilt in petty
cases because they were not salaried but paid from fees ex-
tracted from convicted defendants (Hinsdale 1981, 47-48).

The Bell Committee's recommendations reflected a basic
premise that responsibility for the administration of justice

should be centralized in the chief justice and the state supreme court. The commission's work resulted in a constitutional amendment in 1962 providing a new judicial article. The new article vested all of the state's power in one court—the General Court of Justice—with three divisions: appellate, superior and district. The new article authorized an eight-year period for the legislature to change the judicial system. Between 1963 and 1975, the North Carolina Courts Commission implemented the new structure. The commission abolished the office of justice of the peace and created the office of magistrate (Hinsdale 1981, 49).

The new judicial article also established the Administrative Office of the Courts (AOC). The AOC, which began July 1, 1965, is the administrative and financial arm of the Judicial Department. The AOC is headed by a director appointed by the chief justice of the state supreme court. The chief justice also appoints a director, who serves as administrative assistant to the chief justice. AOC establishes fiscal policies and prepares the budget for the Judicial Department. The AOC's purchasing division purchases equipment and supplies. The personnel division recommends pay and job classifications. The AOC also issues standard court forms; the clerk of superior court in each county operates a statewide record-keeping system maintained by the AOC. The AOC collects and publishes statistics on the work of the appellate and trial courts. The AOC also handles the assignments of superior court judges. Scheduling is worked out by the assistant director of the AOC, who sends each judge information on where the judge will hold court and publishes an annual schedule (Brannon 1994, 16-17).

Since 1960, North Carolina's court system has become a responsibility of state government. Prior to court unification, counties had extensive responsibility for the operation and finance of courts. Now virtually all of the costs of operating the General Court of Justice are paid by the state. The state pays the operating costs of the system along with the salaries of judges, district attorneys, public defenders, magistrates and clerks. Some county responsibilities remain, however. The sheriff office's provide bailiffs. The bailiff opens and closes courts, assists jurors, and generally provides courtroom security (Marcus 1995, 693). Also, the county provides appropriate space and furniture for district and superior courts. In those cities that are not county seats but are seats of district court, the municipality provides physical facilities for courts. A portion of the fees charged in each civil and criminal case is earmarked for court facilities, though these fees do not generate the entire cost. Counties, and a few cities, must meet costs from local revenue (Lawrence 1996, 767).

Court Structure

The judicial article of 1962 divided North Carolina's courts into three divisions: Appellate, Superior, and District.

Appellate Court Division

Appellate courts conduct no trials, hear no witnesses and consider no evidence. Rather, appellate courts decide only questions of law, or in other words, whether the trial court followed the proper procedure in making its decision. Decisions of appellate courts are printed in bound volumes; the decisions have the same force of law as statutes passed by the legislature. The appellate division in North Carolina has two branches: the Supreme Court and the Court of Appeals.

The Supreme Court. North Carolina's Supreme Court is the state's court of last resort. The North Carolina Supreme Court meets in Raleigh for two terms, one begins in February and the other in August. Seven justices, a chief justice and six associate

NORTH CAROLINA COURT SYSTEM

Supreme Court
7 justices—Jurisdiction:
- Direct appeals on judgment of death, life imprisonment
- Appeals from Court of Appeals in cases involving
  constitutional questions or dissent in the Court of Appeals
- Discretionary review of Court of Appeals decisions

*Court of
Last Resort*

↑

Court of Appeals
12 judges—Jurisdiction:
- Appeals as a matter of right from judgments of the
  Superior Court
- Direct appeals from some administrative agencies

*Intermediate
Appellate Court*

↑

*Judgment of death or
life imprisonment*

Superior Court
90 judges—Jurisdiction:
- Original jurisdiction all felony cases
- Civil cases in excess of $10,000
- Appeals from most administrative agencies
- Appeals from District Court (trial de novo)
- Jury trials

*Court of General
Jurisdiction*

↑

District Court
191 judges—Jurisdiction:
- Misdemeanor and infraction cases (non-criminal, traffic)
- Civil cases of $10,000 or less
- Misdemeanor cases except where the charge is joined
  with an indictment for a felony
- Ordinance violations and probable cause hearings
- Juvenile matters, domestic relations, involuntary
  commitments

654 Magistrates—Jurisdiction:
- Accept guilty pleas in certain misdemeanor cases (worth-
  less check)
- Issue arrest and search warrants
- Civil claims of $2,000 or less
- Set conditions for release on bail
- Alcohol, boating, game and fish violations

*Court of Limited
Jurisdiction*

Source: Adapted from Kentucky Judicial Department, *Justice in Our Commonwealth.* Frankfort, KY: Adminstrative Office of the Courts, 1991, p. 42.

justices, are elected to serve on the high court in partisan (Democrat) elections for eight-year terms (Drennan 1989, 477).

The supreme court hears those cases of significance to the state as a whole. It is the ultimate review for all matters concerning interpretation of state law. In two states, Texas and Oklahoma, there are two supreme courts: one for civil cases and the other for criminal cases (Neubauer 1996, 52). In North Carolina and the other states, the supreme court hears both civil and criminal appeals. Cases come to the North Carolina Supreme Court on "right of appeal," on writ of certiorari, or by granting a petition for discretionary review. Cases appealed to the supreme court are "by right" in cases involving constitutional questions, and those for which there has been dissent in the court of appeals. As a matter of right, murder cases in which the defendant is sentenced to death or life imprisonment are appealed directly to the supreme court (Marcus 1995, 690). Criminal cases amount to about half of those appealed to the high court.

According to the state constitution, justices are elected by the people. Most, however, attain office by appointment (Fleer 1994, 140). When a vacancy occurs midterm, the law allows the governor to appoint a justice until the next election. The appointment allows the appointed justice to run for election as an incumbent and as in all elective offices, incumbents usually win. Less than 10% of incumbent judicial candidates in North Carolina are defeated; few judicial races are contested. During 1986, the resignation of Chief Justice Joseph Branch allowed Governor James G. Martin to name Rhoda Billings for the vacancy. In appointing Billings, Martin overlooked the most senior associate justice, James Exum, Jr. and ignored the tradition of governors in the twentieth century of appointing the longest serving member as chief justice. What some observers called "the most bitter campaign election in the history of the state's judiciary" resulted in the election of Exum in November 1986 (Fleer 1994, 142-143).

The Court of Appeals. The general assembly created the North Carolina Court of Appeals in 1967 to relieve the state supreme court. Between 1955 and 1965, North Carolina's Supreme Court was one of the busiest of any state supreme court (Marcus 1995, 689).

The majority of cases to the court of appeals are cases appealed from superior and district courts, although the court hears appeals directly from administrative agencies as well. Twelve judges are elected on the same basis as state supreme court justices, although most of them get the office originally by appointment as is true of the supreme court (and superior court judges). Rarely do the twelve judges of the court of appeals sit together *en banc.* They sit in panels of three, usually in Raleigh, but as facilities become available, also across the state (Drennan 1989, 479).

Superior Court Division

The *superior* court is North Carolina's trial court of general jurisdiction. Superior court is the state's court of original jurisdiction for felony cases. In other states, the felony court is called circuit court, district court, court of common pleas, and in the state of New York, supreme court. Appeals of district court decisions are also decided in superior court which are heard *de novo* (tried anew) by a jury. There is a saying among defense lawyers in North Carolina that as a lawyer "You make your money in district court, you make your reputation in superior court."

The state constitution requires that at least two sessions (of one week each) of superior court be held annually in each county, although the majority of counties hold many more sessions than the constitutional minimum. In larger counties, su-

Figure 9. Superior Court Judge's Office, Kenansville. Formerly the office of L.A. Beasley, a local attorney who was a member of the North Carolina Bar in 1900.

perior court is held every week of the year (Marcus 1995, 692). There are thirty numbered districts divided into four divisions (First-Fourth) although some divisions have been subdivided into about sixty-three subdistricts. Each district ranges from seven counties (District 1, Camden, Chowan, Currituck, Dare, Gates, Pasquotank, Perquimans) to part of one county (District 10A, Wake County). Each subdistrict has either one or two resident superior court judges; there are ninety throughout the state (Marcus 1995, 71). Each district has at least one senior resident superior court judge who has administrative responsibilities. Superior court judges are elected for eight year terms.

North Carolina has a system of *judicial rotation* in which judges "ride circuit." In each rotation, judges rotate among the judicial districts within the division where they reside for six months or longer (depending on the number of judgeships). Rotation has been controversial since 1790 when the general assembly inaugurated the system. The primary argument for rotation is that it maintains judicial impartiality. Rotation also promotes political independence of the judiciary and helps maintain a judicial system that is truly statewide (Campen and Martin 1981, 26). The major arguments against rotation are that it presents an obstacle to efficient court administration and results in fragmented case management; effective case management is complicated by the judge's travel schedule. Overall, this may result in more continuances and makes it difficult to establish accountability for the administration of justice (Campen and Martin 1981, 27; Exum 1988).

District Court Division

The *district court* division represents North Carolina's trial courts of limited jurisdiction. District courts hear misdemeanor and infraction cases (noncriminal, traffic), preliminary stages of felony cases (probable cause hearings), and involuntary commitments to mental hospitals. District court also has original jurisdiction in juvenile cases, both delinquency cases and dependency cases (abuse, neglect, dependency, termination of parents rights). In other states, lower courts are variously called justice of peace, city, county, magistrate and municipal courts (Neubauer 1996, 50).

The majority of North Carolinians with a case filing in state court involve district court. In 1988, the number of cases filed in state court reached 2 million for the first time, and by 2000, that number will likely top 3 million. Of district court cases, about half are related to motor vehicles, either criminal violations or infractions. Criminal cases comprise the bulk of the caseload overall; the bulk of civil cases involve domestic disputes and child support issues (Fleer 1994, 138).

There are forty district court districts; each district covers as few as one or as many as seven counties. The typical district has three to five judges; District 26 (Mecklenburg County) has 14 and District 9B (Warren County and part of Vance County) has only one. There are 191 district court judges (Marcus 1995, 74). District judges are elected in district elections to four-year terms. They are fulltime judges and may not practice law (Drennan 1989, 485). The chief justice of the supreme court appoints one judge in each district as chief district judge who assigns judges to sessions of district court and prescribes times and places for magistrates to conduct court business (Drennan 1989, 486).

Each district court has *magistrates* as well. Magistrates are officers of the district court appointed to two-year terms by the senior resident superior court judge from nominations made by the clerk of superior court. Magistrates may be full- or part-time; few have law degrees. Magistrates serve only in their county of residence; they perform judicial matters and clerical matters; they accept guilty pleas in minor misdemeanor cases (such as writing a check with insufficient funds); and handle small civil claims and minor traffic, alcohol, boating, and game and fish violations. Magistrates may also issue arrest and search warrants, conduct initial appearances, and set conditions for release on bail. Magistrates, which replaced the old justice of the peace system, also conduct marriages (Drennan 1989, 486).

The Adjudication Process

The steps below outline the major steps of *adjudication*—the process of determining guilt or innocence in North Carolina. The steps do not describe what happens to the typical defendant, however. Only a fraction of arrests in North Carolina, as in the United States as a whole, ever lead to a trial. The vast majority of criminal defendants never experience trial by jury. At the same time, there is a great deal of variation across counties. What happens in Charlotte, or Raleigh, is different than what happens in rural counties.

Arrest

Arrest refers to action taken to restrict the freedom of a suspect. An arrest occurs when a law enforcement officer takes a suspect into custody. Patrol officers are responsible, either directly or indirectly, for most arrests. Either they arrest a suspect at the crime scene, or obtain information (description, name of suspect, etc.) from the victim or a witness.

The Fourth Amendment to the U.S. Constitution provides for arrests to occur on the basis of a warrant. An *arrest warrant* is an order from a district judge or magistrate that directs the police to arrest a designated person for a specific offense.[2] The officer must have probable cause to believe that a crime has been committed by the person in question. Most arrests are, however, made without an arrest warrant. The judiciary has recognized that it is not always practical to get an arrest warrant beforehand. So, when a victim or witness reports a crime to a police officer, the officer may, with reasonable grounds, make a warrantless arrest for a crime that is a felony. An officer must view the act in misdemeanor crimes.

Once a suspect has been arrested, the police make an administrative record or *booking*. This process involves recording the suspect's name, address, the time and place of arrest, the charge, and so on. Fingerprints and photographs may be taken at the police department, or the suspect may be transported directly to the jail. Admission to jail usually requires a complaint, arrest af-

---

2. If the judicial officer (judge or magistrate) believes that the defendant will voluntarily appear in court, a summons rather than an arrest warrant may be issued.

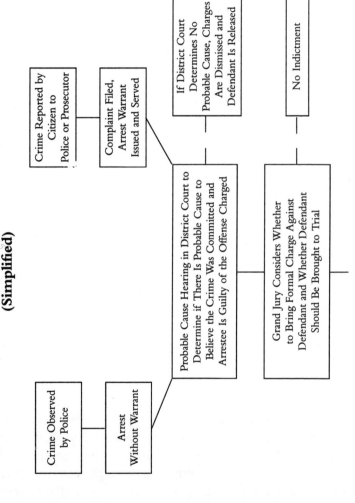

NORTH CAROLINA FELONY CASE PROCESS
(Simplified)

Crime Reported by Citizen to Police or Prosecutor

Complaint Filed, Arrest Warrant Issued and Served

If District Court Determines No Probable Cause, Charges Are Dismissed and Defendant Is Released

No Indictment

Crime Observed by Police

Arrest Without Warrant

Probable Cause Hearing in District Court to Determine if There Is Probable Cause to Believe the Crime Was Committed and Arrestee Is Guilty of the Offense Charged

Grand Jury Considers Whether to Bring Formal Charge Against Defendant and Whether Defendant Should Be Brought to Trial

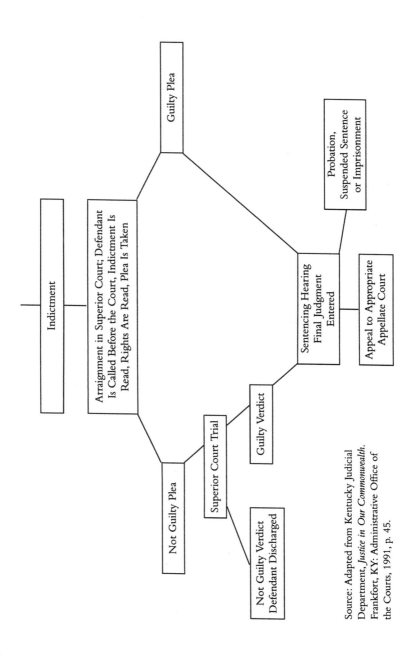

Indictment

Arraignment in Superior Court; Defendant Is Called Before the Court, Indictment Is Read, Rights Are Read, Plea Is Taken

Guilty Plea

Not Guilty Plea

Superior Court Trial

Guilty Verdict

Not Guilty Verdict Defendant Discharged

Sentencing Hearing Final Judgment Entered

Probation, Suspended Sentence or Imprisonment

Appeal to Appropriate Appellate Court

Source: Adapted from Kentucky Judicial Department, *Justice in Our Commonwealth.* Frankfort, KY: Administrative Office of the Courts, 1991, p. 45.

fidavit, or warrant. The police officer prepares a criminal *complaint*, which is a formal, written document specifying the charge, date, crime, time, and circumstances of arrest. The charge on the police complaint is not necessarily the final or formal charge to be filed in court.

At the jail, the suspect must surrender property on their person. Jail staff, usually a deputy sheriff, conducts a preliminary screening to determine if the suspect has any medical problems or needs medical treatment. When the screening is complete, the inmate receives a jail number, and those suspects not eligible for immediate release change from street clothes into jail garb.

At this point, the law requires that the accused be taken before a judicial officer to be formally charged and to be considered for temporary release until trial. After arrest, the police must seek authority from a judicial officer to detain the suspect. If the charge is minor, the police may seek permission from the district court, the magistrate, for a complaint. In this case, the district attorney does not know about the arrest until the police agency files papers with the district court. If the charge is serious, the police are required to request prosecution from the district attorney. Generally, the district attorney is notified within 24 hours of a felony arrest.

Probable Cause Hearing

Defendants who are not released from jail within a day or so appear in district court at a first appearance or *probable cause hearing*. This is a nonadversarial proceeding in district court in which the judge determines probable cause and decides whether to release the accused. At this first appearance, the judge advises the defendant of their rights and informs them of the charges against them. Those charged with misdemeanors are asked to plead; those who plead guilty are sentenced on the spot. If fined, they may pay the fine and leave.

The probable cause hearing is held in district court to determine if there is probable cause to believe the crime was committed and the defendant is guilty of the offense charged. The probable cause hearing is conducted by a judge; lawyers are present who may use the information as part of the discovery process. Both the law enforcement officer that makes a warrantless arrest and the judge who issues an arrest warrant are concerned with whether probable cause justifies the arrest. *Probable cause* refers to the reasonable belief that a crime has been committed; information that would be considered hearsay at trial may be used in developing probable cause. The judge reviews information that includes a copy of the warrant, the officer's report, and any SBI lab reports.[3] While warrantless arrests are routine, police officers are advised to secure a warrant prior to arrest whenever possible; "Get a warrant and the judge goes to court," as the saying goes.

For persons charged with felonies, the decision about whether to release or detain the defendant is made at the initial appearance. A defendant may be released on bond, or released on their own recognizance (ROR). Making *bail* refers to posting of financial security that gives the court sufficient reason to believe that the individual will reappear for subsequent legal proceedings. Some defendants hire bail bondsmen, who in return for a nonrefundable fee, arrange to post bond. Five states,

---

3. The investigating agency sends any materials that need to be tested, such as drugs, blood, and hair to the SBI Laboratory in Raleigh, and when the results are ready, forwards a copy to the District Attorneys's Office. The file also contains an Investigative Report to the District Attorney's Office, the most important part of the file. This report organizes all the information pertaining to a case.

Kentucky, Oregon, Wisconsin, Nebraska and Illinois—-prohibit commercial bail bonds (Neubauer 1996, 186). Kentucky, for example, has a statewide pretrial services system. In North Carolina, bail bondsmen operate in most jurisdictions.

A file is prepared for every case that comes to the District Attorney's Office. Early involvement of the district attorney—before the superior court takes jurisdiction—allows the prosecutor to dismiss a case. If the district attorney decides to prosecute, the suspect is then charged with a specific offense found in the *North Carolina General Statutes*. The charge filed by the district attorney is not necessarily the same as the charge requested by the police. The prosecutor may, on the basis of the evidence, file a less serious charge against the defendant than the police initially requested.[4]

---

4. One of the most sensational murder trials that never happened involved the youngest child of R.J. Reynolds in 1932, founder of corporate giant RJR Nabisco. Z. Smith Reynolds was only seven when his father died, and barely a teenager when his mother, Katharine, died. He quit school to take up flying, and at 18, married Anne Cannon, the daughter of the famous towel manufacturer. He divorced her within a year, and six days later married Libby Holman, a Broadway singer. After a party at the couple's home on July 5, 1932, one of the guests, Abe Walker, heard a muffled gunshot from the second floor. A drunken Libby appeared at the balcony and screamed "Smith's killed himself." The police found Smith sprawled across a bed with a bullet in his right temple. The police ruled the death a suicide, but a coroner's inquest a few days later found that Smith had died "at the hands of a party or parties unknown." In August, the grand jury indicted Libby for murder and Walker as an accomplice. The shooting attracted national attention as reporters poured into Winston-Salem from across the country. Articles appeared about wild parties at the Reynolds home and the couples' flamboyant lifestyle. Will Reynolds, an uncle who had raised the victim, wrote the district attorney that the family would be "relieved" if the charges were dropped. The district attorney complied and Libby never went on trial. After a lengthy court battle over the estate, the Reynolds siblings decided to use his share, about $7.5 million, to start the Z. Smith Reynolds Foundation. The Z. Smith Reynolds Foundation has funded philanthropic projects throughout North Carolina and the South (Tursi 1994, 194).

Grand Jury

In about half the states (and the federal system), the indictment process in felony cases requires a grand jury formally charge or *indict* defendants before they can be put on trial. In some states, the prosecutor can bring the charge solely on the basis of an *information*. This is a written accusation by the state charging the accused with committing a crime, and it is filed with the clerk. In these states, it is common to test the government's case at a preliminary or probable cause hearing. Although not all states using the information use a preliminary hearing, some grand jury states using the information also use the preliminary hearing. North Carolina uses both the probable cause hearing and the grand jury.

The chief function of the *grand jury* is to determine whether the evidence exists to proceed with the prosecution of a person accused of a crime.[5] The grand jury determines whether persons accused of felony crimes likely committed the crimes for which they have been charged. In grand jury proceedings, a jury foreman selected by the judge presides over proceedings which are secret (Brannon 1994, 18). The grand jury consists of eighteen persons; half are drawn from the jurors called for the first criminal session of court after January 1, and half from those called for the first criminal session after July 1. A member of the grand jury serves for twelve months. Grand juries meet at regular intervals, or as needed. In large counties, two grand juries serve concurrently, convening on alternate Mondays, to carry the case load.

Indictment (official accusation by the grand jury) is a necessary prerequisite to a trial in superior court, unless the accused

---

5. Grand juries are authorized to perform other functions. Grand juries may also issue presentments (the results of investigations). The grand jury also has the duty to inspect the county jail and may inspect other county offices (Howard 1990, 75).

waives it. The accused may waive indictment in all cases except those for which the punishment would be death. When a defendant has been bound over for trial in superior court, the prosecutor must submit to the grand jury a bill of indictment stating the charges. The grand jury hears from witnesses called by the prosecutor and may request others. The grand jury then decides whether it is a "true bill of indictment" or "not a true bill of indictment" (Brannon 1994,18). In North Carolina the finding on an indictment, or return of presentment, requires a twelve-member majority.[6]

Arraignment

Arraignment is the first time felony defendants are asked to enter a plea. It is conducted in superior court. Most of the courthouse regulars are in attendance: judge, prosecutor, defense attorney, court clerk, court reporter, and bailiff. The judge reads the charges and informs those defendants without an attorney of their right to counsel. Indigent defendants not appointed an attorney earlier are appointed one now. The defendant can plead guilty (rare at this stage), not guilty (the usual plea) or "nolo contendere," which means the defendant does not admit guilt and will not contest the charges. Once a plea of not guilty is entered, the judge may assign the case to a trial date. Sometime before the trial date, the judge and attorneys confer at a *pretrial hearing* or docket sounding to determine whether the defendant will go to trial or negotiate a plea.

Most cases are plea-bargained, usually sometime between the arraignment and trial date. About 90% of all convictions in felony cases result from a plea. A *plea bargain* amounts to an

---

6. The above steps may be bypassed. The district attorney or attorney general may file a case directly with the grand jury. Presentments may be initiated by the grand jury, by a judge or prosecutor, although this is rare in North Carolina.

agreement between the state and the defendant. The state agrees to lessen the charge to a less serious crime (or the number of counts, or proposes a sentence of community supervision, or something else) in return for waiver of a jury trial and an admission of guilt from the defendant.

Plea negotiations occur around the *discovery process*. The right of pretrial discovery is the right of defendants to inspect certain materials held by the prosecution. Not all states recognize the right of pretrial discovery in a criminal case. In some states, however, the law extends to the prosecution the same rights of pretrial discovery granted to defendants. If the prosecution has provided a list of witnesses, the defense must do the same.

In those cases not resolved by guilty plea, pretrial preparation begins. Cases that go to a jury trial usually involve complex issues to be resolved by the court through a series of *pretrial motions* filed by the litigants. Pretrial motions include motions to suppress evidence (that the defense believes the prosecution obtained illegally), a motion for severance (separate trials for defendants jointly charged for the same offense, which are usually tried together), and incompetency (defendants cannot be tried if they are mentally incapable of consulting with their lawyer or understanding the nature of the proceedings). Change of venue, or relocating the place where the defendant is to be tried, is rare (Myers and Pudlow 1991, 67).

Trial

Trial can be heard by a judge sitting alone (a *bench trial*) or by a jury of citizens. *Voir dire* is the process of jury selection. The objective is to find a dozen citizens who will objectively decide about the facts in the case. Potential jurors may be removed from service by either attorney for cause or peremptory challenge (the removal of members from a jury for not stating a reason or cause).

The trial begins with opening statements by the prosecution and the defense. The judge may give specific instructions to the jury regarding the charge, counts, suppressed evidence, or other issues. Most of the evidence presented during a trial is in the form of witness testimony. The process includes *direct examination* of witnesses (questioning by counsel who introduced them) and *cross-examination* (questioning by opposing counsel). Because the defendant's right to a fair trial could be jeopardized should a witness fail to appear in court, attorneys for both sides *subpoena* witnesses. A *subpoena* is written legal notice requiring a person to appear in court to provide testimony. The prosecution, which bears the burden of proving the state's case to the standard of beyond a reasonable doubt, is the first to call witnesses and enter evidence. The prosecution presents witnesses through the process of direct examination, who are subject to cross-examination by the defense counsel. The defense presents its case, followed by closing arguments. In some states, the prosecution makes the final closing argument, in other states the defense has the final say.

The jury deliberates and the judge renders the verdict. In most states, jury verdicts must be unanimous (a few allow conviction on the basis of ten). If the jury fails to reach a decision, the result is a hung jury, and possibly a new trial in which the case is tried by another jury.

Sentencing

After trial, the defendant, if found guilty, returns to court for *sentencing*. The judge inquires whether there is any reason why sentence should not be pronounced, and if there are none (virtually always so), the defendant has an opportunity to make a statement to the court. Both defense and prosecution may call witnesses to testify at the sentencing hearing. A friend or relative may testify for the defense about the defendant's character or depth of remorse. The victim or a member of the victim's family make a statement or file a statement (Myers and Pudlow 1991, 163). In some states, the judge pronounces the sentence, in other states, the jury makes the decision. A disposition usually involves imprisonment or probation and community service.

During the interval between a defendant's conviction and the sentencing hearing, the court gathers information to enable the judge to impose an appropriate sentence. In the majority of cases, the sentencing decision is based on a *presentence investigation* (PSI). Usually written by a probation officer, the report includes family and employment history, mental or physical health problems, history of alcohol or other substance abuse, and record of previous incarcerations.

Judges are also guided by *sentencing guidelines* that identify sentencing options for each category of offense. North Carolina's structured sentencing legislation, which became effective in 1994, revised sentencing laws for all crimes except drunk driving. The legislation put emphasis on "intermediate punishments," such as a split sentence or special probation in which the offender spends a short part of the probation term in jail. The guidelines were drafted by the Sentencing and Policy Advisory Commission created by the general assembly in 1990 (Brannon, Clarke, and Farb 1995, 82).

Appeal

The vast majority of defendants convicted by jury trial seek appellate court review or an *appeal*.[7] Appeals are based on claims that one or more errors in criminal procedure occurred during the criminal adjudication process. If an appeal is

---

7. Double-jeopardy protection prevents the district attorney from appealing a trial verdict of not guilty.

granted, conviction may be set aside and a new trial ordered. Few of those who appeal are successful. An appellate court will not review a judgement simply because the trial court made an error. Many of the errors brought on appeal are considered harmless errors, and not an error so prejudicial as to invalidate the entire trial (Myers and Pudlow 1991, 203).

In a few states, not North Carolina, a writ of habeas corpus is the principal method of postconviction relief. In habeas corpus proceedings, petitioners claim that their conditions of confinement violate a constitutional right and seek conditional discharge (National Center for State Courts 1994). Although the grounds for habeas corpus relief vary from state to state, the most common are jurisdictional and constitutional. ARTICLE 1, SECTION 21 of the North Carolina constitution specifically states that "the writ of habeas corpus shall not be suspended." Relatively few cases have been decided on this section, however, because the North Carolina Supreme Court has adopted a restrictive interpretation of its meaning. In an early case *In re Schenk* (1876), the North Carolina Supreme Court refused to issue the writ of habeas corpus to a prisoner in the state penitentiary whose sentence may have been erroneous because that sentence was issued by a court of competent jurisdiction. "In other words," Professor John V. Orth explains, "the writ may be used to challenge the authority that imposed the restraint, not its fairness" (Orth 1993, 62).

African Americans in the Judiciary

Formally, the state constitution requires only two qualifications for a judge: the candidate must be a qualified voter of at least 21 years of age and must be duly authorized to practice law in the state. The second requirement was only added in 1981, after a fire extinguisher salesman without a law degree or judicial experience gained nomination as a candidate for chief justice of the supreme court (Fleer 1994, 139).

Traditionally, there have been other criteria. The majority of judges (about 85%) are Democrats. The selection process has traditionally followed a predictable pattern. A Democratic governor nominated a Democratic judge to fill a vacancy until the election; the incumbent judge ran for election unopposed and without campaigning, and election occurred without much notice (Fleer 1994, 141). Most judges come from the Piedmont region of the state. The majority of judges graduated from University of North Carolina at Chapel Hill Law School; another quarter from Wake Forest University Law School. And, the majority of judges are white males. In July 1990, only about 10% of trial judges and appellate judges were African American, less than 8.5% were women (Fleer 1994, 139-140).[8]

In the past decade or so, these informal criteria have begun to weaken. Elections of Republican governors during the 1980s and an increasing number of Republicans in the general assembly, has weakened the hold of the Democratic Party on the state's judiciary. In 1975, North Carolina became the first state to elect a woman as chief justice; Susie Sharpe served from 1975 to 1979 (Fleer 1994, 140). In 1982, Henry Frye, a Greensboro attorney, became the first African-American to serve on the state supreme court (Luebke 1990, 112). In 1956, Frye was denied the right to vote in Ellerbe (eastern Piedmont region) by the local registrar who claimed that despite being a college graduate and a veteran, Frye failed a literacy test. Twelve years later, he became the first African American elected to the general assembly in this century. He was also the sole Black person in the legislature out of 170 representatives

---

8. For an analysis of the politics of judicial campaigns in North Carolina, see Reid 1996.

and senators in a state in which Black people comprise one-fifth of the population (Luebke 1990, 112)

African Americans have served in the North Carolina judiciary since 1967. In that year, Samuel S. Mitchell became the fist Black American to be appointed to the bench. He served in the Raleigh recorder's court. In 1968, Elreta Alexander-Ralston became the first African American to be elected as Guilford County District Court Judge. By 1975, there were five Black district court judges; by 1987, there were fourteen. In 1986, Judge Terry Sherrill, a Charlotte attorney became the second African American in state history to serve on the superior court bench. Prior to Sherrill, only Judge Clifton Johnson, also of Charlotte, had ever been elected to the superior court, although five African Americans had been appointed to serve as special superior court judges (replacing vacancies). Judge Clifton Johnson became the first African American to serve on the court of appeals. In 1990, Judge Allyson Duncan became the first African American woman to serve on a state appellate court (Joyner 1992, 16). As of 1995, 1 of 7 justices on the supreme court is African-American, 1 of 12 on the court of appeals, 13 of 82 on the superior court bench, and 18 of 187 on the district court bench (Commission on Race Relations in the Legal Profession 1996, 71).[9]

---

9. The Futures Commission also found that nearly three-fourths of those polled believed that the courts worked better for the wealthy. More than half (52%) believed that the courts had a very serious or extremely serious problem with treating people differently based on their wealth. Somewhat less than half (42%) thought that bias of judges was a problem: 27% thought judicial bias was an extremely or very serious problem. Generally, the respondents who had been to court were more likely than those without experience in court to believe that treating people differently according to wealth was a serious problem and that judges were biased (Crowell 1996, 33). The Commission on Race Relations in the Legal Profession also uncovered concern about unfairness and bias. The Commission on Race Relations surveyed several hundred attorneys throughout the state. While the majority (83%) of white attorneys reported that they "never" observed discriminatory

References

Brannon, Joan G. 1994. *The judicial system in North Carolina.* Raleigh: North Carolina Administrative Office of the Courts.

Brannon, Joan G., Stevens H. Clarke, and Robert L. Farb. 1995. Law enforcement, courts, and corrections. In *State and local government relations in North Carolina* (Charles D. Liner, ed.). Chapel Hill: Institute of Government.

Campen, Henry C. and Harry C. Martin. 1981. North Carolina's judicial rotation system. *Popular Government* 46: 23-33.

Coates, Albert R. 1976. *Bridging the gap between the law on the books and the law in action.* Chapel Hill: Institute of Government.

Commission on Race Relations in the Legal Profession. 1996. *Final report and recommendations.* Cary: North Carolina Bar Association and North Carolina Association of Black Lawyers.

Crowell, Michael. 1996. What do North Carolinians think of their court system? *Popular Government* 61:31-33.

Drennan, James C. 1989. The courts. In A. Fleming Bell II, *County government in North Carolina.* Chapel Hill: Institute of Government

Exum, James G. 1988. Judicial selection in North Carolina. *North Carolina State Bar Quarterly*35:4-11.

Fleer, Jack D. 1994. *Politics and government in North Carolina.* Lincoln: University of Nebraska Press.

Hinsdale, C.E. 1981. Changes in the North Carolina court system. *Popular Government* 46:47-52.

---

treatment of minority attorneys by judges, only about one third (38%) of minority attorneys reported that they "never" observed discriminatory treatment. In interpreting these findings, the Commission quoted the authors of a study of California courts with similar findings: "From the results, one might conclude that two very different justice systems exist" (Commission on Race Relations in the Legal Profession 1996, 39).

Howard, Lucille. 1990. *North Carolina: Our state government.* Charlotte: League of Women Voters of North Carolina Educational Fund.

Joyner, Irving. 1992. The African American lawyer in North Carolina. *North Carolina State Bar Quarterly* 39:12-19.

Lawrence, David M. 1996. Appendix: County government in North Carolina. In *Municipal government in North Carolina* (David M. Lawrence and Warren Jake Wicker, eds). Chapel Hill: Institute of Government.

Luebke, Paul. 1990. *Tar heel politics: myths and realities.* Chapel Hill: University of North Carolina Press.

Marcus, Lisa A. 1995. *North Carolina manual 1995-1996.* Raleigh: Secretary of State.

McCain, Paul M. 1954. *The county court in North Carolina before 1750.* Durham: Duke University Press.

Myers, Howard and Jan Pudlow. 1991. *The trial: A procedural description and case study.* St. Paul, Minn.: West Publishing.

National Center for State Courts. 1994. *Habeas corpus in state and federal courts.* Williamsburg, Va.: State Justice Institute.

Neubauer, David 1996. *America's courts and the criminal justice system.* Belmont, Calif.: Wadsworth Publishing.

Orth, John V. 1993. *North Carolina constitution with history and commentary.* Chapel Hill: University of North Carolina Press.

Peak, Kenneth J. 1995. *Justice administration: Police, courts and corrections management.* Englewood Cliffs, N.J.: Prentice Hall.

Reid, Traciel V. 1996. PAC participation in North Carolina supreme court elections. *Judicature* 80:21-25.

St. Clair, Kenneth E. 1953. Judicial machinery in North Carolina before 1865. *North Carolina Historical Review* 30:415-439.

Tursi, Frank W. 1994. *Winston-Salem: A history.* Winston-Salem: John F. Blair Publisher.

Chapter 7

Corrections

Although the terms *prison* and *jail* are often used as synonyms, there is a significant difference between the two. Prisons are operated by the state for felons sentenced to serve terms of a year or longer. Those sentenced to death await execution in a state prison. Jails are local detention facilities operated by counties for the confinement of suspects awaiting trial and those convicted of misdemeanors or minor felonies sentenced to terms of less than a year. North Carolina's experience with jails parallels other southern states, reflecting both historical and contemporary challenges of delivering a just system of sanctions.

Prisons are the only public institution expected to pay for themselves. Rather than public tax support, states have since the time of Thomas Jefferson attempted to finance prisons by means of labor. One of the most notorious features of prison systems within the South was the lease system, a system in which the state rented prisoners to private entrepreneurs for labor. Prisoners across the state worked on railroads, in coal mines and turpentine camps (Knepper 1993). North Carolina was the first southern state to use convict labor for extensive farming activities (Zimmerman 1951, 464). So immense were the profits from North Carolina's prison farms in the early twentieth century that they became models for other states. North Carolina developed the most extensive system of chain gangs and road camps. In fact, chain gangs for road work lasted longer in North Carolina than in any other state. Chain gangs

Figure 10. Superintendent and guard at road camp, Wake County, 1919. Chain gang road building, a practice which began in Mecklenburg County in 1901, persisted longer in North Carolina than any other southern state. (Courtesy of the N.C. Division of Archives and History.)

remained a common site on the state's highways until 1972 (Ireland 1991).

The legacy of chain gangs and road camps has left North Carolina with nearly one hundred correctional facilities, the highest of any state. State prisons in other states are much larger than those in North Carolina. New York, for example, operates about half the facilities with a greater inmate population per facility. In 1992, a consultant secured by the general assembly recommended consolidation of thirty of the smallest facilities into four larger prisons, but the legislature did not make a change at that time. Consolidation will remain an issue for some time to come (Brannon, Clarke, and Farb 1995, 85). At the same time, North Carolina sentences many misdemeanants to state prison that would in other states be confined in county jails. Much of the state's prison population would comprise the jail population in other states. Yet given the unusual decentralization of prisons in North Carolina, local facilities develop ties to communities, through work-release and other programs, and through contact between prisoners and their families that resemble the jail experience in other states (Brannon, Clarke, and Farb 1995, 91).[1]

County Jails

Historically, the county's chief role in the criminal justice process was to ensure the safekeeping of defendants after arrest (by city police) and before disposition by the court (to the state department of corrections). Counties have operated jails for this purpose since the colonial era. While cities and police departments operate temporary holding facilities designed to hold persons until arraignment, such as "drunk tanks" and police lockups, *jails* are defined as facilities designed to hold persons who cannot meet the conditions of pretrial release between the time of their arrest and court appearance. Jails also confine those serving short-term sentences, typically less than one year.

Jails are locally operated facilities. In all but a few states, counties operate jails. In Connecticut, Delaware, Hawaii, Rhode Island, and Vermont, jails are operated by the state as part of combined jail-prison systems. Typically, jails are administered by the sheriff's department, although there are exceptions to this as well. In Kentucky, for example, sheriff's do not have responsibility for the county jail. The county jailer is an

---

1. There are also three private adult correctional facilities in North Carolina. Together, these three facilities have a rated capacity of 1,000 (Maguire and Pastore 1997, 93).

elected official distinct from the sheriff (Kentucky Legislative Research Commission 1993, 103).

The term "jail facilities" is used because while the majority of facilities are known as "county jails" there are variations within the state, such as "satellite jail" (Cawtawba County), "jail annex" (Durham County), and "detention center" (Dare County). Seven of these facilities have more than 250 beds, 53 have between 50 and 249 beds, and the remaining 42 have 49 or fewer beds. There are no "mega jails" in the state (jails with 1,000 or more beds) (American Correctional Association 1993, 285). The number of county jails does not correspond exactly with the number of counties because some counties have more than one jail facility and some counties have no jail. Several counties— Mecklenburg, Durham, Guilford—have more than one jail facility; there is the Guilford County Jail in Greensboro, Guilford County Jail in High Point, and the Guildford County Prison Farm in Gibsonville. Other counties have combined to operate a single district jail. The Albemarle Regional Jail in Elizabeth City serves Camden, Pasquotank, and Perquimans Counties and the Bertie-Martin Regional Jail in Windsor serves Bertie and Martin Counties (Dellinger, Farb, and Smith 1989, 502).

Colonial Jails

Jails in the American colonies were modeled after the English county jail. Jails amounted to local lockups for the detention of suspects awaiting trial and convicted lawbreakers sentenced to corporal punishment. They were something like boarding houses; the jailer lived with his family on site, and the prisoner's lot depended on finances or handouts from friends or relatives. In Virginia and other colonies, they were used for short-term confinement (Knepper 1993, 129).

There were, however, no jails in North Carolina before the early eighteenth century. In 1715, the assembly ordered the

Figure 11. Duplin County Jail, Kenansville. Built in 1979, and renovated in 1986, the jail has a rated capacity of 40.

provost marshal (later replaced with the office of sheriff) to use his own house as "the County prison until sufficient Gaols are built" (Spindel 1989, 120-121). Few counties provided adequate facilities and officials in several counties were charged with "keeping a bad prison." One prisoner obtained early release in 1732 due to the "heat of the season and the Loathsomeness of the prison." Other jailers simply did not perform their duties. The Edenton jailer in 1731 simply "left the say'd Charge" at one or two in the morning. In 1739, the keeper of Bath jail was accused of unlawfully confining a merchant and charging him twenty shillings for his release (Spindel 1989, 121).

In 1741, the legislature empowered the counties to levy a tax for the construction of "a Courthouse, Prison, and Stocks." Carteret County prepared to build a jail of sawed logs four inches thick, a double door, and two windows fitted with iron grates. Prisoners were entitled to a daily ration of a pound of bread, two quarts of water, and "dressed meat." However, fines and corporal punishment prevailed. The legislature dealt severely with theft of horses, cattle, and other livestock. The law passed in 1741 prescribed a fine of £10 above the cost of the animal, and forty lashes for a first offense. Second offenders could be forced to "stand in the Pillory Two Hours, and be branded in the left Hand, with a red hot iron, with the letter "T" (Spindel 1989, 122). For counterfeiting, first time offenders could receive forty lashes, two hours in the pillory, and have "both Ears nailed to the Pillory and cut off." Second time counterfeiters faced execution (Spindel 1989, 123).

Jails operated according to the principle that they should not cost the county any money and prisoners received little from the county. In 1816, the general assembly required that jailers clean the rooms used to hold prisoners at least once a day. Not until 1919, however, did the legislature require jailers to provide blankets in winter, along with a supply of water and roasted meat (Smith 1985, 4).

Jails have historically served as "catchalls," as a place for law enforcement to put persons of all sorts until a judge can decide what to do with them. Imprisonment for debt was common in North Carolina until 1844 (Smith 1985, 2). In 1848, social reformer Dorthea Dix traveled the state investigating treatment of insane persons and found many insane persons confined in county jails. Vagrants, public drunks, and runaway youths joined the mix, although with runaway slaves prior to the Civil War and protestors during the Civil Rights movement. When forty-one Black college students carrying picket signs on the sidewalk in front of a F.W. Woolworth store in Raleigh were arrested for "trespassing" during the sit-in period early in the national movement for civil rights, each student was booked and fingerprinted at the Wake County Jail then released on bond. One year after the first sit-ins, "freedom riders," Black and White students, who traveled by bus through Virginia, North Carolina, South Carolina, Georgia, and Alabama to challenge segregation in bus terminals, "jail—no bail" became a Congress of Racial Equality (CORE) tactic. They were charged with trespassing, fined, and they elected to be taken to jail rather than pay the fine (Crow, Escott, and Hatley 1992, 188, 193).

Jail Administration

Responsibility for the county jail in North Carolina is divided between the sheriffs and the board of county commissioners. The commissioners build, maintain, and finance the jail, and the sheriffs administer them. In counties with small jails (less than fifty beds), the sheriff directly administers the jail; in counties with larger facilities, the sheriff appoints a chief jailer or administrator to run the jail.

In addition to safekeeping defendants awaiting trial, state statutes require counties to provide jail space for some convicted defendants. The Local Confinement Act (1977) required that prisoners with sentences of six months or less be confined in county jails. All misdemeanants sentenced to a term of imprisonment of 180 days or less, are assigned to a local confinement facility (county jail) unless it is filled to capacity. In that case, prisoners may be assigned to a Department of Correction institution (N. C. Gen. Stat. §148-32.1). The State Department of Correction must reimburse each county jail at a set rate for the cost of providing food, clothing, and medical services for those prisoners serving thirty days or more (Dellinger, Farb, and Smith 1989, 503). At the end of 1995, there were 1,350 inmates in county jails that had been adjudicated, waiting to come to the Division of Prisons but for which there were no available beds (Division of Prisons 1996).

Mandatory standards have been set in about half of the states; other states have voluntary jail standards or no minimum standards. In the majority of states with minimum standards, the Department of Corrections operates the jail inspection service (Mays and Thompson 1991, 19-20). Grand juries in most states are constitutionally or statutorily mandated to inspect jails (Mays and Thompson 1991, 6).

North Carolina has established mandatory minumum standards for jails. Under authority of state statute (N.C. Gen Stat. §153A-221), the state promulgates minimum jail standards (N.C. Administrative Code, Title 10, Subchapter 3J). In 1990, the Department of Human Resources issued new standards for jail construction, operation, classification, programs, and other aspects of jail operation, including the physical condition of confinement and provision for the health and safety of inmates. The county commissioners must provide sufficient jail personnel able to provide continuous supervision. In addition, the commissioners must develop a plan for medical care for the inmates. The local director reviews the commissioners' plan and approves it if it meets the need to provide for inmates health and welfare (Dellinger, Farb, and Smith 1989, 502). The Division of Facilities Services, within the Department of Health and Human Resources (DHHR), conducts a jail inspection service. State statutes require this jail standards agency to inspect every jail twice a year to see that the standards are met. The secretary of the DHHR may order corrective action or close a jail that fails to meet the standards.

Voluntary standards are also set by the American Jail Association (AJA). The AJA is a national organization of jail administrators, sheriffs, local government officials, and private companies affiliated with the American Correctional Association (ACA). The AJA was organized in 1981 as the result of a merger of the National Jail Association and the National Jail Managers Association. Permanent headquarters were established for the organization five years later. While jail standards issued by the AJA have no constitutional or statutory authority, they are seen by many as a basis for sound jail administration and a strategy to avoid litigation.

History and Organization of State Corrections

Institutional Corrections

The first prison in the United States was established in Philadelphia in 1790. By 1800, an additional four states had authorized prison construction including New York, New Jersey, Virginia, and Kentucky (Knepper 1993). By the outbreak of the Civil War, all the states had constructed prisons except for three: Florida, South Carolina, and North Carolina (Hawkins 1985, 191). Instead of constructing a state prison, North Carolina developed a system of convict leasing, chain gangs, and prison farms. Variants of these practices remained until 1960, and modified forms continue today (Hawkins 1985, 191).

The 1868 Constitution of North Carolina abolished all forms of corporal punishment and substituted "imprisonment with or without hard labor" in the state prison or a county jail. Recognizing the inadequacy of county jails for long-term confinement, the constitution directed the general assembly to "make provision for the erection and conduct of a state prison or penitentiary" (Smith 1985, 2). The legislature enacted legislation providing for prison construction that year. Two years later a site near a large prison farm in Wake County was purchased, but political opposition to the idea of a penitentiary delayed construction (Coates 1976, 315). Using inmates who were confined to a wooden palisade to quarry stone on site, the Central Prison finally opened in 1884. The primary building, constructed from granite on site, is divided into interior cell blocks based on the Auburn plan. Central Prison in

Raleigh remains the only prison in North Carolina with a granite wall.[2]

The 1868 Constitution also provided that institutions of punishment be "self-supporting" (Coates 1976, 333), which led to creation of the chain gang. North Carolina's practice of chain gang road building persisted longer than in any other state. Legislation enacted in 1867 allowed superior court judges to place offenders on county chain gangs. By 1887, use of inmate labor developed into a complex county-state system. Convicts who would otherwise have been confined in a state prison were kept by counties (and cities) to work on local projects, such as highway construction. Special county road commissions emerged to control use of inmate labor and occasionally the legislature directed the counties to make their prisoners available for large-scale construction projects. Mecklenburg County linked jail sentencing to road construction in 1901 and had one hundred convicts crushing stone for roads around Charlotte. Within a year, about 25 counties worked prisoners on roads according to the Mecklenburg Plan (Ireland 1991,

---

2. While Central Prison is considered the state's first, North Carolina did authorize and open another prison prior to 1868. During the Civil War, North Carolina converted an old cotton factory at Salisbury into a prison beginning in December 1861. Major John Henry Gee, the commandant of Salisbury Prison in 1864 was arrested and tried for crimes against Union prisoners following the war. The prison held Union prisoners, probably the most famous of which was Robert Moffat Livingstone of the 3rd Regiment of New Hampshire volunteers; he was the oldest son of Dr. David Livingstone, the missionary doctor and African explorer. The prison held civilian prisoners including hostages, deserters, Quakers and other conscientious objectors who had not provided substitute or paid the $500 tax. All African Americans were classified as prisoners of war. In March 1865—three weeks before Lee's surrender at Appomattox and two years after the Emancipation Proclamation of January 1, 1863—fifteen Black men and women, boys and girls from the prison were auctioned in front of the Salisbury courthouse (Brown 1980).

128). Others were sentenced to state supervision and leased by the state to railroads and other contracts who operated prison industries, state public works, or prison farms. The state purchased Caledonia Prison Farm in 1899, and Polk Prison Farm in 1920 (Hawkins 1985, 191).

Nearly half of North Carolina counties worked prisoners on roads before the county-controlled prison system ended. In 1931, the general assembly directed the State Highway Commission to maintain all 4,500 miles of county roads and the state took control of all 3,500 county convicts to work on them. Later, the Highway Department automatically received all prisoners sentenced to thirty days or more and built one hundred new prison camps to hold the influx (Smith 1985, 5). State controlled road crews followed from the "Good Roads and Good Men" campaign of Joseph Hyde Pratt, a University of North Carolina at Chapel Hill geologist and later a member of the Highway Commission. Pratt viewed state control of chain gangs as a reform measure that would reduce abuses under the county system (Ireland 1991). Many counties had thrown together temporary workhouses and road camps along highways to house prisoners, others stuffed prisoners into wheeled cages that were rolled from one location to another (Smith 1985, 3).[3]

---

3. One of those prisoners fortunate enough to avoid the chain gang was prisoner number 17758, David Marshall Williams. Williams became famous in the MGM movie *Carbine Williams* (1952), in which Jimmy Stewart played the title role. Williams had been convicted of second degree murder in 1921 for the killing of Deputy Sheriff Al J. Pate in a raid on Williams's still near Fayetteville. In 1992, Williams began serving time at Caledonia Prison Farm, and after a run-in with Captain H.T. Peoples, spent some time in solitary. While in "the box," Williams had the idea for the "floating chamber" which became the basis for the caliber carbine. Williams manufactured tools (secretly at first) and later made three firearms while working in the prison's blacksmith shop (he test fired them in the old prison cemetery). The Colt Patent Firearms Company heard about the new rifle from a local newspaper

In 1933, the general assembly transferred control of the state's three prisons to the State Highway and Public Works Commission. The merger of highways and prisons resulted from the sagging economy during the Depression. During this arrangement, prisoners were supported by the Highway Fund while employed extensively on road construction (Marcus 1995, 336). The Division of Prisons remained under control of the Highway and Public Works Commission until 1955, when the general assembly formed the Prison Reorganization Commission to study the arrangement. The reform effort resulted in separation of the two systems in 1957 and creation of a new State Prison Department. Also in 1957, North Carolina became the first state to implement work release statewide: prisoners were allowed to work at private employment during the day and return to confinement in the evening (Marcus 1995, 337). The State Prison Department was, however, required to furnish the Highway Department with inmate labor for road maintenance until 1973, when the "road quota" was eliminated.

In 1974, the State Prison Department was renamed the Department of Correction. The department was established in 1972 by authority of the Executive Reorganization Act of 1971 as the Department of Social Rehabilitation and Control. The act joined the Probation Commission, the Board of Paroles, and the Department of Youth Development, to form the Department of Social Rehabilitation and Control. In 1975, the Division of Youth Development was transfered to the De-

---

article and helped Williams obtain a pardon in 1929. At a parade in New York City honoring Williams in 1951, General Douglas MacArthur autographed Williams's M-1 carbine and said, "The carbine was one of the strongest single contributing factors in our victory in the Pacific." Captain Peoples published an article in *Reader's Digest* magazine that year entitled "My Most Unforgettable Character" (Beard 1977).

partment of Human Resources, leaving the Department of Correction as currently organized.

Community Corrections

Probation began in Boston Municipal Court in 1841, when John Augustus became the first probation officer. Augustus, a reformer of the temperance movement, intervened in the case of a public drunk about to be sentenced to a six-month term in the Boston House of Correction. Augustus asked the judge to release the man under his supervision, and he would guarantee his reappearance in three weeks. Augustus paid court costs, the judge released the man, and Augustus returned with the man as promised. So impressed was the judge with the man's reformation that he suspended the original jail sentence and substituted a small fine (Silverman and Vega 1996, 495). Augustus continued his work until 1858, supervising more than two thousand probationers. After his death a year later, Massachusetts enacted the first probation legislation. During the first decades of the twentieth century, additional states enacted probation statutes. By 1920, every state permitted juvenile probation, and thirty-three states authorized adult probation. By 1954, probation was available to offenders in all states (Silverman and Vega 1996, 495).

North Carolina enacted its first probation statute in 1919 although the law limited probation to first-time prostitution and certain juvenile offenders. In 1937, the legislature extended the law to adults and allowed an adult to be placed on probation at the discretion of the court for any period of less than five years. Conditions of probation specified that the prisoners must "avoid injurious or vicious habits," "places of disreputable or harmful character," and meet the probation officer as directed. Probationers also had to find suitable employment, pay court costs, make restitution, and support their families (Coates 1976,

336–337). That same year, the general assembly formed the Probation Commission to supervise a statewide network of male and female offenders reporting to probation officers. The Probation Commission disbanded in 1972 when the Division of Adult Probation and Parole was formed (Marcus 1995, 337).

Beginning in 1974, probation officers in North Carolina began carrying caseloads of both probationers and parolees. Probation officers today assigned to field services carry probation caseloads for the most part, although they also supervise dual cases (cases that are both probation and parole) (Marcus 1995, 337)

Parole comes from the French phrase *parole d'honneur,* which means "word of honor." The French used the phrase to denote release of a prisoner for good behavior based on the convicts' word of honor that the law would be obeyed in the future. In the United States, use of parole can be traced to the governor's power to commute or pardon inmates. Following Zebulon Brockway's experiment with conditional release at Elmira Reformatory in 1876, parole became a popular concept. By 1900, about twenty states had parole statutes; by 1944, every state had a parole system (Silverman and Vega 1996, 501).

North Carolina's original constitution in 1776 conferred to the governor the power to grant clemency and governors created a system for processing requests. This system was maintained in the Reconstruction constitution of 1868, and in 1919, the general assembly created an Advisory Board of Paroles, which made recommendations to the governor. In 1925, the governor received the assistance of a full-time pardon commissioner. In the late 1920s, the governor appointed a commission to visit all state prisons, interview those who had served at least half of their terms, and release those who could be turned loose without a threat to public safety (Coates 1976, 337). By 1933, the position of pardon commissioner had developed into a pardon and parole commission. The commission's staff searched records of those eligible for parole or pardon rather than waiting for prisoners to request such an investigation. In 1935, legislation was enacted reducing this board to the Commissioner of Paroles and creating the position of parole officer under the supervision of the commissioner (Dorris 1946; Marcus 1995, 337).

A constitutional amendment in 1954 transferred the power to parole from the governor to the Parole Commission, organized within the Department of Correction (Orth 1993, 97). The constitution empowers the governor "to grant reprieves, commutations, and pardons, after conviction, for all offenses" but specifies that "the terms reprieves, commutations, and pardons shall not include paroles" (ART. III, SEC. 5, subsection 6). In 1974, the General Assembly enlarged the commission to five full-time members and transferred administration of parole officers to the Division of Adult Probation and Parole. The commission grants paroles (early release from prison subject to certain conditions) and advises the governor concerning commutations and pardons (Marcus 1995, 337).

The Department of Correction

The North Carolina Department of Correction is responsible for the care, custody and supervision of all individuals sentenced after conviction for a felony or serious misdemeanor. Major divisions include the Division of Prisons and the Division of Adult Probation and Parole.

The department is headed by a secretary, who is appointed by the governor. The secretary is responsible for administering the state system, including planning, financial, records, and personnel functions. Major sections have been created for planning, grants, fiscal operations, personnel, staff development and training, and management information and research.

Division of Prisons

The Division of Prisons provides direct supervision and care of inmates. The division operates about 93 prison institutions across the state that confine about 30,000 inmates; 26,800 felons and 2,600 misdemeanants (Division of Prisons 1996). The division receives felons and misdemeanants sentenced to terms ranging from six months to life.

Classification within the system is based on the seriousness of the crime, the willingness of the inmate to abide by institutional rules, and the potential for escape. The prison facilities within the division provide one or more levels of security (Marcus 1995, 339):

Maximum custody for prisoners who have demonstrated through their behavior to present a clear and present danger to society and other prisoners. Privileges are limited and security precautions are extensive.

Close custody for prisoners who require security but to a lesser extent than those in maximum security. Basic education, counseling, and work programs are available to those in close custody institutions.

Medium custody for prisoners able to participate in programs and activities operating under supervision of armed security. Programs include academic and vocational instruction, drug and alcohol abuse treatment, psychological and other counseling programs, and various work assignments.

Minimum custody are misdemeanants and those felons that have little time remaining to serve or who have been determined not to present high security or escape risk. These units do not have gun towers nor the security measures of other institutions (several of the advancement centers do not have fences.)

In 1978, the state began development of a central inmate transfer and classification system to monitor assignment of very serious offenders (Reed 1979, 3). Central Prison serves as a support institution for the Division of Prisons; the institution provides services that assist the other ninety or so prison facilities in North Carolina. Central Prison in Raleigh, reconstructed in 1987, has a capacity of 1,215. Central Prison serves as a reception center for male felons sentenced to terms longer than 20 years and has a medical and psychiatric hospital. The prison also houses all death row inmates (American Correctional Association 1995, 330). Located near downtown Raleigh, Central Prison occupies twenty-nine acres of land, most of it enclosed by a double fence topped with razor wire. It is the state's only maximum security prison. In addition to regular population inmates, the prison houses other inmate populations including protective segregation, disciplinary segregation, and those needing medical treatment.

Central Prison housed both men and women from 1884 to 1931. In 1938, construction began on the North Carolina Correctional Center for Women. About 95% of the state prison population is male. The Division of Prisons operates five institutions for women; the North Carolina Correctional Institution for Women at Raleigh is the largest (544 capacity). The division also operates nine facilities for youthful offenders (under 23) who have been tried and sentenced as adults; Foothills Correctional Institution (664 capacity) and Western Youth Institution (676 capacity) at Morganton are the two largest (American Correctional Association 1995, 338). Southern Correctional Institution serves as a reception center for all male felons with sentences of twenty years or less and houses close custody youth.

The ACA is an important national organization which affects North Carolina. Founded in 1870, the ACA seeks to shape the development of corrections policy and promote professional development in all areas of corrections.

Youth Command. Youthful offenders under age 23 who are tried and sentenced as adults are committed to the Division of Prisons, Youth Command. Within the Youth Command, these offenders are segregated from the adult population, and segregated by age and seriousness of offense. Felons between ages 18 and 23 sentenced to medium custody are sent to Polk or Morrison Youth Institutions; minimum custody felons and misdemeanants between ages 18 and 23 are assigned to Sandhills Youth Center or Burke Youth Center; and felons and misdemeants under age 19 are assigned to Western Youth Institution at Morganton (American Correctional Association 1995, 338-339).

What became the Western Youth Institution began in 1967, when State Commissioner of Corrections V. Lee Bounds initiated a plan to build high-rise prisons across the state. The legislature perceived the high-rise concept as untried and agreed to fund only a single facility, which was located in Burke County. The sixteen-story prison facility in Morganton, a unique architectural structure within North Carolina's prison system, opened in 1969 as Western Correctional Center. The institution was designated as a youth facility in 1972, and Western Youth Institution began receiving offenders under age 21 from Polk Youth Center and Harnett Center. Western Youth Institution has offered GED programs to youthful offenders through Western Piedmont Community College, in addition to other programs. The Explorer Post, an off-site program featuring community service projects and overnight camping trips began in 1973. At this same time, Burke Youth Center opened to house the large numbers of offenders under age 18 who were sent to the institution. The BRIDGE program began after a fire swept through the South mountains in 1985; BRIDGE activities include fighting fires, planting trees, and clearing access

Figure 12. Western Correctional Center, Morganton, 1969. The only "high rise" prison in the state, it was designated as an institution for youthful offenders in 1972. It has rated capacity of 676. (Courtesy of the N.C. Division of Archives and History.)

roads. BRIDGE expanded to about fifty youthful offenders from Burke Youth Center in 1987, and completion of Blue Ridge Youth Center has expanded the program. In 1992, Western Youth Institution's average daily population increased to over eight hundred and became the second largest correctional institution in the state at the time, second only to Central Prison in Raleigh (Western Correctional Center 1997).

Division of Probation and Parole

The Division of Probation and Parole is responsible for supervision of more than 109,000 convicted offenders within the community. Most of these offenders have been sentenced by the court to probated sentences and are supervised by officers who offer counseling and job development services.

Headquartered in Raleigh, the division is headed by a director who is ultimately responsible to the secretary of the Department of Correction. The division is divided into twelve field branches that cover geographical areas across the state comprised of between one and eighteen counties. Charlotte-based Field Branch L, for example, covers only Mecklenburg County. Field Branch A, on the other hand, covers eighteen western counties from a headquarters at Asheville. The Division of Probation and Parole operates one treatment facility, the DWI Parole Treatment Facility, which opened in 1989 at Goldsboro. The facility provides residential parole substance abuse treatment for DWI offenders (American Correctional Association 1995, 338-340).

The Division of Probation and Parole is also responsible for supervising those offenders released by the Parole Commission. The Mutual Agreement Parole Program (MAP) involves a binding agreement between the offender, the two divisions, and the Parole Commission. The agreement provides for 12 to 18 months of vocational instruction prior to a specified release date. In order to be released on that date, the offender must participate in vocational training as assigned, and maintain under supervision without infraction or escape. The Division of Prisons provides the requisite vocational training and provides for release on the specified date (Marcus 1995, 340-341).

Since 1989, the Division also administers the Intensive Motivational Program of Alternative Treatment (IMPACT). IMPACT is a "boot camp" program for males ages 16-25 designed to instill self-confidence, discipline, and work ethic. Correctional administrators may recommend placement of those convicted of misdemeanors and nonserious felonies as part of presentencing or as an alternative to revocation, but only judges may order placement (Jones and Ross 1997, 52).

The American Probation and Parole Association's (APPA) members are involved in the design, management and delivery of probation, parole, and community-based sentences for adult and juvenile offenders. The association issues policy statements and organizes training programs.

The Death Penalty

Since the federal government began collecting execution statistics in 1930, more than four thousand legal executions have been carried out in the United States. About half of these occurred in eleven southern states. Only four states have executed more people than North Carolina, although nine states currently have a higher number on death row. In fourteen states, there is no death penalty (Stephan and Snell 1996, 1,11). Nationwide, there are about 2,700 prisoners under sentence of death (Stephan and Snell 1996, 7). Currently, there are about one hundred and sixty men and three women on death row in North Carolina.

During the colonial period, the sentence of death was authorized for a wide variety of offenses. Blackstone found one hundred and sixty offenses in 1765 declared by parliament to be felonies punished by "instant death." While not all those who committed such offenses actually received the sentence, counties did carry out public executions along with whippings and other bodily punishments. North Carolina's statutes reduced the number to less than thirty in 1837, to less than twenty in 1854, and

Figure 13. Execution of Wilfred Roseboro, Iredell County, 1903. The hanging of Tom Dula, which inspired the folk song "Hang Down Your Head Tom Dooley," occurred here in 1868. (Courtesy of the N.C. Division of Archives and History.)

to four by 1868. The constitution of that year reserved the death sentence for four crimes: murder, arson, burglary, and rape.

In 1910, the general assembly transferred the power to execute criminals from the counties to the state. On March 18 of that year, Walter Morrison became the first man to die in the state's electric chair. An African American from Robeson County, Morrison had been convicted of rape and sent to Central Prison. Between 1910 and 1997, North Carolina executed another 369 persons (Department of Correction 1997, 7). North Carolina has executed 80 White men, 282 Black men, 2 Black women, 1 White woman, and 5 American Indian men (Central Prison 1997, 4).

The arbitrary and capricious nature in which the death penalty had been applied in Georgia led to the landmark *Furman v. Georgia* case in 1972. In this case, the majority held that the death penalty as currently implemented was unconstitutional given the "arbitrary and capricious" nature of decision making. The case resulted in a moratorium on executions across the country until 1977, when the U.S. Supreme Court reinstated the death penalty in *Gregg v. Georgia* (1977). In response to the *Furman v. Georgia* decision, the North Carolina Supreme Court ruled that the death penalty would be mandatory for certain crimes. Following the North Carolina Supreme Court's decision, the number of death row inmates climbed to 120, the highest in the nation. The U.S. Supreme Court overturned North Carolina's mandatory death provision in *Woodsen v. North Carolina* (1976). The Court vacated the sentences of North Carolina's death row inmates. Many received new trials and life sentences (Department of Correction 1997, 7).

In 1977, North Carolina's revised capital punishment law became effective. The revised law restored the death penalty for first degree murder, defined as wilful killing, deliberate and premeditated killing, or killing while committing another felony (N.C. Gen Stat. § 14-17). In 1986, the North Carolina Supreme Court examined 199 death and life imprisonment cases tried under the new statute. James G. Exum, Jr., then an associate justice and later chief justice of the North Carolina Supreme Court, wrote that while personally opposed to the death penalty, the death penalty is clearly constitutional. "It is the duty of the criminal justice system to enforce our capital punishment laws which the people have demanded with as much fairness...and with as many reasonable safeguards as we can humanely devise," writes Exum, "I believe our system in North Carolina is genuinely striving for this goal." Adam Stein, first director of the Office of Public Defender, believed that North Carolina's system remained arbitrary and "stained with racism." Stein, who argued that the North Carolina Supreme Court's analysis overlooked those life imprisonment cases not appealed to the North Carolina Supreme Court, explained that "two-thirds of the people on death row are black. No fancy analysis can explain that fact away for me" (Exum 1985, 12-14).

The electric chair was used until 1936, when the state began using the gas chamber. Lethal gas served as the method of execution until 1983, when the general assembly enacted legislation allowing death row inmates the option to choose death by lethal injection. If the inmate does not agree to lethal injection by writing at least five days prior to the execution, the gas chamber will be used to carry out sentence. Since then, six men and one woman have requested lethal injection (Department of Correction 1997, 9). Lethal injection is the most common means of execution in the United States, although the majority of states authorize two methods of execution. In most states with death penalty statutes, condemned inmates may choose between lethal injection, electrocution, and lethal gas. Four states authorize hanging, one state (Utah) authorizes firing squad (Stephen and Snell 1994, 5).

The men on death row are sentenced to Central Prison, the women to the North Carolina Correctional Institution for Women. Death row conditions are similar for men and women. Death row inmates are housed in single cells within the maximum security area of the prison. The cells open into a day-room that has a television. Death row inmates receive an hour a day for recreation and showers; they may also participate in weekly religious services.

When all appeals have been exhausted, the inmate moves to the death watch area of Central Prison three to seven days prior to the execution date. The death watch area is under 24 hour surveillance by correctional officers. The inmate remains in the death watch area until receiving a stay or an escort to the execution chamber (Department of Correction 1997, 13).

Race, Roads and Convict Labor

Convict leasing, the most notorious feature of prison systems in the South, raises serious questions about the rationale for corrections. Convict leasing in the South has been described as a thinly-disguised effort to preserve slavery. In truth, convict leasing was not a uniquely southern institution; about half the states used convict leasing at one time or another. What is true about southern leases is the color of convict labor (Knepper 1995).

Darnell F. Hawkins, formerly at the University of North Carolina-Chapel Hill and now Professor of African-American Studies and Sociology at the University of Illinois-Chicago, examined shifts in the ratio of Black and White imprisonment rates in North Carolina between 1870 and 1980. Until about 1890, in North Carolina and other southern states, leasing convicts to railroad companies was the major form of convict labor. Black offenders comprised as many as 90% of those sentenced to the state prison system during the closing decades of the nineteenth century, during a time when courts demonstrated a reluctance to sentence White convicts to prison. Work on railroads was considered "Black work," and resulted in disproportionate numbers of Black convicts being assigned to railroads. Most White convicts were assigned to other work projects (Hawkins 1985, 198). Black prisoners laid virtually every mile of the 3,582 miles of railroad track laid in North Carolina between 1876 and 1894 (Hawkins 1985, 199).

By 1890, when the availability of railroad leasing began to decline, state prison officials turned to the prison farm. Officials argued that since the majority of North Carolina convicts came from rural backgrounds, farm labor would be more suitable than industrial trades common in northern prisons. The race-related pattern of work continued. White convicts were assigned to agricultural labor while Black convicts received chain-gang labor on roads, quarries, canals and other work projects. This dual system of prison labor-White prison farms and Black road camps—continued until 1930 when the number of White convicts equaled the number of Black convicts for the first time. After consolidation of state and county systems in 1933, and the demise of traditional farming in the South and elsewhere, the state shifted convict labor to build and repair the expanding network of state highways. In the decades between 1930 and 1960, up to 90% of the state prisoners were sentenced to road camps (Hawkins 1985, 199-200).

The worst features of convict labor have ended, and North Carolina has made progress in avoiding the excesses of inmate labor. In 1957, North Carolina became the first state to implement a statewide work-release program when the general assembly enacted legislation authorizing inmates to work at private employment during the day and return to confinement in the evening (Marcus 1995, 337). Since 1965, work release has been a major program of North Carolina's prison population (Reed 1979, 4). While other states have developed similar programs, North Carolina has the largest work-release population (Marcus 1995, 337). The state's prison population, however, continues to be disproportionately African American. While Blacks comprise about 20% of the North Carolina population, they make up 65% of the state's prison population (Division of Prisons 1996).

Many African Americans have also replaced the exclusively white staffs of correctional facilities. By 1994, there were more than four thousand Black correctional officers in North Carolina; about one-third of the total staff population. Of ninety superintendents in the state, there were about twenty of African ancestry (Maguire and Pastore 1995, 96,94). Exactly who was the first African American to head a prison in North Carolina is a matter of some debate because it depends on what is meant by prison administrator. Two of North Carolina's prisons are headed by administrators designated as wardens: Central Prison in Raleigh and the North Carolina Correctional Center for Women, also in Raleigh. James B. French, the current warden at Central Prison, is the first African American warden in North Carolina. When Lewyn M. Hayes took charge of the Raleigh Youth Center for Negroes in 1952, he became the first Black superintendent in North Carolina. The facility relocated to Cherry Hospital in Goldsboro and became the Goldsboro Youth Center for Negroes (McQuillan 1998). Robert L. Reese was among the first superintendents at an integrated facility. After Reese was hired in 1961, Prisons Director George Randall dispatched Reese and fourteen other Black employees to form an all-Black staff at an all-Black prison, the minimum custody facility for youthful offenders at McLeansville. Reese was later transferred to Charlotte Correctional Center and became the only minority at most staff meetings. After working at several other facilities, Reese became superintendent of Charlotte Correctional Center in 1973 (McQuillan 1998).

References

Ashman, Allan. 1968. North Carolina jails and prisons: A brief history. *Popular Government* 33:1-6.

American Correctional Association. 1993. *National Jail and Adult Detention Directory 1993-1995.* Laurel, Md.: American Correction Association.

American Correctional Association. 1995. *Directory: Juvenile & Adult Correctional Departments, Institutions, Agencies and Paroling Authorities.* Laurel, Md.: American Correction Association.

Beard, Ross E. 1977. *Carbine: The Story of David Marshall Williams.* Lexington, S.C.: The Sandlapper Store.

Brannon, Joan G., Stevens H. Clarke, and Robert L. Farb. 1995. Law enforcement, courts and corrections. In *State and local government relations in North Carolina* (Charles D. Liner, ed.). Chapel Hill: Institute of Government.

Brown, Louise A. 1980. *The Salisbury prison: A case study of confederate military prisons 1861-1865.* Wendell: Avon Books.

Central Prison. 1997. *Central prison.* Raleigh: Central Prison.

Crowe, Jeffrey J., Paul D. Escott, and Flora J. Hatley. 1994. *A history of African Americans in North Carolina.* Raleigh: North Carolina Division of Archives and History.

Dellinger, Anne M., Robert L. Farb, and Michael R. Smith. 1989. The criminal justice system. In *County government in North Carolina* (A. Fleming Bell, II, ed.). Chapel Hill: Institute of Government.

Department of Correction. 1997. *The death penalty and the North Carolina Department of Correction.* Raleigh: North Carolina Department of Correction.

Division of Prisons. 1996. *Offender population utilization system (OPUS) computer system information.* General Information

Fact Sheet, January 31, 1996. North Carolina Department of Correction, Office of Research and Planning.

Dorris, Jonathon T. 1946. Pardoning North Carolinians, *North Carolina Historical Review* 23:360-401.

Exum, James G. 1985. The death penalty in North Carolina, *Campbell Law Review* 1-28.

Hawkins, Darnell F. 1985. Trends in black-white imprisonment: Changing conceptions of race or changing patterns of social control? *Crime and Social Justice* 24:187-209.

Ireland, Robert E. 1991. Prison reform, road building, and southern progressivism: Joseph Hyde Pratt and the campaign for 'good roads and good men'. *North Carolina Historical Review* 68:125-157.

Jones, Mark and Darrell Ross. 1997. Is less better? Boot camp, regular probation and rearrest in North Carolina, *American Journal of Criminal Justice* 21:147-162.

Kentucky Legislative Research Commission. 1993. *A citizen's guide to the Kentucky constitution.* Frankfort, Ky.: Legislative Research Commission.

Knepper, Paul. 1995. The Kentucky penitentiary at Frankfort and America's first convict lease system, 1798-1840. *Filson Club History Quarterly* 69:41-66.

_____. 1993. Thomas Jefferson, criminal law reform, and the founding of the Kentucky penitentiary at Frankfort. *Register of the Kentucky Historical Society* 91: 129- 149.

Maguire, Kathleen and Ann L. Pastore. 1995. *Sourcebook of criminal justice statistics 1994.* Washington, D.C.: U.S. Department of Justice, Office of Justice Programs.

_____. 1997. *Sourcebook of criminal justice statistics 1996.* Washington, D.C.: U.S. Department of Justice, Office of Justice Programs.

Marcus, Lisa A. 1995. *North Carolina manual 1995/1996.* Raleigh: Secretary of State.

McQuillan, Patty. 1998. Reese retires: First African American hired by department, *North Carolina Department of Correction News.*

———. 1996. Gaither receives minority pioneers top honor, *North Carolina Department of Correction News.*

Orth, John V. 1993. *North Carolina constitution with history and commentary.* Chapel Hill: University of North Carolina Press.

Reed, Amos E. 1979. The North Carolina department of correction: Problems, progress, and plans. *Popular Government* 44:1-7.

Silverman, Ira J. and Manuel Vega. 1996. *Corrections: A comprehensive view.* St. Paul, Minn.: West Publishing.

Smith, Michael R. 1985. History of jails in North Carolina. *Jail Law Bulletin* 7:1-5.

Spindel, Donna J. 1989. *Crime and society in North Carolina, 1663-1776.* Baton Rouge: Louisiana State University Press.

Stephan, James and Tracy L. Snell. 1996. *Capital punishment 1994.* Washington, D.C.: Bureau of Justice Statistics.

Thompson, Joel A. and G. Larry Mays. 1991. *American jails: Public policy issues.* Chicago: Nelson-Hall.

Zimmerman, Jane. 1951. The penal reform movement in the south during the progressive era, 1890-1917. *Journal of Southern History* 17:462-492.

Chapter 8

Juvenile Justice

Juvenile justice refers to the collection of state and local programs reserved for a category of lawbreaker defined as a juvenile by state statute. Most states define a juvenile under the original jurisdiction of the juvenile court system as persons under age 18; about a dozen states define the upper limit for original juvenile court jurisdiction at age 15 or 16. Since Illinois organized the first juvenile court in 1899, juvenile justice has occupied an uncertain place at the crossroads of what to do about crime. Between 1992 and 1995, legislatures in forty-seven states have redefined the role of juvenile courts, including changes in jurisdictional authority, sentencing authority, confidentiality, victim's rights, and correctional programming (Torbet *et al.* 1996). Asked to consider the future of juvenile justice, Professor Carl E. Pope at the University of Wisconsin at Milwaukee writes that the "major consideration as we move into the twenty-first century is whether there will, in fact, be a separate system of juvenile justice" (Pope 1995, 268).

In North Carolina, juvenile court jurisdiction extends to persons who are at least age 6, but younger than age 16. North Carolina law identifies two categories of juveniles. An *undisciplined juvenile* is unlawfully absent from school; is beyond disciplinary authority of his parents; is regularly found in places where it is unlawful to be; or who has runaway from home. A *delinquent juvenile* has committed a crime or infraction under state law (including motor vehicle laws) or under ordinance of local government. Responsibility for juvenile justice is divided between the executive branch and the judicial branch. The Juvenile Services Division, Administrative Office of the Courts (AOC), provides court intake, probation, and aftercare services. The Division of Youth Services, Department of Health and Human Services, administrates community-based programs, juvenile detention centers, and training schools.

As is true elsewhere in the country, North Carolina's juvenile justice system is changing. In September 1997, Governor James Hunt named a nineteen-member Commission on Juvenile Crime and Justice to review the juvenile code and make recommendations for improving juvenile justice. The commission had four subcommittees: juvenile code, prevention, disposition, and agency reorganization. The commission held public hearings throughout the state during fall 1997. The commission's recommendations are to be considered at the special session of the general assembly during 1998. North Carolina's juvenile justice system is subject to change.[1]

The Beginnings of Juvenile Justice

The concept of juvenile justice originated at the end of the nineteenth century when Chicago established a separate court for juveniles. In 1899, the Illinois legislature established the first juvenile court with the Juvenile Court Act. Many social re-

---

1. The Juvenile Justice Reform Act, enacted by the general assembly in October 1998, made several changes in juvenile law. These had to do with extended jurisdiction, law enforcement records, training schools, open hearings, and conditions of probation. The act also created a cabinet-level juvenile justice agency which merged Juvenile Services, Administrative Office of the Courts; Division of Youth Services, Department of Health and Human Services; and the Center for the Prevention of School Violence, Governors Crime Commission. In January 1999, Governor Hunt announced that George Sweat, formerly chief of the Winston-Salem Police Department, would lead the new agency.

formers concerned with child welfare in Chicago enjoyed a national reputation and the Juvenile Court Act became a model for similar legislation in other states. By 1917, juvenile court legislation had been passed in all but three states, and by 1932, there were over six hundred independent juvenile courts in the United States (Platt 1977, 10). The Chicago Juvenile Court Act emphasized that juveniles were salvageable human beings who needed treatment rather than punishment, and that a separate court would protect the juvenile from the stigma of criminal proceedings. The act provided for limited courts of record for all persons under age 16 and for the care of abused and neglected children who had been abandoned and in need of state care. Also, the act prohibited judges from confining juveniles under age 12 in a jail or police station. Young offenders were assigned to probation officers who would see to their needs temporarily (Champion 1992, 250).

There were separate institutions for juveniles prior to 1899. The New York House of Refuge, established in New York City by the Society for the Prevention of Pauperism in 1825, was established to deal with runaways and unruly children. The New York House of Refuge was part orphanage for abandoned children and part training school for delinquent children. Houses of refuge opened in Philadelphia, Boston and other cities. Beginning about midcentury, reform schools began to appear. One of the first appeared in Westboro, Massachusetts in 1848. By the end of the century, all states had reform schools of one sort or another. These institutions were characterized by strict discipline and vocational labor. After 1865 children orphaned by the Civil War were sent to reform schools, not because they needed reform but because they were vagrants.

North Carolina's juvenile court began with the North Carolina Constitution of 1868. The constitution established the framework for a separate court system for juveniles with a provision that the state provide for the "poor, the unfortunate and the orphan" (Alley and Wilson 1994, 2). Despite these provisions, children were often confined with adults. In 1870, the North Carolina Board of Public Charities investigated jails and charitable institutions within the state. The board was disturbed by the practice of confining juveniles with adults in county jails: "Every offender, or even one accused of crime—the boy of twelve, put in for a street fight, or some slight misdemeanor, and the hardened criminal, deep dyed in infamy, are all thrown together in filth and idleness, thereby making the jail a seminary of crime and corruption" (Ashman 1968, 2). In about 1904, the Ladies of Public Charities visited Central Prison in Raleigh and found many young children there.

Development of the County System

In 1919, the general assembly enacted the Juvenile Justice Statute, which provided statewide juvenile courts for delinquent, dependent, and neglected children ages 16 or younger. The statute did not appropriate state funds for a separate court. Rather, the legislature revised the state's welfare statutes to structure a county administered program under the supervision of the State Board of North Carolina (which later became the North Carolina State Board of Charities and Public Welfare). The counties designated their own juvenile officers. The clerk of superior court acted as juvenile judge and the county director of public welfare acted as chief juvenile probation officer.

Problems with the organization of juvenile justice remained. In 1934, the State Board commissioned a study of the county juvenile justice system. The board counted 108 juvenile courts in North Carolina. There were the Domestic Relations and Juvenile Court of the City of Charlotte and County of Mecklenburg; other large cities, including Greensboro, Raleigh, Wilmington, and Winston-Salem funded their own courts, and the remaining counties used the clerk of the superior court. Only three juvenile courts had detention facilities approved by the State Board; eight counties had created separate sections for juveniles within the county jails, five used the county homes, and a few relied on private homes. In most counties, juvenile probation was part of the duties of the staff of the county welfare department, appointed and compensated without the approval of the State Board of Charities and Public Welfare (Alley and Wilson 1994, 8).

Development of the State System

The state system began to take shape with the Judicial Department Act of 1965. The act abolished all courts inferior to superior court and phased in the statewide district court. District court had jurisdiction in all cases affecting the family, except adoption. District court now had jurisdiction of juvenile matters, including delinquent, dependent, and neglected children (Alley and Wilson 1994, 36-37). In February 1971, Governor Scott appeared before the North Carolina Bar Association to request a study of juvenile corrections (Alley and Wilson 1994, 48). The bar's report recommended a unified system of probation and aftercare services to allow for state juvenile court services in all counties. At that time, the services of twenty-seven urban counties were supported by the AOC and programs in twelve other counties received federal funds (Alley and Wilson 1994, 55).

In 1974, the general assembly created the Division of Juvenile Services within the AOC in order to standardize intake services in all judicial districts. In 1975, the legislature transferred responsibilities for juvenile detention to the Department of Human Resources, creating for the first time one division responsible for all areas of juvenile detention (Alley and Wilson 1994, 62). The legislature also designated the Department of Human Resources

North Carolina's Juvenile Justice System (Simplified)

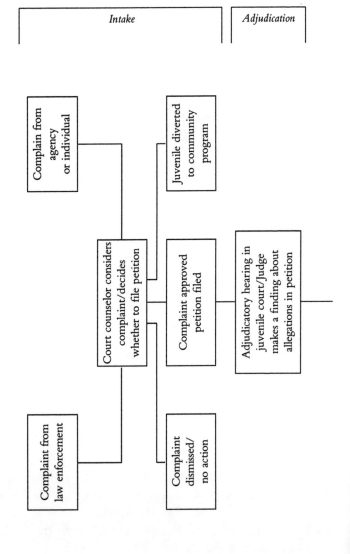

Intake

Adjudication

Complaint from agency or individual

Complaint from law enforcement

Court counselor considers complaint/decides whether to file petition

Juvenile diverted to community program

Complaint approved petition filed

Complaint dismissed/ no action

Adjudicatory hearing in juvenile court/Judge makes a finding about allegations in petition

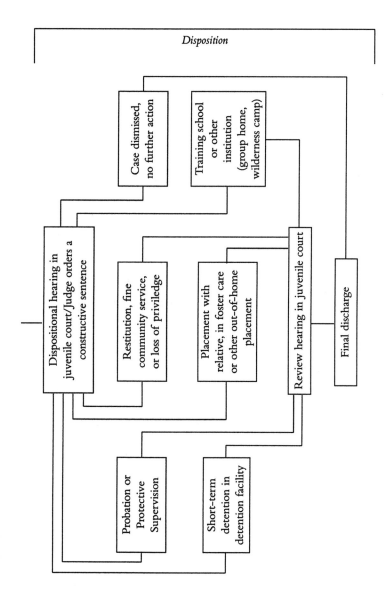

for development of community-based alternatives to training schools (Alley and Wilson 1994, 60). In 1978, the legislature created a youth services advisory committee to advise the secretary of the Department of Human Resources on youth services programs and the operation of training schools, and consolidated management authority over training schools and development of community based programs within the Department of Human Resources (Alley and Wilson 1994, 65).

The easiest way to understand North Carolina's juvenile justice system is to consider the institutions at each major stage of the juvenile justice process: intake, adjudication, and disposition (Hargrove and Mason 1998). The state also offers delinquency prevention programs designed to prevent youth from entering the juvenile justice system.

Delinquency Prevention Programs

In 1974, the primary goal of federal juvenile justice legislation became prevention, to alter the pathway toward delinquency before delinquent behavior becomes a fact. The Juvenile Justice and Delinquency Prevention Act introduced several major strategies to reduce juvenile crime, including financial and technical assistance to state and local delinquency prevention efforts. Many delinquency prevention efforts are school-based programs. The DARE program is an example of a national delinquency prevention program that operates in North Carolina; the Center for Prevention of School Violence and the Support Our Schools programs are examples of state efforts.

DARE. One of the most popular recent approaches to delinquency prevention is Drug Awareness Resistance Education or DARE. DARE programs operate throughout North Carolina. Created by the Los Angeles Police Department in

1983, DARE has become the "largest and most widely implemented drug and violence prevention program in the world." By 1995, more than 22,000 police officers from 7,000 communities had delivered the program to more than 25 million elementary students. DARE is a collaborative program between schools and law enforcement. Uniformed police officers, typically from community policing projects, deliver a copyrighted curriculum designed to prevent substance abuse and develop resistance to drugs and violence. Officers receive training from DARE America, a nonprofit corporation that operates five regional training centers funded by grants from the Bureau of Justice Assistance (Bureau of Justice Assistance 1995).

Center for Prevention of School Violence. North Carolina's delinquency prevention efforts received a boost from the general assembly in 1993 when the Center for Prevention of School Violence opened as part of the Governor's Crime Commission. The Governor's Crime Commission is located within the Department of Crime Control and Public Safety. The Center for Prevention of School Violence aims to reduce school violence through technical assistance to student-focused programs, distribution of prevention oriented information, and evaluations of violence prevention programs in schools. The center, located in Raleigh, is a partnership with the North Carolina State University College of Education and Psychology.

The center's approach is based on the "safe schools pyramid," a collection of violence prevention programs with physical design and safety at the top, and the school resource officer at the base. Programs include teen/student courts, conflict resolution and peer mediation programs, and law-related education programs. School Resource Officers (SROs) are law enforcement officers permanently assigned to cover a school or set of schools. They received special training to be law enforcement officers, law-related counselors, and law-related teachers. Most SROs are sheriff's deputies; about one third are employed by city police departments. Most began working in schools (Center for Prevention of School Violence 1997, 1-10).

Support Our Students. Support Our Students (SOS) programs are designed to prevent juvenile crime by providing enrichment activities during after-school hours. Proposed by Governor James Hunt as part of his crime package in 1994, SOS programs target children in grades K-9. The programs are coordinated by the Division of Youth Services. Adult volunteers and teenagers work with children to improve school performance and enhance self-esteem. In 1997, there were SOS programs at 175 sites across North Carolina (Division of Youth Services 1997, 2).

Intake

Intake is the first step for defendants in juvenile court. At intake, the decision is made whether to begin formal proceedings. Although the decision may be made by the juvenile court judge or prosecutor, most states employ a designated intake officer. Intake officers have different names, depending on the state, and they may be employed by the state Department for Social Services, the AOC, or a separate juvenile department within the executive branch. In North Carolina, juvenile intake officers are called *juvenile court counselors* (Hargrove and Mason 1998, 7-8). North Carolina's juvenile justice procedures require that when a police officer takes a juvenile into temporary custody, the officer (1) release the juvenile without making a complaint, (2) release the juvenile and make a complaint to the court counselor's office, or (3) hold the juvenile, make a complaint to the court counselor's office, and request a secure or nonsecure custody order (Administrative Office of the Courts 1991, 67).

Juvenile Services

Court counselors work for *Juvenile Services*, a division within the AOC. Juvenile Services is responsible for the administration of a statewide, uniform system of juvenile intake, probation, and aftercare services for juveniles before district courts for delinquency and undisciplined matters. The administrative head of the Division of Juvenile Services is the Administrator for Juvenile Services, appointed by the director of the AOC. The administrator is responsible for planning, organizing, and administering juvenile probation and aftercare services statewide. The AOC establishes uniform procedures, conducts staff development and training, and is responsible for appointing a chief court counselor in each district.

The AOC operates a uniform court counselor program statewide. Each district court is assigned three or more court counselors; there are more than 350 court counselors statewide (Brannon 1994, 20). The program is called *intake counseling* and its aim is to divert juvenile cases from the courts to appropriate community-based agencies when possible (Brannon 1994, 20). Court counselors conduct prehearing studies of children alleged to be delinquent or undisciplined. Counselors also arrange detention for those juveniles who require detention before or after a hearing. Court counselors are appointed by the chief court counselor in each district. Chief court counselors direct the program of juvenile probation and aftercare in each district under supervision of the administrator of Juvenile Services. The counties provide office space for the court counselors (Hargrove and Mason 1998).

Juvenile Detention

State law provides for *detention*, or temporary custody, of juveniles who need to be detained prior to adjudication or disposition. In some states, juveniles are simply confined in county jails; usually they are kept separate from adults. In North Carolina, juveniles are not held in county jails, but rather in regional juvenile detention centers or in a nonsecure detention program.

Detention centers provide a safe and secure environment as an alternative to adult jails. In 1978, the first state-operated juvenile detention center opened in Cumberland County. In 1984, all children in North Carolina being held for a criminal offense were removed from adult jails and holding facilities. The Division of Youth Services, Department of Health and Human Services, operates eight regional secure detention centers located in Buncombe, New Hanover, Wake, Cumberland, Gaston, Granville, Pitt, and Wilkes Counties. Nonsecure detention programs are for those children who do not present a danger to the community or themselves. These programs meet the needs of children who require supervision rather than secure custody. There are about twenty nonsecure detention programs in operation across the state.

Adjudication

Some juvenile courts, such as Denver's, are mandated by state constitution, but that is the exception. Most are statutory courts. State statutes specify the type of juvenile cases that can be brought to juvenile court, the age of youth whose cases can be heard, the procedures in processing delinquents, and the authority of judicial officers at each stage of proceedings. Local governments enact curfew and traffic ordinances whose violations are heard in juvenile court but state law determines the court's primary subject matter (Rubin 1996, 41).

Juvenile court structure differs by state, and by county within some states. Juvenile courts exist as special jurisdiction trial courts in some states, are located within the state's general jurisdiction trial courts in others, and within the trial courts of limited jurisdiction in others (Rubin 1996, 42). Juvenile court may occur in a freestanding courthouse or juvenile court center. Juvenile court centers, primarily located in suburban areas, typically include the office of juvenile probation and a juvenile detention center (Rubin 1996, 47). In most states juvenile court is typically held in the central, downtown courthouse where other courts are held. Juvenile cases are docketed for one afternoon a week, a day a week, or more frequently depending on the size of the jurisdiction. Because juvenile proceedings are confidential, no one unrelated to the case may be present in the courtroom. In these situations, when the judge is ready to hear the juvenile docket, the bailiff clears the courtroom and the judge announces the first juvenile case.

In North Carolina, juvenile court is located within the district court. District court has jurisdiction of cases concerning children under age 16 who are delinquent or undisciplined. Delinquents have committed acts, that if committed by an adult, would be a crime or infraction. Undisciplined children are those who are beyond parental control, truant from school, or both (Drennan 1989, 487). Cases involving serious felonies, such as rape or murder, may be transferred to superior court (Administrative Office of the Courts 1991, 99-103). Proceedings in juvenile court are initiated by *petition*, the equivalent of an indictment in a criminal case. The petition is filed by the District Attorney's Office (Administrative Office of the Courts 1991, 77-86). In large counties, an assistant district attorney may specialize in juvenile prosecutions. In others, assistant district attorneys handle juvenile cases as part of their regular caseload.

The hearing on the petition, conducted by a judge, is less formal than in a criminal case. No juvenile cases are heard by a jury. Juveniles do possess rights guaranteed by North Carolina's

Juvenile Code; however, and these include the right to counsel. In any proceeding which involves an allegation of delinquency, the judge appoints counsel for the juvenile (unless the juvenile arranges for a private attorney). In some counties, public defenders are used to represent juveniles. In others, an attorney is assigned from a panel or list of attorneys from the community who have expressed an interest in representing children in juvenile court (Administrative Office of the Courts 1991, 77-98).[2]

The chief district judge determines which judge will hear juvenile court cases. There are no specific requirements concerning training or qualifications. Judges must possess a law degree, although there are still a few judges holding juvenile court without a law degree. In some districts, district judges choose to hear juvenile cases and specialize as juvenile judges. In others, there are judges that choose not to hear any (Powers, Wells, and Coleman 1996, 19).

State law (N.C.Gen Stat § 7A-147(c)) requires that the AOC develop a plan to enable district court judges to increase their qualifications to hear juvenile cases. A juvenile court certification process has been established and certification training is provided by the AOC and the Institute of Government at the University of North Carolina at Chapel Hill. Training topics include juvenile law, child development, educational issues, family dynamics, and medical signs of abuse and neglect. Certification also requires that the judge preside over at least one hundred juvenile hearings within twelve months of completing the training. There is no provision for renewing this certification (Powers, Wells, and Coleman 1996, 19).

---

2. Juvenile court also has jurisdiction in dependency, abuse and neglect cases. These concern children under age 18. A *dependent* child is one who is dependent on the state and is placed into the state foster care system. To assist in these cases, the state operates a statewide guardian ad litem program. See chapter 11.

Disposition

Disposition in juvenile court parallels sentencing in adult court, except that "disposition" means more than "sentence." Theoretically, it is the point at which the court decides "what is to be done" with the child. Practically speaking, the range of facilities and programs and the participation of both public and private agencies distinguishes juvenile corrections from adult corrections. In the juvenile system, delinquents, status offenders, voluntary admissions, and dependent children may be housed in the same facilities. Many of these facilities are private organizations, either nonprofit agencies or for-profit businesses, which contract for services with the state.

Administrative organization of juvenile disposition varies by state. Juveniles adjudicated delinquent are placed under the supervision of a Department of Juvenile Justice or the Division of Social Services. Juveniles who receive a disposition of supervision within the community are placed on probation similar to adults. Yet the juvenile court may go further in regulating the lifesyle of juveniles on probation; the judge may order juveniles to live in certain locations, attend school, and participate in programs intended to alter their behavior. In some states, juvenile intake officers also serve as juvenile probation officers; in others, social workers within the Department of Social Services assist the court in arranging aftercare services for children, including counseling, community supervision, or residential services. Residential services include day treatment, group homes, and clinical detention facilities. Juveniles who receive a disposition of detention are held in a range of custody facilities. These include detention centers, training schools, reception and diagnostic centers, shelters, ranches, forestry camps and farms.

Before a hearing to determine the child's disposition in North Carolina, a court counselor or social services worker may investigate the matter alleged in the petition and the child's background, and make findings for the judge's consideration. The judge's authority in delinquency cases ranges from placing children on probation to confining them in a training school (Drennan 1989, 487; Administrative Office of the Courts 1991, 119-137).

Probation and Parole

The Juvenile Services Division of AOC is responsible for probation and aftercare. Juvenile probationers are supervised by court counselors with the court counselor's office. The conditions or length of probation may be modified by the judge at any time provided the juvenile and parents give notice and a hearing is held. Juveniles alleged to have violated a condition of probation may be required to return to court. If the allegations are true, the judge may assign another disposition, including confinement in a juvenile institution (Administrative Office of the Courts 1991, 135).

There is no juvenile parole board in North Carolina. The release date for each juvenile is determined by staff at the institution in consultation with aftercare counselors unless the court specifies a release date in deciding the term of commitment.

Community Services

Juveniles who receive a disposition other than probation are the responsibility of the Division of Youth Services (DYS). The DYS is headed by a director who is appointed by the secretary of the Department of Health and Human Services. Administrative services provided by the DYS include fiscal management, staff development, planning, technical assistance, and data management.

Community Based Alternatives. In 1975, the general assembly provided for the creation of community-based alternatives to training school commitment with the intention of reducing the number of status offenders within youth development institutions. Status offenders are those juveniles guilty of offenses that would not be violations of the law if committed by an adult, such as running away and truancy. The legislation funded Community-Based Alternative (CBA) programs.

Located in each county approved for funding, CBA program staff assist in the planning and organization of community programs for youth. More than 390 locally-operated programs aimed at prevention and intervention are organized through the CBA program (Marcus 1995). These are locally directed by a CBA Youth Services Advisory Committee (YSAC), which is mandated by statute to annually review the needs of troubled juveniles within the county. The DYS develops and implements uniform standards for the operations of CBA programs. The Secretary of the Department of Health and Human Resources oversees a grant program in which local governments received matching state funds for community-based programs for juveniles.

Counties receive money from the state of North Carolina for CBA program grants based on the number of young people in the population. The county board of commissioners allocates state funds and matching county funds to community programs based on the recommendations of the YSAC. The YSAC develops a planning process, which includes needs assessment and monitoring of existing CBA funded programs, to make its annual recommendations. The YASC's role is to improve coordination between the schools, juvenile court, department of social services, and the community mental health agency. The YSAC also develops a comprehensive plan of services for the at-risk youth population. YSAC members are appointed by the county commissioners.

Figure 14. Dobbs School, Kinston. Opened in 1944, Dobbs is a training school for delinquent boys. It has a rated capacity of 162.

Institutional Facilities

The DYS also has responsibility for institutional facilities. These include six regional detention centers, three schools, and six multipurpose homes. Regional detention centers are located at Asheville, Fayetteville, Dallas, Greenville, Raleigh and Wilkesboro. Multipurpose homes are located at Edenton, New Bern, Winton, Franklin, Lumberton, and Goldsboro. C.A. Dillon School in Butner and Dobbs School in Kinston hold boys ages 18 or younger; Stonewall Jackson School in Concord holds felons. Samarkland Manor in Eagle Springs holds girls (felons and misdemeanants) and the Juvenile Evaluation Center at Swannanoa provides services to both girls and boys (American Correctional Association 1995, 340-341).

Training Schools. In 1969, North Carolina had 2,595 admissions to training schools, the highest number of juveniles in training schools in the United States. Since then, the state has reduced the number of admissions to training schools and the number of training schools. There are five training schools currently in operation; three of the eight operating since1969 have been transferred to the Department of Correction.

North Carolina's first training school opened in 1909. Stonewall Jackson Training School, North Carolina's first and largest correctional institution, opened after a campaign by James P. Cook. Cook, editor of a newspaper in his hometown of Concord, became a lifetime advocate of a state reform school for wayward boys after witnessing the sentencing of a 13-year-old boy who received a three-and-a-half year sentence of hard labor for stealing $1.30. In 1907, the citizens of Concord raised $10,000 toward the purchase of a farm near Concord, and in 1908, the King's Daughters, a woman's club, raised $5,000 toward construction of the first cottage. By 1951, the school had more than five hundred boys, and a program featuring trades in machine shop, shoe shop, sewing, printing, barbering, textiles, dairying, along with an academic school and gymnasium.

In 1974, North Carolina, along with other states, began diverting juveniles away from training schools and towards community-based programs. In 1997, the DYS implemented a revised treatment program for the five training schools operated by the state. All schools operate under one treatment manual and a uniform code of conduct (rules and sanctions for misbehavior). The overall mission of the schools is to provide appropriate treatment according to the needs of juveniles committed by the court. These services include educational, clinical, medical vocational, and recreational programs. Program requirements depend on classification group, length of stay ranging from nine months to sixty days across five treatment categories. In August 1995, all five training schools were reaccredited by the American Correctional Association.

Multipurpose Juvenile Homes. In 1993, the state opened six multipurpose juvenile homes with eight beds in each. The homes operate under contract with private providers: North Carolina Methodist Homes for Children and Mountain Youth Resources. These homes serve juveniles identified by juvenile court as in need of either secure detention or training school commitment. A major goal of these homes is to reduce training school commitments by providing realistic program options for court-referred youth, particularly in rural areas of the state with few alternative programs. Five of the homes are located in eastern North Carolina, the other in Macon County. Each home serves one or two judicial districts (Division of Youth Services 1997, 14).

Eckerd Theraputic Wilderness Camping Program. In 1977, the Eckerd Wilderness Educational System of Florida approached the state of North Carolina willing to invest $400,000 over a three-year period for theraputic wilderness camps. Eckerd Theraputic Wilderness Camps are for young people ages 8 to 15 with behavioral problems or who have had encounters with the law. North Carolina foundations, Babcock, Duke, and Z. Smith Reynolds, matched the Eckerd offer and the general assembly authorized additional funds. Four theraputic camps opened between 1977 and 1979, one in each region of the Department of Human Resources. Each camp was designed to treat sixty boys, ages 7 to 17, who live for about twelve months in small residential groups of ten campers and two counselors. Girls groups were at two of the camps in 1983 and 1984 (Alley and Wilson 1994, 65). The Eckerd Theraputic Wilderness Camping program is a partnership between Eckerd Family Youth Alternatives, a private nonprofit foundation, and the DYS.

Death Penalty

The death penalty for juveniles generates considerable controversy within the legislature and the public in general. Across the country, however, few persons have been executed in recent years for crimes committed while being a juvenile. In North Carolina, despite legal authorization to execute persons as young as age 14, there have been no executions of persons for crimes committed while under age 18 since 1973 (when current statistics began).

Juvenile death penalty statutes vary by state. In about eight states, there is no minimum age for the death penalty. In most states that specify a minimum age for the death penalty, the minimum is set at ages 16 or 18. (There is no death penalty in about thirteen states.) In *Sanford v. Kentucky* (1989), the U.S. Supreme Court decided that the Eighth Amendment to the U.S. Constitution does not prohibit the death penalty for crime committed at ages 16 or 17. Despite legal provision for the death penalty, imposition of the death penalty for crimes committed at age 17 or younger is rare. From 1973 to 1996, 143 death sentences were handed down to 130 persons who were younger than age 18 at the time of their crime. Youth under 18 represented about 2% of persons sentenced to death during that time (Office of Juvenile Justice and Delinquency Prevention 1997, 44).

In North Carolina, age 17 is the minimum age for the death penalty unless the offender was incarcerated for murder when a subsequent murder occurred; then the age may be 14 (Bureau of Justice Statistics 1996, 5).[3] Four of 130 offenders across the nation sentenced to death for crime committed before age 18 were sentenced in North Carolina. Texas and Florida accounted for about one third of the total. During the same time period, nine executions occurred. All offenders had been age 17 at the time of offense, they ranged between age 24 and age 31 at the time of execution. On average, executions took place twelve years after

---

3. Effective 1994, North Carolina's criminal procedure allows, only by order of a judge, admission of a defendant's juvenile record as evidence in either the guilt phase or to prove an aggravating factor at sentencing (N.C. Gen. Stat. § 1, 7A-675(a)).

initial death sentences were imposed. Five of the nine executions occurred in Texas; there were none in North Carolina.

Meeting the Needs of African American Youth

The founders of North Carolina's juvenile justice system overlooked youth of African ancestry. Providing for African American juveniles began with efforts of African Americans. N. Yolanda Burwell, Associate Professor of Social Work at East Carolina University, has uncovered historical evidence of self-help efforts among Black North Carolinians. By collecting pennies, nickels and dimes from "friends," African Americans paid the salaries and expenses of the first "colored" social workers in rural North Carolina (Burwell 1995). Lawence Oxley, an early African American social worker, used the politics of self-help to change public welfare activities and influenced the course of juvenile justice in North Carolina (Burwell 1996).

In 1925, the State Board of Charities and Public Welfare created the Bureau of Work among Negroes. It was the first of its kind in the nation and became a model for other states in the South and Midwest (Burwell 1996). The bureau was funded by a $60,000 grant from the Laura Spelman Rockefeller Memorial Fund and money from local African American commuties. The grant allowed the state to set up pilot programs for social services in selected counties; in 1926 there were only thirteen Black social workers in the entire state. The bureau was headed by Lawrence A. Oxley, who later left for a career in the U.S. Department of Labor. By the time Oxley left the bureau, welfare services for Blacks had been organized in 35 counties (Crow, Escott and Hatley 1992,137; Burwell 1996).

Oxley centered his efforts on broken homes, truants, and delinquent children, along with providing medical and other services to industrial workers. Focusing on Appalachia, Oxley found that no Black youths had been declared wards of the county and the delinquent Black children were sent home to be whipped by their parents, a disposition never given with youth (Alley and Wilson 1994, 6). In 1929, Oxley's agency received funds from the Rosenwald Foundation to study child welfare among blacks. Oxley conducted a survey of local officials across the state to uncover White attitudes toward Blacks after legal enfranchisement. Few of those surveyed desired Blacks to achieve an education or receive anything other than farm laborers. The clerk of court in Burke County put it this way, "The white people should not be taxed in order to put money into something that is of no value. 'Educate' a negro and you ruin a good servant" (Crowe, Escott and Hatley 1994, 138).

Not surprisingly, North Carolina's Black citizens saw a pressing need to establish educational institutions for themselves. Palmer Memorial Institute, in Sedalia, was among the most well known. Founded by Dr. Charlotte Hawkins Brown in 1902, Palmer Memorial Institute offered both elementary and high school education. Brown, the granddaughter of former slaves, directed Palmer Memorial Institute from one that emphasized agricultural and industrial pursuits to an accredited junior college by the end of the 1920s (Crow, Escott, and Hatlley 1994,157-158). In 1925, the State Federated Negro Women's Club, led by Brown, set up the Efland Home for Girls near Hillsboro. The home housed twenty girls, including twelve committed there by the juvenile court, although the institution was not state supported. The home offered instruction in sewing and domestic science. Oxley helped club members lobby the legislature to take over the home, but the state provided only a small appropriation and it was forced to close in 1942 (Alley and Wilson 1994, 7).

In 1990, federal legislation guiding the distribution of federal funds under the Juvenile Justice and Delinquency Prevention Act required participating states to determine whether a disproportionate number of minority children are in state custody. Research conducted by Charles Dean and Robert Brame of the Office of Justice Research at University of North Carolina at Charlotte, found that about half of the juveniles referred to intake were African American although African Americans comprised about one-forth of the juvenile community. The racial distribution of those juveniles adjudicated was similar to those of juveniles referred for intake; African Americans made up about two-thirds of the population of juveniles committed, although they made up less than half of those referred to intake and those adjudicated. The authors concluded by emphasizing the need for further research and suggesting that the same pattern did not vary by county. "In short, [the data] indicate that minority overrepresentation is less of a problem at the level of court referral decision making while it may be more of a problem when decisions about confining juveniles to training school facilities... The court referral stage appears to largely pass along the racial distribution that it receives" (Dean and Brame 1994, 11).

References

Alley, Betty G. and John T. Wilson. 1994. *North Carolina juvenile justice system: A history 1868-1993*. Raleigh: North Carolina Administrative Office of the Courts.

Administrative Office of the Courts. 1991. *Juvenile justice procedures*. Raleigh: North Carolina Administrative Office of the Courts.

American Correctional Association. 1995. *Directory of juvenile and adult correctional departments, institutions, agencies and paroling authorities*. Laurel, Md.: American Correctional Association

Ashman, Allan. 1968. North Carolina jails and prisons: A brief history. *Popular Government* 33:1-6.

Brannon, Joan G. 1994. *The judicial system in North Carolina*. Raleigh: North Carolina Administrative Office of the Courts.

Bureau of Justice Assistance. 1996. *Capital punishment 1994*. Washington, D.C.: U.S. Department of Justice, Office of Justice Programs.

Bureau of Justice Assistance. 1995. *Drug abuse resistance education (D.A.R.E.)*. BLA Fact Sheet. Washington, D.C.: U.S. Department of Justice, Office of Justice Programs.

Burwell, N. Yolanda. 1995. Shifting the historical lens: Early economic empowerment among African Americans. *Journal of Baccalaureate Social Work* 1:25-37.

_____. 1996. Lawrence Oxley and locality development: Black self-help in North Carolina, 1925-1928. In *African American community practice models: Historical and contemporary responses* (Iris Carlton-LaNey and N. Yolanda Burwell, eds.). New York: Haworth Press.

Center for Prevention of School Violence. 1997. The North Carolina high school strategy survey: The center's safe school pyramid and other strategies for ensuring safety and security. *CenterLink Research Bulletin* 1:1-10.

Champion, Dean J. 1992. *The juvenile justice system: Delinquency, processing and the law*. New York: Macmillan.

Crow, Jeffrey J., Paul Escott, and Flora J. Hatley. 1994. *A history of African Americans in North Carolina*. Raleigh: North Carolina Division of Archives and History.

Dean, Charles W. and Robert Brame. 1994. *The effect of minority group membership on juvenile case dispositions: An assessment of the evidence from ten North Carolina counties*. Charlotte: Office of Justice Research, University of North Carolina-Charlotte.

Division of Youth Services. 1997. *Sourcebook 1997*. Raleigh: North Carolina Department of Health and Human Services.

Drennan, James C. 1989. The courts. In *County government in North Carolina* (A. Fleming Bell, II, ed.). Chapel Hill: Institute of Government.

Hargrove, Donn and Janet Mason. 1998. North Carolina's juvenile court counselors, *Popular Government* 62:3-11.

Marcus, Lisa A. 1995. *North Carolina manual 1995/1996.* Raleigh: Secretary of State.

Office of Juvenile Justice and Delinquency Prevention. 1997. *Juvenile offenders and victims: 1997 update on violence.* Washington, D.C.: Office of Juvenile Justice and Delinquency Prevention.

Platt, Anthony M. 1977. *The child savers: The invention of delinquency.* Chicago: University of Chicago Press.

Pope, Carl E. 1995. Juvenile justice in the next millenium. In *Crime and justice in the year 2010* (John Klofus and Stan Stojkovich, eds.) Belmont, Calif.: Wadsworth Publishing.

Powers, Linda, Susan Wells, and Emily Coleman. 1996. *Child protection proceedings in North Carolina juvenile courts.* Research Triangle Park: Research Triangle Institute.

Rubin, H. Ted. 1996. The nature of the court today. *The Future of Children* [The David and Lucille Packard Foundation] 6:40-52.

Torbet, Patricia *et al.* 1996. *State responses to serious and violent juvenile crime.* Washington, D.C.: Office of Juvenile Justice and Delinquency Prevention.

Chapter 9

The Federal Presence

Criminal justice is chiefly the function of state and local government. Federal law enforcement agencies make far fewer arrests than local police, federal courts try a fraction of the criminal cases tried by state courts, and federal prisons confine a small number compared to those in state prisons. Of spending by all levels of government for criminal justice activities in the United States, the federal government spends about 14%, state governments 32%, and local governments 53% (Maguire and Pastore 1995, 5).

While state and local criminal justice activities originated in colonial government, federal criminal justice developed more recently. Federal courts began with the founding of the American nation. The Judiciary Act of 1789, the first bill introduced in the U.S. Senate, divided the country into thirteen judicial districts. The U.S. Supreme Court first assembled in 1790 in New York City (then the nation's capital). Some federal law enforcement organizations, such as the U.S. Marshal's Services, began about this same time but a number of others developed more recently. The Federal Bureau of Investigation (FBI), for example, did not begin until 1935; it developed from the Bureau of Investigation under the U.S. Attorney General, created by executive order in 1908. The Federal Bureau of Prisons was not organized until 1933. The federal prison on Alcatraz, nicknamed the "The Rock," opened that

Figure 15. United States Courthouse and Federal Building, Raleigh. The building houses the U.S. District Court for the Eastern District of North Carolina including offices of the senior judge, clerk, and U.S. attorney.

year as well. Alcatraz had been the Army's Pacific Branch Military prison in since 1907.[1]

Nevertheless, there are two criminal justice systems in North Carolina: the state system and the federal system. The federal system includes each major aspect of criminal justice: law enforcement, prosecution, adjudication, and corrections. For the most part, the federal and state systems are parallel systems.

---

1. The expense of ferrying water, fuel, food, and supplies made Alcatraz about twice as expensive to operate as any other federal prison. Attorney General Robert Kennedy closed the prison in 1963. In 1972, Alcatraz Island became a national park administered by the National Park Service.

Federal and State Jurisdiction

The two criminal justice systems are a product of shared powers of the federal and state governments. The operation of two parallel court systems, a state system and the federal system, is known as a *dual court system*. Once a case enters either federal or state courts, it is unlikely to move from one system to the other. Exceptions are cases tried in superior court and appealed to the North Court Supreme Court, involving a substantial question of federal law. This case could be appealed to the U.S. Supreme Court.

Most criminal cases constitute violations of state law and can be tried only in state courts. All federal courts are courts of limited jurisdiction. They are empowered to hear only those cases that fall within federal judicial power, as defined by the U.S. Constitution, and entrusted to them by the U.S. Congress. For criminal activity to be within federal jurisdiction, it must arise under a specific criminal statute passed by U.S. Congress. Some crimes, such as counterfeiting, racketeering, blackmail, treason, mail fraud, and illegal immigration are prohibited by federal law and can be tried only in federal courts.[2] Some crim-

---

2. In *United States v. Ensbrook Breeze*, the defendant was charged with stealing government funds an illegally making $20 bills. Breeze was involved in a scam in which he assured undercover agents of the U.S. Secret Service that he could make $20 bills out of $1 bills. As part of the investigation, the agents provided Breeze with a quantity of money for conversion. Breeze decided to take the money and run. At his trial in U.S. District Court for the Middle District of North Carolina, Breeze defended himself by informing the jury that he was an experienced con man. He claimed to be so good, in fact, that the U.S. Secret Service had offered him a $60,000 a year position if he could fool other Secret Service agents. Breeze claimed to be auditioning for the job when he was caught. The jury remained unimpressed, however, and returned a verdict of guilty. Prior to the trial, Judge Hiram H. Ward had advised the jury in his preliminary instructions that actual trials are not like

inal acts, however, violate both state and federal laws and can be tried in either state or federal courts. It is also possible for a person to be prosecuted in both state and federal courts for a single act. Prosecution in both court systems does not violate the prohibition against double jeopardy because the two systems are sovereign systems; killing a person, for example, is defined and punished differently (Glick 1993, 49).

Practically speaking, how a case winds up in federal court or state court depends on which prosecutor, federal or state, files the case. If the case is developed by a state or local law enforcement agency, and a district attorney decides to file the case, the crime will be prosecuted in state court. If a federal law enforcement agency develops the case, and a U.S. attorney decides to prosecute, the case will be a federal case. Which cases prosecutors receive depend on the cases law enforcement organizations investigate and develop. Federal and state law enforcement coordinate in the investigation of some criminal activities; in others areas, law enforcement organizations have traditionally developed particular areas of emphasis. Therefore, motor vehicle theft would likely be investigated by municipal police or the sheriff's department and prosecuted in state superior court. Auto theft involving organized crime and interstate activity would be handled by the FBI and prosecuted in U.S. District Court.

Sometimes a case, which has been investigated by a state law enforcement agency, will be prepared for prosecution in federal court. The "task force" concept, for example, combines the expertise and resources of state and local agencies with federal agencies. In 1992, President Reagan announced creation of the

---

the interesting, unusual drama as seen on television. After Breeze had given his testimony and the verdict had been returned, the judge apologized to the jury and retracted his earlier statement (Executice Office of U.S. Attorneys 1989, 123).

Organized Crime Drug Enforcement Task Force (OCDETF) Program. The program created regional networks of local, state, and federal law enforcement agencies to combat drug trafficking and organized crime. A case investigated primarily or exclusively by the SBI may be prosecuted in federal district court when the U.S. Attorney's Office, in consultation with the SBI and the state attorney general, decide that federal court is more appropriate. So long as federal jurisdiction exists—that is, if it can be proven that violation of federal law occurred—the case becomes federal. The state law enforcement agencies then assist the U.S. Attorney's Office in preparation and presentation of the case (Mckenzie Cole 1998, 14).

Law Enforcement

Many federal agencies possess law enforcement responsibilities of one sort or another. There are about twenty federal agencies employing five hundred or more full-time officers with authority to carry firearms and make arrests (Maguire and Pastore 1995, 60).[3] These include the U.S. Capitol Police, U.S. Forest Service, and U.S. Fish and Wildlife Service. In North Carolina, seven federal agencies are the most active.

Alcohol, Tobacco and Firearms Bureau

The Bureau of Alcohol, Tobacco, and Firearms (ATF) enforces federal laws regulating the sale, distribution, and posses-

---

3. Not including law enforcement personnel of the U.S. Armed Forces or the U.S Coast Guard.

sion of firearms, explosives, alcohol and tobacco products. Special agents investigate such matters as illegal trafficking of cigarettes and firearms across state lines, arson-for-profit schemes involving explosive devices, and criminal and domestic terrorist groups in illegal possession of firearms and explosives. The ATF began as an investigative branch within the U.S Department of Treasury with the "Whiskey Rebellion" of 1794 and grew during prohibition (as the Bureau of Prohibition) as Elliot Ness received national attention. ATF agents, or "revenuers," searched the woods of North Carolina for whiskey stills. Today, ATF activities include violations of firearms laws, illegal use of explosives, arson, and illegal trafficking in cigarettes. There are five ATF field offices in North Carolina: Charlotte, Fayetteville, Raleigh, Wilmington, and Winston-Salem.

Federal Bureau of Investigation

The Federal Bureau of Investigation (FBI) is one of the best known law enforcement organizations in the world due to the efforts of its first director, J. Edgar Hoover. The FBI has broad jurisdiction that covers a range of cases including kidnapping, bank robbery, fraud, organized crime, civil rights violations, illegal banking practices and espionage. Located within the U.S. Department of Justice, the FBI is divided into fifty-six divisional offices across the country with a headquarters in the J. Edgar Hoover Building in Washington, DC. The FBI operates a forensic laboratory and the National Crime Information Center. The FBI has a field office in Charlotte, and resident agencies at Asheville, Hickory, Greensboro, Elizabeth City, Greenville, Wilmington, Raleigh/Durham, and Fayetteville. The FBI has investigated cases in North Carolina involving public corruption, illegal banking, gambling, white-collar fraud, interstate transportation of stolen property, civil rights violations, and election fraud.

Drug Enforcement Agency

The Drug Enforcement Agency (DEA) enforces federal laws concerning drugs. Located within the U.S. Department of Justice, DEA agents enforce the registration provision of federal drug laws, combat illicit narcotics traffic, and the distribution of dangerous drugs. Although more than one third of DEA agents are stationed in Florida, Texas, and California, the DEA is one of the largest regulatory agencies within the federal government. The DEA regulates the entire controlled substances industry, including the dispensing of controlled substances by doctors and pharmacists. President Richard Nixon created the DEA in 1973 with an executive order consolidating the Bureau of Narcotics and Dangerous Drugs, the Office of Drug Abuse Law Enforcement, and the Office of National Narcotics Intelligence into a single agency. The (Federal) Bureau of Narcotics, the oldest DEA ancestor, was created in 1930 when President Herbert Hoover appointed Harry J. Ainslinger the first Commissioner of Narcotics. Today, the DEA has twenty field divisions throughout the United States. The Atlanta Division has four subdivisions in North Carolina: Charlotte, Greensboro, Raleigh, and Wilmington.

U.S. Customs Criminal Investigation

The Criminal Investigation Division (CID) of U.S. Customs investigates smuggling of goods in and out of the country. The U.S. Customs is charged with enforcing nearly four hundred federal laws, including laws intended to guarantee payment of revenue for incoming goods, to protect the health and safety of citizens, and to protect trademark and patents of U.S. companies. U.S. Customs was organized in 1789 to protect tax revenue. It was placed, as it is today, within the U.S. Treasury Department. The U.S. Congress authorized a Special Service

Agency, forerunner of the U.S. Custom's Office of Investigations, in 1870. Today, the agency has 17,000 employees; most are deployed at 300 points of entry along the Mexican and Canadian borders and at international airports throughout the United States. The states with the most U.S. Customs agents are Texas, California, New York, and Florida.

Internal Revenue Service Criminal Investigation

The Internal Revenue Service (IRS), the largest bureau within the U.S. Treasury Department, seeks to encourage voluntary compliance with the tax revenue system. The CID of the IRS investigates cases to determine if sufficient evidence exists to recommend prosecution for wilful attempts to violate federal tax laws. CID special agents investigate cases concerning tax fraud schemes, illegal tax protest groups, and money laundering. There are about 2,800 special agents located within 7 regional offices and 63 district offices. The IRS CID district office for North Carolina is located in Greensboro.

U.S. Secret Service

The U.S. Secret Service is best known for its role protecting the President of the United States. U.S. Secret Service agents provide security for the president, the vice president, former presidents and their families as well as visiting heads of foreign governments and, at the direction of the president, other foreign visitors to the United States. More than two thousand agents provide security for the White House, Treasury Building, and the embassies of foreign governments in the United States. The Uniformed Division, also known as the White House Police Force, was organized in 1922. Congress created the U.S. Secret Service in 1865 for the sole purpose of suppressing counterfeit currency. In 1901, Congress directed the

Secret Service to protect the president after the assassination of President William McKinley. The Secret Service protects coins and securities of the federal government, and investigates cases of counterfeiting including credit card fraud. Agents also investigate computer fraud, automated teller machine fraud, cellular and long distance telephone fraud, and electronic fund transfer fraud. There are U.S. Secret Service field offices located in Charlotte and Raleigh

U.S. Postal Inspection Service

The U.S. Postal Inspection Service has responsibilities related to the security of the postal system. Postal inspectors enforce eighty-five postal-related laws. They investigate losses of mail and property owned by the U.S. Post Office, robberies of post offices and vehicles, fraudulent schemes perpetrated by means of the mail, and sending prohibited items through the mail such as narcotics and explosives. More than 2,000 postal inspectors are organized into 150 field offices across the country; postal inspectors are authorized to carry firearms and make arrests. There is a field division office for the U.S. Postal Inspection Service located in Charlotte.

Immigration and Naturalization Service

The Immigration and Naturalization Service (INS) enforces the immigration and naturalization laws of the United States. INS officers conduct investigations concerning entry of illegal aliens, review applications for visas, gather information about residence of those convicted in federal court, and gather information for civil and criminal hearings related to deportation. The chief duty of the Border Patrol—a highly-mobile, uniformed force component of INS—is to detect and prevent illegal entry of persons into the United States. Border Patrol agents inspect commercial carriers across international borders, question suspects at terminals and ports of entry, and carry out deportation actions. The INS operates in North Carolina from a district office located in Atlanta, Georgia.

U.S. Marshal's Service

The U.S. Marshal's Service executes commands of the federal courts. Deputy U.S. Marshals provide protection for federal judges and juries, transport federal prisoners, seize property under court order, retrieve federal probation violators, and other duties. The U.S. Marshal's Service operates the witness protection program, which protects, relocates and issues "new identities" to government witnesses in organized crime cases. Also, the U.S. Marshal's Service carries out the extradition of fugitives in foreign countries in coordination with the International Police (INTERPOL). There are 94 U.S. marshals appointed by the president and about 2,500 deputy marshals. There are U.S. marshals in North Carolina located in Raleigh, Greensboro, and Asheville; districts coincide with federal court districts.

Prosecution and Defense

United States Attorney

Federal prosecutors are known as U.S. attorneys. Upon receiving arrest reports from the ATF, FBI, or other law enforcement agency, the U.S. attorney decides whether to file criminal charges. The prosecutor must decide what federal laws and been violated and exactly what charges to file. Federal prosecutors are obliged to follow policies established by the Justice Department in Washington, DC, and those of the Executive Office for U.S. Attorneys. The Executive Office for U.S.

Attorneys was established by order of the U.S. Attorney General in 1953 "to provide general executive assistance and supervision to the offices of the United States Attorneys." But as a practical matter, U.S. attorneys tend to identify as local law enforcement officials (Glick 1993, 210). As is true with most violations of federal law, U.S. attorneys have broad discretion to initiate, pursue, and decline criminal prosecutions.

When the U.S. Congress created the federal court system, it also created the office of U.S. attorney. The Judiciary Act of 1789 directed the president to appoint in each federal judicial district "a person learned in the law to act as an attorney for the United States." The first U.S. attorneys, who were appointed by President George Washington, were paid on a fee system. In 1861, the U.S. Congress authorized supervision of the U.S. attorneys by the U.S. Attorney General and in 1870, the attorney general became head of the Department of Justice. In 1896, Congress abolished the fee system and established the salary system.

Before the Civil War, U.S. attorneys prosecuted only cases mentioned specifically in the Constitution. These were piracy, counterfeiting, treason, perjury, bribery, and arson (Executive Office for U.S. Attorneys 1989, 2). Over the years, caseloads have changed. Cases involving the great Brink's robbery, the trial of Aaron Burr, the Chicago Seven, Al Capone, and civil rights murders in Mississippi have all been handled by U.S. attorneys (Executive Office for U.S. Attorneys 1989, 5).

Presently, there are ninety-three U.S. Attorneys and their staffs. U.S. Attorneys are appointed by the president, although the politics surrounding the selection process usually results in appointment of an attorney with a local background. Assistant U.S. attorneys are appointed by the U.S. attorney general upon the recommendations of the U.S. Attorney. Both U.S. attorneys and assistant U.S. attorneys are salaried and prohibited from engaging in private law practice while in office (Mckenzie Cole 1998, 3).

In the Eastern District of North Carolina, the permanent staff of a U.S. attorney's office includes the U.S. attorney, full-time assistant district attorneys, paralegal specialists, an administrative officer, and clerical staff. The office is headquartered in Raleigh, the location of all permanent staff. Unstaffed office space is maintained in Elizabeth City, Fayetteville, Greenville, New Bern, and Wilmington for use when staff members are attending court in those divisions. The office is divided into a civil division and a criminal division. The criminal division is headed by an assistant district attorney. The criminal division works along side the grand jury, in session for two days a month, and investigative law enforcement agencies, which investigate cases for prosecution.

As one of the original thirteen states, North Carolina became one of the first districts assigned a U.S. attorney. The first appointee was John Sitgreaves, commissioned in 1790 for the district of North Carolina. Sitgreaves, who had distinguished himself in the North Carolina Militia during the Revolutionary War, served as a delegate to the Continental Congress in 1784 and 1785. Another North Carolinian, Charles B. Aycock, became U.S. attorney for the Eastern District of North Carolina in 1893; in 1899, he was elected governor of North Carolina. In 1893, Robert B. Glenn became U.S. attorney for the Western District; he was elected to the North Carolina Senate in 1899 and in 1904, was elected governor of North Carolina.

Federal Public Defender

Pursuant to the Criminal Justice Act, the federal public defender is appointed by the court to represent indigent criminal defendants who desire, but cannot afford to retain an attorney to represent them. The court determines a defendant's financial eligibility. Once appointed, the federal public defender represents clients through all stages of the process, from pre-trial through the first postconviction appeal (Webb 1998).

The federal public defender represents clients charged with committing any offense designated as a felony or Class A misdemeanor under the U.S. Criminal Code. Cases range from "street crimes" to "white collar crimes" of fraud. In addition, the office represents all juveniles alleged to have committed an act of delinquency, persons charged with violating probation and supervised release, persons subject to hearings involving mental condition, persons subject to extradition to the United States, persons in custody as material witnesses, and persons who otherwise face a loss of liberty in a case where federal law requires appointment of legal counsel (Webb 1998).

The Federal Public Defender program is administered through the Administrative Office of U.S. Courts. In the Eastern District of North Carolina, the Office of the Federal Public Defender includes a first assistant public defender, nine assistant federal public defenders, a staff of investigators, a paralegal, legal secretaries, and a research and writing specialist. Two of the assistant public defenders are assigned all criminal appeals, two others represent clients during the pretrial, trial, and sentencing phases. The Federal Public defender may also assign cases to attorneys from the private bar. These *panel attorneys* are assigned to avoid any violation of the rules of professional ethics. When the public federal defender is appointed to represent a person charged with conspiracy, the office cannot represent any other person alleged to have participated in the same offense (Webb 1998).

Courts

Although the U.S. Supreme Court meets in the nation's capital, the major trial and appellate courts within the federal court system are spread across the country. Despite their federal label, trial and appellate courts are organized on a local and regional basis so that federal courts hear those cases over disputes arising within their area. Federal courts take on a local or regional flavor (Glick 1993, 28).

The federal court system began with the Judiciary Act of 1789. The law created a federal court system comprised of the U.S. Supreme Court, U.S. Circuit Courts, and U.S. District Courts. U.S. Congress designed regional jurisdiction to reflect local cases. There are no federal districts that cross state boundaries and no districts in which cases arise in areas other than that part of the state.[4] Federal judges are required to reside within their district. They are appointed by the president and approved by the U.S. Senate. This process means that senators from the state in which the appointment is made influence the selection. Federal judges are typically, born, raised, educated and are part of the politics of their home state or region (Glick 1993, 53).

The Supreme Court

The U.S. Supreme Court sits in the Supreme Court Building (completed in 1935), across from the U.S. Capitol Building, in Washington, D.C. Etched in the marble above the main entrance is the phrase "Equal Justice Under Law." Nine justices wearing black robes sit for sessions beginning the first Monday in October for a term which usually last until June or July.[5] Cases are heard *en banc*, meaning that all the justices sit together

---

4. Federal prosecutorial districts follows the geographical divisions of federal district courts.

5. When the court is in session, the Marshal announces the entrance of the justices at 10 o'clock. At the sound of the gavel, the audience rises to hear "The Honorable, Chief Justice and the Associate Justices of the Supreme Court of the United States. Oyez! Oyez! Oyez! All persons having business before the Honorable, the Supreme Court of the United States, are admonished to draw near and give their attention, for the court is now sitting. God save the United States and this Honorable Court!"

in open court. There are about 6,500 cases on the court's docket per year. About 150 cases or so are considered cases of great national significance and are granted plenary review with oral arguments by attorneys. About three-fourths of these decisions are announced in full published opinions.

Eight associate justices and the chief justice comprise the court. Members of the court are appointed by the president, subject to U.S. Senate confirmation, which until recent years, amounted to a rubber stamp. Two North Carolinians have served on the nation's highest court. James Iredell, appointed by President George Washington, served from 1790 to 1799. Iredell, who studied law under Samuel Johnston, had been collector of the Port of Edenton, judge of the North Carolina Supreme Court, and attorney general of North Carolina. Alfred Moore, appointed by President John Adams to replace Iredell, served from 1800 to 1804. Moore, of New Hanover County, served in the North Carolina General Assembly following service in the First North Carolina Regiment during the Revolutionary War. While attorney general of North Carolina, Moore argued the case of *Bayard v. Singleton* (1787), one of the earliest and fullest discussions of the doctrine of judicial review.

Courts of Appeal

The U.S. Courts of Appeal are the primary intermediate appellate court in the federal court system. There are eleven numbered circuits, plus the federal circuit and the Washington, D.C. Circuit. Congress created the Circuit Court of Appeal in 1891 to hear appeals from district courts (and old circuit courts of appeal which were originally organized as trial courts; the old circuit courts were abolished in 1911 and their powers transferred to district courts). The act also permitted the U.S. Supreme Court to become more selective (Glick 1993, 56).

The courts of appeal hear appeals from district courts located within the circuit. Criminal cases and prisoners' petitions make up about one-third of those cases in district courts, but about half of all cases in courts of appeals. Appeals in criminal cases, particularly drug cases, have increased the most since 1980 (Glick 1993, 35). Since very few cases are decided by the U.S. Supreme Court, courts of appeals are the last stop for nearly all litigants in federal courts (Glick 1993, 35).

Each circuit contains a different number of states and judges. As with district court districts, no circuit cuts across a state line. The ninth circuit includes California, Nevada, Oregon, Washington, Idaho, and Montana. The ninth circuit has been nicknamed the "California Circuit," however, because appeals from district courts in California equal as many as the other states combined (Glick 1993, 34).

Cases appealed in federal courts located in North Carolina are appealed to the 4th circuit court of appeals. The fourth circuit covers North Carolina, along with South Carolina, Virginia, West Virginia, and Maryland. The U.S. Court of Appeals, Fourth Judicial Circuit, sits in Richmond, Virginia, the first full week of each month, October through June (Marcus 1995, 957). There are ten circuit judges, a senior judge, and a chief judge.

District Courts

District courts are the trial courts of original jurisdiction within the federal court system. There is at least one district court in each state, and states with larger populations have two or more district courts. States along the eastern coast, midwestern states, and those on the western coast are divided into two or more districts. Most districts have several judges and those districts in large cities have as many as thirty judges.

Federal district courts may hear any cases involving federal law. Federal courts also have jurisdiction over cases in which the federal government is a party to the case, either as plaintiff or defendant (Glick 1993, 29). In recent years, the percentage of criminal cases in district courts has increased relative to civil cases. Many categories of federal crime have increased, including weapons violations, fraud, and especially drug offenses. The Anti-Drug Abuse Act of 1988 increased the number of ATF and border patrol agents by over 300 and the number of assistant U.S. attorneys by 1,240. Since then, the U.S. Congress has raised the penalties for drug-related crimes which has also promoted prosecution of drug cases (Glick 1993, 33).

There are about 160 federal district judges and 475 federal magistrates. U.S. magistrates have trial jurisdiction in cases involving misdemeanors and petty offenses. They also conduct preliminary proceedings in serious cases, including search warrants, initial appearances, bail reviews, grand jury returns, arraignments, evidentiary hearings, and pretrial conferences (Maguire and Pastore 1995, 73).

The U.S. Congress created the original District of North Carolina in 1790; it covered all of what is presently the state of North Carolina. It was administered by a single judge, John Sitgreaves, who was nominated by President George Washington.[6] In 1801, the U.S. Congress subdivided the District of

---

6. Washington first nominated William R. Davie, a delegate to the Constitutional Convention. Davie declined to serve however, because the pay was "too paltry." He was later appointed as a Brigadier General in the U.S. Army and later became governor of North Carolina in 1798. Washington turned next to John Stokes of Rowan County, who had lost part of his arm in the Battle of Waxhaw during the Revolutionary War. Stokes used a silver cup at the end of his amputated arm as a gavel to get the attention of the court. Stokes fell ill and died within two months of his appointment, which makes John Sitgreaves the first sitting federal judge in North Carolina (United States District Court n.d., 1).

North Carolina into three local districts: the Albemarle, Pamptico, and Cape Fear districts with courts at Edenton, New Bern, and Wilmington. This division remained until legislation in 1872 carved out the Western District of North Carolina. Since 1927, when the U.S. Congress added the Middle District, North Carolina has been divided into three judicial districts: Eastern, Middle, and Western. There is a headquarters for each district as well as divisional offices—other statutory places of holding court. The Eastern District is headquartered at the federal building in Raleigh; there are additional seats of court at Greenville, Elizabeth City, Fayetteville, New Bern, and Wilmington. The Eastern District contains forty-five eastern counties. The Middle District, has a headquarters at the U.S. Courthouse in Greensboro: there is an additional seat of court at Winston-Salem. The Middle District covers twenty-eight counties in the Piedmont. The Western District is headquartered at Charlotte, and has additional seats at Statesville and Asheville. The Western District consists of twenty-eight counties in the mountains of western North Carolina.[7]

Each district has between four and seven judges. After passage of the Omnibus Judgeship Act of 1979, the U.S. District Court for the Western District of North Carolina became one of the three busiest courts in the federal system. In 1993, the

---

7. In 1994, reorganization of the federal courts moved a divisional office for the Eastern District from New Bern to Greenville. The General Services Administration, which acquires and maintains buildings for the federal government, leases the building because the agency would need U.S. Congressional approval to build a new courthouse. This process takes years. The courthouse now has a 2800 square foot courtroom, the largest in the Eastern District, necessary for the growing number of multidefendant criminal cases. The building is equipped with state-of-art security and evidence presentation technology. The building also houses offices of the U.S. attorney, federal public defender, U.S. probation office, district judge, and the clerk of court for the Eastern District of North Carolina. The Eastern District court used to occupy a building next door which had been a post office until 1990. The old post office building now houses offices of the U.S. magistrate and U.S. pre-trial services.

U.S. District Court for the Western District of North Carolina had the second highest number of cases filed per judgeship of any federal district; the Western District had 135 criminal cases per judgeship. Only the U.S. District Courts for the Southern District of California and the Virgin Islands had higher ratios of 169 and 185 (Maguire and Pastore 1997, 63).

Corrections

Institutional Corrections

There were no federal prisons until 1891.[8] In order to comply with the Judiciary Act of 1789, the Justice Department contracted with state and local facilities to confine federal prisoners. Due to the financial rewards involved in contract prison labor, many states offered to confine federal prisoners free of charge. In 1887, however, the U.S. Congress enacted legislation prohibiting contract labor with federal prisoners and the attorney general recommended construction of a federal peniten-

---

8. Federal prisons began in the western United States during the last half of the nineteenth century. Unlike the states along the eastern coast, which started out as colonies, the states of the far west started out as territories. U.S. Congress established prisons across the west as part of its territorial policy. An 1867 act set aside proceeds from the internal revenue collected in federal territories for prison construction in the territories of Washington, Nebraska, Colorado, Idaho, Montana, Dakota, and Arizona. (The territories of Utah and New Mexico received appropriations under separate legislation in 1853, as had Oregon Territory in 1855.) Under this legislation, territorial legislatures designated sites and the Secretary of the Interior supervised construction. Once these prisons opened, U.S. marshals in the territories (who answered to the attorney general in Washington, D.C.) acted as wardens, and the U.S. government collected a fee from the territorial governments to confine territorial prisoners. In 1873, Congress transferred control of these prisons to the territories and by 1885, most federally-established prisons were under control of states and territories (Knepper 1992, 237-238).

tiary. In 1891, the U.S. Congress passed an act authorizing the purchase of three sites for U.S. penitentiaries at Leavenworth, Kansas; McNeil Island, Washington (off Puget Sound); and Atlanta, Georgia. The three-prison act did not include appropriations and it took several years before all three prisons actually opened. Atlanta Federal Penitentiary, the site selected for the southern prison, opened in 1902 (James 1990, 5).

In 1907, the U.S. attorney general created the position of superintendent of prisons within the Department of Justice. For some years, the department had employed a general agent and one or two examiners responsible for overseeing conditions at federal facilities. Robert V. Ladow served as the first superintendent of prisons. Federal legislation after 1920 (the Prohibition Act, the Harrison Narcotic Act, and the Automobile Theft Act) rapidly increased the number of federal prisoners, and nine years later the House Special Committee on Federal Penal and Reformatory Institutions drafted a report recommending creation of a central agency for administration of federal facilities. In 1930, the U.S. Congress created the Federal Bureau of Prisons (BOP) within the Department of Justice and charged it with overseeing all federal prisons (Keve 1991, 91-93).

In 1996, the BOP administrated eighty-five federal prison facilities located across the country. BOP facilities are divided into one of five security levels that are distinguished by the presence of external patrols, gun towers, fencing, type of housing, internal security features, and the inmate to staff ratio. These include several high-security U.S. penitentiaries, medium- to low-security correctional institutions, minimum security prison camps, and minimum-security satellite camps (adjacent to main facilities). Additionally, there are metropolitan correctional and detention centers (jails) located in major cities (Federal Bureau of Prisons 1996). The BOP organizational structure divides the country into six regions; North Carolina falls within the BOP's Mid-Atlantic Region.[9] There are federal facilities in North Carolina located at Seymour Johnson Air Force Base and Butner. Federal Prison Camp-Seymour Johnson, located on Seymour Johnson Air Force Base near Goldsboro, is a minimum-security facility with capacity for 576 males. Federal Correctional Institution-Butner, located near the Research Triangle area, includes both medium- and low-security facilities. Low security for males has a capacity for 992, medium security for males has a capacity of 513 (although in recent years the daily population has averaged over 700). There is also an adjacent minimum-security camp for 296 females (Federal Bureau of Prisons 1996).

The Federal Correctional Institution at Butner, North Carolina, which opened in 1976, began with James V. Bennett, who became BOP director in 1937. Bennett felt that the federal system needed a specialized prison with psychiatric services to diagnose and treat emotionally disturbed, violent prisoners. Bennett received congressional authorization but left the BOP before such an institution could be built. After Norman Carlson became director in 1970, plans for the institution were completed, and the contract for construction at Butner was approved in 1972. The BOP planned to call the new institution the Center for Behavioral Research and selected a psychiatrist, Dr. Martin Groder, to be the warden. After Groder began to recruit staff, opposition to the center started. The experience with the Tuskegee Study, in which hundreds of Black men with syphilis were left untreated for the purpose of federally-sponsored research, left concern. The Commission on Racial Justice, a church-based civil rights organization, attracted national attention to the BOP's plans for Butner (Keve 1991, 220).

---

9. This region also includes South Carolina, Virginia, West Virginia, Kentucky, Ohio, Indiana, Michigan, Maryland, and Delaware.

The Commission on Racial Justice study succeeded in redirecting the programmatic plans for Butner. The BOP renamed the institution and altered the programmatic design to apply the ideas of Norval Morris, a law professor at the University of Chicago. In an influential book, Morris had argued that behavior control schemes for forced rehabilitation do not work; the violent prisoners sent to Butner should voluntarily agree to undergo treatment at Butner. Staff training emphasized the need to allow prisoners to freely express hostile feelings so long as no assaultive action followed. Prisoners were allowed to move freely among the buildings inside double-fencing and perimeter security involving motion detectors, as recommended by Morris. Additionally, the institution followed another of Morris's suggestions and hired a high proportion of women on the staff. When Margaret Hambrick was appointed at Butner in 1981 she became the first woman to be warden of a prison for men (Keve 1991, 242). The prison has continued to serve federal courts as a place for temporary holding and clinical study prior to sentencing. Despite its population, the facility has operated with relatively few problems. It has become "recognized worldwide as an innovative prison concept" (Keve 1991, 220-221).

Probation and Parole

During the first few decades of this century, the National Probation Association campaigned for a federal probation system. Sanford Bates, the Federal Bureau of Prisons' first director favored parole and probation laws, as did Attorney General George W. Wickersham. But FBI Director J. Edgar Hoover opposed it, as did Minnesota congressional leader Andrew Volstead, who feared that bootleggers and moonshiners would take advantage of the law and undermine the prohibition act. Not until after Volstead left Congress in 1923 did Congress create a federal probation law (Keve 1991, 156; Evjen 1997).

The U.S. Congress enacted legislation to create a federal probation system in 1925. President Calvin Coolidge, whose home state of Massachusetts had created the first probation system decades earlier, signed the legislation into law. Probation services had no central directorship until 1930, when Congress gave the U.S. attorney general authority to set standards and administer combined probation and parole services. The attorney general delegated this responsibility to the director of the BOP, who subsequently hired Colonel Joel R. Moore to be supervisor of probation and parole. The legislation that created federal probation also abolished institutional parole boards and established the U.S. Bureau of Parole within the BOP. The BOP administered probation and parole until 1940, when the system was transferred to the Administrative Office of U.S. Courts, which had been created a year earlier (Keve 1991, 156; Evjen 1997).

Federal Probation and Pretrial Services employs about 3,300 federal probation officers and 439 pretrial services officers nationwide. Probation officers write presentence investigation reports, which contain recommendations for sentencing, and carry out supervision of federal offenders released conditionally in the community. Depending on the level of supervision assigned, probation officers regularly interview probationers in person, by telephone, or both. Officers also monitor probationers sentenced to home confinement, with and without electronic monitoring, make mental health referrals, and carry out requirements concerning drug screens. Pretrial services officers write pretrial services reports, which provide the information needed for decisions to release or detain suspects prior to adjudication (Storm 1997). Pretrial services officers interview defendants shortly after arrest about family, employment, prior criminal record, length of residence in the community, and results of post-arrest drug tests. Persons determined to be good risks by a U.S. magistrate are released on their own recognizance. Defendants charged with serious, violent offenses or drug trafficking are not eligible. Following release, pretrial services officers contact the defendants to ensure the defendant will appear for court (Wolf 1997).

Both probation officers and pretrial services officers carry out investigations and are also authorized by federal law to carry firearms in the performance of their duties. Most chief probation and pretrial services officers—with the approval of their district judges—have implemented firearms programs in their districts and have selected officers to serve as firearms instructors. These instructors are trained and certified at schools conducted by the Federal Corrections and Supervision Division of the Administrative Office of U.S. Courts (Wooten 1997).

Federal Assistance to States

Nationalization of crime control policy in the United States advanced with the Law Enforcement Assistance Administration (LEAA), intended to be the federal government's major entity to combat crime. In 1964, President Lyndon Johnson created the President's Commission on Law Enforcement and the Administration of Justice and pushed for legislation to create a program of federal grants to state, local, and private agencies. In 1968, the U.S. Congress passed the Omnibus Crime Control and Safe Streets Act and created the LEAA. LEAA provided funds to states (based on population) and directly to organizations for support of crime reduction strategies.

In an effort to avoid adding to the federal bureaucracy, LEAA congressional sponsors set a structure for decentralizing the agency. The largest portion of federal funds were dispersed through block grants. To receive these funds, each state had to create a state planning agency to develop a comprehensive plan for using the money. The state planning committees then allocated the money for state and local projects. Members of the state planning committees generally interpreted "law enforcement assistance" to mean assistance to police departments, and in its early years, LEAA funding emphasized state and local law enforcement. Considerable funds went for hardware and technical approaches, which led to concerns about wasteful government spending. In some cases, vendors virtually wrote grant applications for purchase of their own equipment. In later years, LEAA funds financed projects ranging from state computer crime networks to juvenile diversion programs. But by the time the Carter Administration took over, the very idea of federal assistance to local crime problems raised the specter of big government and federal interference in local issues. Congress withdrew funding for LEAA in 1980 (Walker 1980, 238).

LEAA did, however, establish a role for federal assistance to the states. Currently, the Office of Justice Programs (OJP) carries out much of what the LEAA did in the area of federal leadership. Congress created the OJP in 1984 as part of the Comprehensive Crime Control Act. The act reestablished research and statistics units within the Justice Department, and required that financial and technical assistance be provided to state and local government. The act created five bureaus headed by an assistant attorney general:

> *Bureau of Justice Statistics.* The Bureau of Justice Statistics (BJS) collects, analyzes, publishes and distributes statistics concerning crime, crime victims, criminal offenders and the operation of the justice system at the local, state, and federal levels.

> *Bureau of Justice Assistance* The Bureau of Justice Assistance (BJA) administers grant programs to improve state and local criminal justice systems. The Anti-Drug Abuse Act, for example, provides federal funding to local, state, and units of the federal government to combat drugs. BJA carries out the Edward Byrne Memorial State and Local Law Enforcement Assistance Programs to assist

state and local governments in improving their criminal justice systems as well as enhancing drug control efforts.

National Institute of Justice The National Institute of Justice (NIJ) funds research to increase knowledge of criminal behavior and improve criminal justice. NIJ provides financial assistance for evaluations of programs and various demonstration projects across the country.

Office of Juvenile Justice and Deinquency Prevention. Congress created Office of Juvenile Justice and Delinquency Prevention (OJJDP) with the Juvenile Justice and Delinquency Prevention Act of 1974 to help state and local governments improve their juvenile justice services. OJJDP also provides grants for research dealing with missing and exploited children.

Office for Victims of Crime. The Office for Victims of Crime (OVC) administers the Victims of Crime Act of 1984, including a state compensation and assistance program (a grant program providing direct assistance to victims). The fund is financed by fines and penalty assessments on defendants convicted in federal courts.

African Americans and the Federal System

Clarence Thomas, whose nomination to the position of associate justice by President George Bush in 1991 raised a firestorm of controversy during Senate confirmation proceedings, became the second African American to serve on the U.S. Supreme Court. Thomas took the seat left open by the retirement of Thurgood Marshall, the first African American U.S. Supreme Court Justice. Marshall, the great grandson of a slave and the son of a dining car waiter, earned a bachelor's degree from Lincoln University and graduated first in his class at

Howard University Law School in 1933. Marshall worked full-time for the National Association for the Advancement of Colored People (NAACP) and argued the case of *Brown v. Board of Education* (1954) decided in Marshall's favor. President John F. Kennedy appointed Marshall to the U.S. Court of Appeals for the Second Circuit in 1961; two years later, President Lyndon Johnson appointed Marshall as an associate justice of the U.S. Supreme Court. Marshall remained a champion for civil rights throughout his life (Bloch 1992, 427-528).

Few African Americans gained appointment to the federal judiciary until the Presidency of Jimmy Carter. It was Carter who appointed Henry M. "Mickey" Michaux to serve as U.S. attorney for the Middle District of North Carolina. Michaux served from 1978 to 1982, the first Black American to serve as a federal prosecutor in North Carolina. In 1966, Henry Frye became the first African American to be hired as an assistant U.S. attorney in North Carolina. Carter also appointed the first Black American to serve as a U.S. district court judge in North Carolina. Richard C. Erwin of Winston-Salem joined the Middle District of North Carolina in 1980 (Joyner 1992, 16).

In 1971, Lee B. Jett became the first black warden of a federal prison. Jett took charge of Englewood Federal Correctional Center (FCI). Opened in 1940, Englewood FCI was one of only three integrated federal prisons at the time of the landmark *Brown v. Board of Education* desegregation case in 1954 (Keve 1991, 207). J. Edgar Hoover, whose activities directed at African Americans included an effort to undermine Dr. Martin Luther King Jr., likely hired some of the first African Americans in federal law enforcement. During the Black Scare of 1918-1921, when Hoover was in charge of the Justice Department's General Intelligence Division, he used two Black agents as informers to capture Marcus Garvey. Garvey, whom Hoover considered "the foremost radical among his race," pushed for return of Blacks to Africa before he was convicted on a mail fraud charge, sentenced to five years in the Atlanta penitentiary, and deported. James Wormley Jones, confidential agent "800," infiltrated the Garvey's Universal Negro Improvement Association. James E. Amos, a special agent, assembled evidence against Garvey and prepared witnesses for trial (Hill 1984, 227).

References

Bloch, Susan L. 1992. Marshall, Thurgood. In *The Oxford companion to the supreme court of the United States* (Kermit L. Hall, ed.). New York: Oxford University Press.

Evjen, Victor. 1997. The federal probation system: The struggle to achieve it and its first 25 years. *Federal Probation* 61:81-92.

Executive Office for United States Attorneys. 1989. *Bicentennial celebration of the United States attorneys.* Washington, D.C.: Office of the Attorney General.

Federal Bureau of Prisons. 1996. *State of the bureau: Accomplishments and goals.* Washington, D.C.: U.S. Department of Justice.

Glick, Henry R. 1993. *Courts, politics and justice.* New York: McGraw-Hill.

Hill, Robert A. 1984. 'The foremost radical among his race': Marcus Garvey and the black scare, 1918-1921. *Prologue* 16:215-231.

James, Barbara G. 1990. The Atlanta federal penitentiary, 1902-1970, *Atlanta History* 34:5-23.

Joyner, Irving. 1992. The African American lawyer in North Carolina, *North Carolina State Bar Quarterly* 39:12-19.

Keve, Paul W. 1991. *Prisons and the American conscience: A history of federal corrections.* Carbondale, Ill.: Southern Illinois University Press.

Knepper, Paul. 1992. The women of Yuma: Gender, ethnicity and imprisonment in frontier Arizona, 1876-1909. *Criminal Justice Review* 17:235-257.

Maguire, Kathleen and Anne L. Pastore. 1997. *Sourcebook of criminal justice statistics 1996.* Washington, D.C.: U.S. Department of Justice, Office of Justice Programs.

Marcus, Lisa A. 1995. *North Carolina manual 1995/1996.* Raleigh: Secretary of State.

McKenzie Cole, Janice. 1998. *The office of the United States attorney.* Raleigh: United States Attorney, Eastern District of North Carolina.

Storm, John P. 1997. What United States probation officers do. *Federal Probation* 61:13-18.

Walker, Samuel. 1980. *Popular justice: A history of American criminal justice.* New York: Oxford University Press.

Webb, William. 1998. Letter to the Author, January 20, 1998. Raleigh: Federal Public Defender, Eastern District of North Carolina.

Wooten, Evey B. 1997. Firearms instruction. *Federal Probation* 61:32.

Wolf, Thomas J. 1997. What United State pretrial officers do. *Federal Probation* 61:19-24.

United States District Court. 1997. *United States District Court: Eastern District of North Carolina.* Raleigh: U.S. Courthouse and Federal Building.

Chapter 10

Education and Training

Criminal justice includes several distinct professions. While the term criminal justice professional is used to refer to those who work in the criminal justice system, the professionals themselves do not always agree that they have much in common. Police officers, attorneys, judges, and correctional officers have developed their own professional identities and do not necessarily see themselves as coworkers in the administration of justice.

At the same time, criminal justice includes several academic disciplines. Sociology, philosophy, and psychology all contribute theories of criminality, and law, political science, and social work have something to say about the administration of the criminal justice system. While courses in law and justice have been offered at colleges and universities for hundreds of years, degree programs in criminal justice have developed in the past three decades or so. Courses in criminal justice courses are taught by professors with degrees in sociology, political science, criminal justice and other disciplines.

In addition, the professional credentials of those who work in the criminal justice system include some combination of education and training. Basic training, not a four-year college degree, is required for most entry-level positions in law enforcement and corrections. Police officers and correctional officers complete basic training, begin work, and may complete a two-year, four-year, or graduate degree to earn a promotion. There are also those who complete a four-year college degree prior to basic training and entry into a police or corrections profession. Alternatively, there is no basic training prior to becoming a defense attorney, prosecutor, or judge. Prosecutors, defense attorneys and judges complete a four-year degree, then a three-year law degree to obtain a law license. They begin prosecuting cases, defending clients, or trying cases without any specialized training. All of the above do, however, complete training after beginning their chosen profession—in-service training for police and corrections, continuing legal education (CLE) for lawyers.

Basically, *training* refers to specialized instruction specific to a particular job responsibility. Training is intended to be up-to-date and task-specific, such as following a particular policy or applying new technology. *Education*, on the other hand, is meant to communicate a broad base of conceptual knowledge in order to produce individuals who can communicate effectively, analyze information, and solve problems. A person with a college degree in criminal justice has received a base of knowledge about criminal justice issues and procedures, but also knows something about art, science, literature, and so on. Entering a police or corrections professions with a criminal justice degree is something like entering the banking or brokerage professions with a degree in economics—one has a broad understanding of the overall system, but still needs to learn the specifics of a particular job tasks.

Preservice Training

Some states have training academies for law enforcement. Local law enforcement may receive entry-level training from the state police academy, or some other central academy for statewide education. In North Carolina, each agency is responsible for their own training. In North Carolina, law enforcement training remains a cooperative effort; larger departments provide much of their own training as do state law enforcement agencies. Smaller departments rely on state agencies or local community colleges (Brannon, Clarke, and Farb 1995, 87). There are about sixty-five agencies that provide law enforcement training throughout the state.[1]

Early Training Efforts

New York City initiated a training program for police officers in 1853, which became known as the School of Instruction. The thirty-day program included on-the-job instruction. By 1914, the curriculum had expanded to include refresher courses in laws and regulations for senior officers, and specialized training for officers assigned to bicycle, motorcycles, and traffic duty (Palmiotto 1997, 263). In 1908, August Vollmer, chief of police in Berkeley, California, started a "police school" for his officers that earned a national reputation. Vollmer's curriculum covered a variety of practical as well as theoretical topics: police procedures, fingerprinting, first aid, criminal law, public health, photography, and occasional lectures on topics such as psychiatry and criminology. By 1917, the school expanded to a three-year

---

1. The Federal Law Enforcement Training Center (FLETC) at Glynco, Georgia, is an interagency training facility serving over seventy federal law enforcement organizations representing eighteen executive departments, the U.S. Congress, the Supreme Court, and other independent organizations. The center provides basic, advanced and specialized training at the Georgia site, as well as at satellite training centers located in Tucson, Arizona, and Artesia, New Mexico. State and local officers may also enroll in specific programs, such as questioned documents, court security, financial investigation, interviewing child witnesses, and many other topics.

course of study emphasizing criminalistics, criminal law, and police administration (Douthit 1975, 102).

Several universities opened training programs; most of these provided training and certificate programs for police officers. The Graduate School at Harvard established the Bureau of Street Traffic Research program in 1923; the Traffic Institute at Northwestern University in Evanston, Illinois, opened in 1936; and the Southern Police Institute at the University of Louisville, opened in the 1950s. One of the first training schools for correctional officers was developed by the Federal Bureau of Prisons.

The Federal Bureau of Prisons (BOP) opened a staff training school in New York in 1930 under the leadership of Jesse Stutsman. Sanford Bates, Director of the BOP, had heard about the British staff training school at Wakefield at the 1925 International Prison Congress in London. As designed by Bates and Stutsman, the training program in New York emphasized broad behavioral science themes rather than daily security practices. Bates and Stutsman wanted correctional officers to learn "methods of controlling men by intelligence and leadership rather than by force" (Keve 1991, 104). Stutsman, however, died in 1933 and the BOP cut funding for the New York school. Beginning in the late 1930s, the BOP designated six prisons as regional training centers for correctional officers and by 1940, expanded the courses to include nonsecurity personnel. In 1982, the BOP became one of the participating federal agencies at the training center in Glynco, Georgia (Keve 1991, 236-237).

In North Carolina, the State Highway Patrol became one of the first law enforcement organizations to require formal training. After the general assembly enacted legislation creating the North Carolina Highway Patrol in 1929, the State Highway Commission selected ten men for two-weeks training at the Pennsylvania State Police Academy in Harrisburg, Pennsylva-

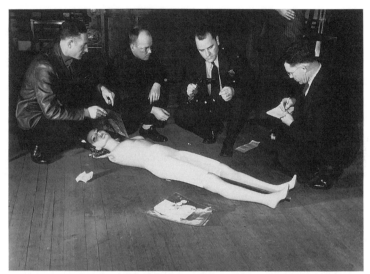

Figure 16. Police school crime scene, 1946. The training topic is search/evidence preservation. The location might be the Institute of Government, UNC–Chapel Hill. (Courtesy of the N.C. Division of Archives and History.)

nia. The Pennsylvania Police Academy, one of the first state police academies in the country, enjoyed a national reputation during the 1930s.[2] These ten, the commander and nine lieutenants, returned to conduct North Carolina's Basic Patrol School. The first training school began in May 1929 at Old Camp Glen near Morehead City. The thirty-seven men selected for the new law enforcement organization, many of whom had military experience, became the first patrol officers to attend the school (State Highway Patrol 1979, 168).

---

2. The FBI established the Police Training School in 1935 for local and state police officers, which later became the National Academy. The FBI National Academy offers an eleven-week training program that enrolls about one thousand municipal, county, and state police officers each year. Participants can receive college credit for the National Academy Program through the University of Virginia.

Municipal police departments had to develop their own training programs. The Raleigh Police Department had no police training until 1949, when the department opened the first Police Academy in Raleigh. Under the direction of Chief Ralph R. Hargrove (1947-1952) the academy offered a two-week basic training program for new officers (Raleigh Police Department, n.d.). Today, Raleigh police officers are trained at the John H. Baker, Sr. Training Center. The center provides all basic and in-service training, and conducts three classes a year. Raleigh officers may also complete courses at the center from instructors of Wake Technical College.

Development of a State System

Law enforcement training in North Carolina began at the Institute of Government. The Institute of Government, under the direction of Albert Coates, offered training courses for law enforcement in 1921. In the 1940s, the state began funding the Institute of Government, a department within the University of North Carolina-Chapel Hill, and it has become the largest and most diverse university-based training and research organization in the United States. The Institute offers more than two hundred specialized courses, conferences and schools annually. From the beginning, criminal justice has been a major emphasis of the Institute (Dellinger 1996, 3).

Standardization of law enforcement training curriculum throughout the state came in 1963, when a group of local law enforcement executives and state agency personnel agreed to sixty-hour basic curriculum. Training efforts received a boost when the state began to create a comprehensive system of two-year colleges in the 1960s, and the community colleges quickly assumed the major role in law enforcement training. North Carolina's training initiative received federal support when the U.S. Congress enacted the Omnibus Crime Control and Safe

Streets Act in 1967. The President's Commission on Law Enforcement and the Administration of Justice issued its report that same year, as law enforcement organizations across the country examined their training efforts. North Carolina Governor Dan Moore urged the general assembly to create the Governor's Law and Order Committee as required by the federal initiative (Justice Academy 1986, 12).

Governor Moore's Law and Order Committee led to creation of a Criminal Justice Training Council and development of statewide training standards for entry into the law enforcement profession. In 1971, legislation mandated that basic curriculum be approved by a state agency, now known as Criminal Justice Education and Training Standards Commission. In 1983, the legislature established a similar, separate commission for deputy sheriffs (who had been formally trained by the Criminal Justice Education and Training Standards Commission), the North Carolina Sheriff's Education and Training Standards Commission. The minimum number of hours required to be certified as an officer has grown to 432 for local police and 444 for deputy sheriffs (Brannon, Clarke, and Farb 1995, 87).

The Governor's Committee also recommended creation of a centralized training academy (Justice Academy 1986, 12). In 1973, the general assembly enacted legislation creating the North Carolina Criminal Justice Education and Training Center, now known as the North Carolina Justice Academy, a unit within the Department of Justice. In 1974, the state acquired the ninety-five-acre campus of Southwood College, a private community college that folded in Salemburg. That same year, Attorney General James Carson recommended appointment of J. Perry Powell, Jr. as the permanent director of the academy. Powell had been a staff member at the Institute of Government and legal advisor to the Charlotte Police Department. The Department of Correction became the first agency to train employees on the campus. The first class ate meals in the cafeteria, but had to stay in hotels in Dunn, North Carolina, until dormitory space could be constructed (Justice Academy 1986, 12). Officers must be certified by successfully completing 160 hours of training. A 40-hour refresher course is required yearly.

As the academy's facilities have grown, additional agencies initiated training programs on the campus, including the State Bureau of Investigation, the Alcohol Law Enforcement Division, and Division of Marine Fisheries. The purpose of the academy is to develop and conduct training courses for local criminal justice agencies and to provide the resources and facilities for training various state agencies. The academy, a unit of the North Carolina Department of Justice, develops and maintains mandated certification programs in basic law enforcement training, basic jailer training, criminal justice instructor training, radar and other advanced areas (Marcus 1995, 270).[3]

Several universities within the University of North Carolina system have additional resources for training criminal justice personnel. The Appalachian Regional Bureau of Government, housed within the Department of Political Science and Criminal Justice at Appalachian State University in Boone, provides training, technical assistance, and evaluation services for local law enforcement and other local government officials. North Carolina State University in Raleigh offers a public administration program to train law enforcement personnel, city and county managers, and other elected officials. The Administrative Officers Management Program is a multiweek program for midlevel managers in state and local law enforcement agencies. Western Carolina University in Cullowhee offers a local government training program linked to the Institute of Government at University of North Carolina at Chapel Hill.

---

3. On September 16, 1998, Attorney General Michael F. Easley dedicated the North Carolina Justice Academy-West. The facility, located at Edneyville, provides training for officers based in the western portion of North Carolina.

Certification and Accreditation

The Criminal Justice Standards Division, established by the general assembly in 1971, administers programs of the North Carolina Criminal Justice Education and Training Standards Commission. The commission was formed in 1979 when the legislature consolidated the original Criminal Justice Council and the Justice Academy's Council into a single commission. The Commission establishes and enforces minimum employment, training, and retention standards for law enforcement officers as well as corrections officers, local detention officers, criminal justice instructors, and schools. The Criminal Justice Standards Division administers seven criminal justice certification programs encompassing 27,000 certified officers, in addition to a speciality certification program in radar operation (Marcus 1995, 275).

Sixteen law enforcement agencies in North Carolina have received national accreditation; about 380 agencies are accredited in the United States and Canada. In 1986, Greensboro became the first, followed by fifteen others within the next ten years. National accreditation is awarded by the Commission on Accreditation for Law Enforcement Agencies (CALEA), a private, nonprofit corporation established in 1979 by four major law enforcement organizations: International Association of Chiefs of Police (IACP), the Police Executive Research Forum (PERF), the National Organization of Black Law Enforcement Executives (NOBLE), and the National Sheriff's Association (NSA). Accredited agencies must meet standards in six major areas: (1) the agency's role, responsibilities, and relationships with other agencies; (2) organization, management, and administration; (3) personnel administration; (4) law enforcement operations, operational support, and traffic law enforcement; (5) prisoner and court-related services, and (6) auxiliary and technical services (Ennis 1996, 15).

College Education

Early College Programs

While criminal justice programs at colleges and universities are relatively recent, university courses in criminal justice topics are not. The historical antecedents of criminal justice extend to eighteenth century England, where William Blackstone, "Solicitor General to Her Majesty," offered a series of lectures at Oxford to undergraduates who would later sit as justices of the peace in the counties. Criminology continues in Britain, where criminology degrees are attached to law schools. In the United States, the rise of proprietary law schools during the eighteenth and nineteenth centuries weakened the study of law in undergraduate curriculum (Gee and Webber 1986).

In the United States it was August Vollmer, the police chief who began the nation's first police training program, who also advanced college education for police officers. Vollmer teamed up with a member of the law faculty at the University of California at Berkeley to offer a degree program in criminology. Berkeley awarded the nation's first baccalaureate degree in 1923 (Palmiotto 1997, 254). Vollmer's appointment in 1929 as the nation's first police professor culminated a decade of his efforts to establish police education in colleges and universities. In 1931, Vollmer helped organize the first college-level education for law enforcement in the country at San Jose State College (now San Jose State University). The program at San Jose began a two-year law enforcement curriculum in 1930. The San Jose curriculum emphasized Vollmer's belief in a broad education for police officers, including courses in sociology, political science, public health, psychology, and chemistry. Vollmer said that "the mechanics of the profession are less important than a knowledge of human beings," and that the police officer's role required "a broad cultural, scientific, and technical background" (Douthit 1975, 120).

Figure 17. Dormitory Building, N.C. Justice Academy, Salemburg. Created in 1973, the Justice Academy trains thousands of criminal justice personnel each year at the Salemburg campus and across the state.

By 1949, there were twenty-six colleges and universities offering degree programs in criminal justice. These included Michigan State University, Florida State University, Texas A&M University, Northwestern University, and Ohio University. The programs established during this period were primarily designed for police personnel (Palmiotto 1997, 255).

College degrees in criminal justice became much more common with the Law Enforcement Assistance Administration's (LEAA) Law Enforcement Education Program (LEEP). In 1967, the President's Commission on Law Enforcement and the Administration of Justice recommended a baccalaureate degree as the minimum educational standard for law enforcement. The commission believed that college-educated officers would provide more insightful, more comprehensive police service, and as college-educated officers rose through the ranks of police organizations, they would explore new approaches with more creativity and enhanced planning. A provision of the Omnibus Crime Control and Safe Streets Act of 1968, the U.S. Congress used LEEP to encourage criminal justice personnel to attend college.

LEEP was the best thing and the worst thing that happened to criminal justice higher education. LEEP provided millions of dollars in loans and grants to students for college criminal justice courses and led to the creation of departments of criminal justice at a number of universities. Colleges and universities began to develop law enforcement and criminal justice degree programs, and police departments began to establish incentive pay, educational leave, and other policies to facilitate completion of college degrees (Carter and Sapp 1990, 60). The number of colleges offering bachelor's degrees in criminal justice rose from 39 in 1967 to 376 in 1977. On the other hand, LEEP led to rapid expansion of college programs with great variation in quality; some were little more than training programs for college credit. A report commissioned by the Police Foundation in 1978 found that a number of these programs had succeeded only in providing a "shallow, conceptually narrow" education (Walker 1980, 238).

Criminal Justice as an Academic Major

In the past few decades, criminal justice has developed into an academic social science discipline. While criminal justice programs are administratively housed in a range of academic departments within universities, criminal justice is not an "applied" program of some other discipline. *Criminal justice* is the study of crime and of the administration of justice in society; a discipline in its own right. Criminal justice has its own journals of research, its own academic associations, its own doctor of philosophy (Ph.D.) programs, and a growing number of academics who identify as criminal justice specialists—all the signs of a social science discipline.

Currently, there are about one thousand associate degree programs and about seven hundred baccalaureate programs in criminal justice nationwide. The majority of associate degree programs are offered at community colleges, although some colleges and universities offer both associate and baccalaureate programs. Associate degree programs follow the vocational model; "criminal justice," "criminal justice technology," "law enforcement," and "law enforcement technology" are four of the most common two-year degree programs (Macmillan 1995). The first year curriculum in associate degree programs typically includes general education courses in English, psychology, sociology and government, followed by specialized courses including introduction to law enforcement/criminal justice, police operations and organization, juvenile delinquency and criminal law. During the second year, students complete general education courses in math, the humanities and social sciences and additional specialized courses in criminal investigation, criminal evidence, police community relations, and criminalistics (Stinchcomb 1991, 89).

At the baccalaureate level, these programs vary from liberal arts programs in "justice studies and public policy" and "criminology," to more vocationally-oriented programs in "criminal justice technology" and "law enforcement" (Macmillan 1995). Curriculum varies with the philosophy, organization, and history of the program. Typical core requirements are introduction to criminal justice, criminal justice research methods, criminology and criminal law. The most commonly-offered electives are introduction to corrections, introduction to juvenile justice/delinquency, criminal investigation, and criminal behavior. Many programs offer independent study and internship courses (Southerland 1991, 61). During the first two years of a four-year degree, students generally complete general edu-

Figure 18. Firearms Training Simulator, N.C. Justice Academy, Salemburg. Located adjacent to the firing range, this equipment is used along with traditional "target practice" firearms instruction.

cation requirements in English, mathematics, laboratory science, social sciences, humanities, fine arts, history, and speech communication.

In North Carolina, there are about fifty associate degree programs in "criminal justice," "criminal justice technology," "law enforcement," and "law enforcement technology." There are about twenty baccalaureate programs in criminal justice; two of them in "justice and public policy" (Macmillan 1995, 569). At some universities in the state, criminal justice is a separate department (University of North Carolina-Charlotte and North Carolina Central University, for example). At others, criminal justice degree programs are administratively housed with political science (Appalachian State University), social work (East Carolina University), or other social sciences (University of North Carolina-Wilmington and Elizabeth City State University).

Since fall 1997, all community colleges in North Carolina converted to a semester system. The University of North Carolina General Administration has initiated a process for transfer of credit between two-year and four-year campuses within the state system.

Graduate School

There are about one hundred master's degree programs and about twenty doctorate (Ph.D.) degree programs in criminal justice throughout the United States. Geographically, the South has the most master's degree programs (thirty-three), followed by the Northeast (twenty-nine). About half of the doctorate programs are located in the Northeast (Academy of Criminal Justice Sciences 1995, 7).

Early graduate programs began in California and New York. The University of California at Berkeley opened a school of criminology offering graduate degrees in 1951. In 1955, the New York City Police Department initiated programs at the Baruch School of Business and Public Administration, City University of New York, leading to a master of public administration degree. By 1959, more than one hundred officers took courses toward the graduate degree and the program moved to the John Jay College of Criminal Justice, which began in 1965 (Johnson and Wolfe 1996, 225).

Two universities in North Carolina offer master's degree programs in criminal justice: University of North Carolina–Charlotte and North Carolina Central University.[4] The Department of Criminal Justice at University of North Carolina–Charlotte initiated a master's program in 1984 and awards the

---

4. Appalachian State University recently added a criminal justice track to its Master of Arts in Social Sciences (MASS) degree program.

Master of Science (MS) in Criminal Justice degree. The program, which began with an emphasis on management, was intended to enhance management skills within criminal justice settings. The curriculum features core courses in the criminal justice system, crime theory, criminal justice research, and criminal justice and social control. Faculty specializations include victimology, juvenile justice, court administration, police administration, evaluation research, and statistics. The University of North Carolina-Charlotte's Criminal Justice Department includes the Office of Justice Research. The office analyzes crime, corrections statistics, and conducts evaluation research for local governments in areas of crime prevention, policing, and court administration.

North Carolina Central University's master's program is designed to prepare persons for leadership positions in criminal justice agencies and develop personnel with skills in administration, research, program planning, and evaluation. The Master of Science (MS) in criminal justice program features core curriculum in crime, law and social control, management, statistics, research methods, and areas of specialization in law enforcement administration and correctional administration. There are seven full-time faculty and several adjunct faculty members. North Carolina Central University's program is located in the Whiting Criminal Justice Building on the campus in Durham, across from the College of Law.

Presently, there are no doctorate programs in criminal justice in North Carolina. Two doctorate programs nearby are at the University of Maryland at College Park and American University, both in the Washington, D.C. area. Florida State University at Tallahassee granted a Ph.D. in criminology in 1963, and may have been the first. Michigan State University at East Lansing, Sam Houston State University in Huntsville, and the State University of New York at Albany began conferring doctoral degrees in criminal justice in the early 1970s. The John

Jay College of Criminal Justice, City University of New York, which graduated its first master's degree student in 1970, graduated its first criminal justice Ph.D. in 1985 (Flanagan 1990, 199).

Law School

The educational credentials of an attorney seeking practice in criminal courts as an assistant district attorney or public defender (or a trial judge, for that matter) are not fundamentally different from other law school graduates who practice civil law, such as real estate or family law. In effect, one may specialize in the practice of criminal law, not in preparation for the practice of criminal law.

Beginnings of the Legal Profession

During the early colonial period, the practice of law was forbidden. In 1669, the Lords Proprietors asked John Locke to draw up the Fundamental Constitutions of Carolina. The law prohibited "all manner of comments...on any part of the common or statute laws of Carolina" according to the rationale that the "multiplicity of comments, as well as of laws, have great inconveniences, and serve only to obscure and perplex" (Wettach 1947, 1-2). Only the family relative could plead a case before a judge in open court (Wettach 1947, 2).

Locke's provision was, however, ignored. The laws of 1715 provided a schedule of attorney's fees. The colony's first lawyers had practiced law in England. License to practice law was granted by the colonial governor, a power that created some criticism. In 1760, the assembly criticized the granting of licenses to persons "who are ignorant even of the rudiments of that science [the practice of law]" (Wettach 1947, 5). The assembly changed the licensing procedure to provide that persons seeking a law license would first need to be examined in their legal knowledge by the superior court judges. There were 49 attorneys licensed in 1877, 66 in 1900, and 139 in 1920. There were about 2,500 practicing lawyers in North Carolina in 1950 (Wettach 1947, 7).

Law Practice in Criminal Courts

Generally speaking, lawyers who work in criminal courts receive a baccalaureate degree, complete law school, and bar exams. While political science and English are traditional undergraduate majors for those seeking careers in the law, there is no required "pre-law" curriculum for a person seeking a law career in criminal courts. At the same time, there is no specific track for law students seeking a career in criminal law. Law schools offer the same curriculum. The first year curriculum is uniform; courses in civil procedure, constitutional law, contracts, criminal law, property law, torts, and legal research and writing. Law students may specialize, to some extent, during the second and third years, by completing elective courses and clinical experiences.

The judiciary of each state has been responsible for setting standards for admission to the state bar. Although standards for admission vary by state, in virtually every state a law school graduate must satisfy two standards: the candidate must pass the bar examination and must demonstrate the requisite moral character. In almost every state, bar applicants must graduate from a law school accredited by the American Bar Association (American Bar Association 1992, 273).

In order to practice law in North Carolina, one must be admitted to the North Carolina State Bar. This organization, through its Board of Law Examiners, licenses attorneys who wish to practice law in the state. In order to receive a law license one must successfully pass the state bar exam. Many of those who take the exam each year are recent law school graduates, although there are those who possess degrees from law schools outside the state or other law school graduates seeking a law license for the first time. Not only is the North Carolina State Bar empowered to license attorneys in the state, it is the official organization to discipline lawyers for unethical practice of law (Blackwelder 1957). The Code of Professional Responsibility, issued by the North Carolina State Bar, defines the conduct that the public may expect from attorneys. This code is published in North Carolina General Statutes (Appendix VII, Vol. 4A). The state bar has a committee that investigates any complaint of unethical practice, and if a violation is found, initiates disciplinary action which may involve suspension of the law license (Brannon 1994, 26).

There are five law schools in North Carolina: North Carolina Central School of Law, Durham; Duke University School of Law; Campbell University School of Law, Buis Creek; Wake Forest University School of Law, and the University of North Carolina School of Law at Chapel Hill. The North Carolina Bar Association, a private organization, provides several continuing legal education programs each year. Continuing legal education programs (CLEs) are offered by a variety of local bars and other organizations as well. Local bar associations exist in a number of North Carolina cities and counties including Durham, Asheville, Forsythe, Cumberland, Mecklenburg and Greensboro.

North Carolina is among seven states that requires specific training for new attorneys as a special part of mandatory CLE. CLE is an in-service training requirement for attorneys in which attorneys must complete a certain number of hours of course work (about 8 to 15 hours) per year and regularly report their compliance (every 2 or 3 years) to the state authority.

Failure to comply may result in suspension from practice. North Carolina requires nine hours of practice skills in each of the first three years of practice (American Bar Association 1992, 298).

The Institute of Government at the University of North Carolina-Chapel Hill provides training for court personnel. The institute provides more than twenty seminars or short courses per year for judges, clerks, district attorneys, public defenders, and magistrates. It also publishes various articles, memoranda, and guides to aide court personnel in their work (Brannon 1994, 29).

Career Opportunities

Criminal Justice Careers

More than forty thousand people are employed by the city, county and state agencies that make up North Carolina's criminal justice system (Maguire and Pastore 1997, 29). This number does not include those employed by the federal government, nor those who work for nonprofit and other private sector organizations related to criminal justice.

Police. Most of the nineteen thousand persons employed for police protection work for local government in North Carolina. There are careers in municipal police departments and county sheriff's offices. The greatest range of law enforcement careers exists at the state and federal levels. Positions in state law enforcement include state trooper, highway patrol officer, wildlife conservation officer, park ranger, inspector, and investigator. Positions in federal law enforcement are connected with the Justice and Treasury Departments. A few of the many federal law enforcement organizations are the Drug Enforcement Agency; U.S. Customs Criminal Investigation; U.S. Park Police; Postal Inspection Service; Bureau of Alcohol, Tobacco and Firearms; and the U.S. Marshal's Service.

Courts. About 5,800 individuals are employed in courts, prosecution, legal services, and public defense in North Carolina. The most prominent positions of judges and attorneys require law degrees, but there are careers in state courts systems for those with baccalaureate degrees. These careers are generally connected with court management and services, such as court administrator, juvenile intake officer, and pretrial officer. Other positions in dispute mediation and victim services are found within offices of state attorneys general and prosecuting attorney's offices.

Corrections. The most rapidly expanding sector of the criminal justice system, corrections, employs more than 15,400 people in North Carolina. Careers in institutional corrections are located within federal and state prisons as well as county and municipal jails. These include correctional administrator, correctional officer, and jailer. There are also careers within state and federal governments in community corrections as probation or parole officers, in addition to community-based programs such as half-way houses and juvenile treatment centers.

Career Staircase

Given the range of possible jobs and possible employers in criminal justice, it is virtually impossible to provide a comprehensive list. The types of careers may be thought of a series of educational steps from high school diploma to doctorate degree. Generally, those with high school degrees are engaged in providing direct services to individuals. Those with college degrees are more likely to work in supervisory, management, and other administrative positions, along with evaluation research, policy analysis, and other systems support. Individuals with

Criminal Justice Career Staircase

Degree*	Possible Job Titles	Possible Employers
Ph.D.	Policy analyst, university professor, agency administrator, statistician, research analyst	Institute of Government, UNC-Chapel Hill, Research Triangle Institute, U.S. Sentencing Commission, Rand Corporation, Shaw University
J.D.	trial judge, public defender, assistant district attorney, defense attorney, investigator	Superior Court Division, N.C. Administrative Office of the Courts, Federal Bureau of Investigation, Office of Public Defender, Pamlico Sound Legal Services, U.S. District Court, Administrative Office of U.S. Courts, Office of the Attorney General, N.C. Department of Justice
M.S., M.A., M.P.A., M.S.W.	probation officer, investigator, trial court administrator, assistant superintendent, classification and treatment officer, community college instructor, police chief, research analyst, program administrator	Federal Probation, Administrative Office of U.S. Courts, Office of Research and Planning, N.C. Department of Correction, N.C. Administrative Office of the Courts, Pitt Community College, U.S. Customs Criminal Investigation Division, Henderson Police Department, Onslow County Department of Social Services

Degree*	Possible Job Titles	Possible Employers
B.S., B.A.	police officer, juvenile court counselor, victim's assistance specialist, probation officer, program administrator	Low Security Correctional Institution–Butner, Juvenile Services, N.C. Administrative Office of the Courts, Community Based Alternatives, Division of Youth Services, Winston-Salem Police Department, Mecklenburg County Sheriff's Department, Stonewall Jackson School, Division of Probation and Parole, N.C. Division of Prisons, State Bureau of Investigation
A.A.S, A.A.	police officer, deputy sheriff, detention officer, correctional officer	N.C. State Highway Patrol, New Havover County Jail, Buncombe Regional Juvenile Detention Center, Durham County Sheriff's Office
H.S. diploma	police officer, deputy sheriff, detention officer, correctional officer	N.C. State Highway Patrol, Bertie-Martin Regional Jail, Forsythe County Sheriff's Office

* Ph.D. which refers to "doctor of philosophy," is the generic title for the most advanced degree in many academic disciplines. At a minimum, it typically requires five years in addition to a baccalaureate degree for completion (two years for a master's degree, three years for the doctoral degree). J.D. which refers to "juris doctor," is the law degree required to practice law. At a minimum, it requires three years in addition to a baccalaureate degree for completion. MS refers to "master of science," M.A. to "master of arts," M.P.A. to "master of public administration," and M.S.W. "master of social work." These programs typically require three semesters/two years for completion (although advanced standing in some MSW programs, for example, allows students to complete them in one year).

graduate degrees in criminal justice (M.S. or Ph.D.) and related social sciences work for a variety of public and private organizations in administration, evaluation, planning, research, and teaching.

The criminal justice career staircase provides examples of career possibilities for each level of education. The fact that an agency appears at the high school level, for example, does not mean the agency only hires those with high school degrees. At the same time, the agencies listed at the baccalaureate level are not the only agencies that hire those with baccalaureate degrees. The staircase is intended to suggest the range of possible positions for each level of educational credentials and suggest a few potential employers.

Career Planning

The description above includes only a small sample of the career possibilities in criminal justice. To assist in making a career choice, obtain as much information from many sources as early as possible in your academic career.

1. *Begin where you are.* Students have excellent access to information about careers and job openings. Look for information regarding career opportunities on bulletin boards on campus, and ask professors. Also, contact career services on your campus. Career Services assists students in their job search, resume preparation, and developing presentation skills.

2. *Contact a federal job information center.* Federal Job Information Centers (FJICs) are located across the country to provide information about positions within federal government, along

with testing and application procedures. There is an FJIC in Raleigh.[5]

3. *Request information from the criminal justice agencies nearby.* A brief letter sent to nearby criminal justice agencies asking for information about current job openings will yield a wealth of information. Addresses for corrections, law enforcement, the attorney general's office, and other state criminal justice agencies can be found at any library. State and federal agencies have informational web sites that can be accessed through the internet.

4. *Visit local government agencies.* Stop by county courthouses, city and county administration buildings, and other government offices to learn about openings in local criminal justice agencies. Openings at jails, police departments, sheriff's departments, and juvenile facilities are typically posted in public buildings.

5. *Peruse professional journals and magazines.* Magazines of professional organizations in criminal justice will help direct you toward a better understanding of your career objectives. These periodicals can be found in any university and college library, as well as in most city and county libraries.

Academic Organizations

There are several academic organizations within the field of criminal justice. These organizations encourage student membership, offer paper competitions and other scholarship opportunities for students.

American Society of Criminology. The American Society of Criminology began in 1941 when August Vollmer and some of

---

5. Federal Job Information Center, Federal Building, 310 New Bern Ave., P.O. Box 25069, Raleigh, NC 27611.

his students formed the National Association of College Police Training Officials. As membership grew and began to diversify, the organization renamed itself the Society for Advancement of Criminology in 1946 and became the American Society of Criminology (ASC) in 1957 (Sorensen, Widmayer, and Scarpitti 1994, 150). Today, ASC membership includes academics, policy makers, and practitioners. Membership includes academic and government officials from around the world. ASC publishes the journal *Criminology*, an "interdisciplinary [journal] devoted to the study of crime, deviant behavior, and related phenomena, as found in the social and behavioral sciences and in the fields of law, criminal justice and history." The ASC sponsors an annual conference, usually in November, in cities in the United States and Canada.[6]

Academy of Criminal Justice Sciences. In 1963, some members of the ASC split off to form the International Association of Police Professors. In 1970, this organization became the Academy of Criminal Justice Sciences (ACJS) (Sorensen, Widmayer, and Scarpitti 1994, 150). The ACJS is comprised of academics, criminal justice professionals, and state and local government officials. ACJS publishes two journals of research, *Justice Quarterly* and the *Journal of Criminal Justice Education*. Each year, ACJS members meet for a national conference at a city within the United States.[7]

American Criminal Justice Association-Lambda Alpha Epsilon. The American Criminal Justice Association-Lambda Alpha Epsilon (ACJA-LAE) began as a professional organization for in-service law enforcement personnel. ACJA-LAE originated in 1937 at San Jose State College following the California Techni-

---

6. For membership information write: American Society of Criminology, Ohio State University Research, 1314 Kinnear Rd., Suite 212, Columbus, OH 43212.

7. For membership information write: ACJS Secretariat, Suite 101, 1500 N. Beauregard St., Alexandria, VA 22311.

cal Institute for Peace Officer Training. Membership expanded and in 1964, ACJA-LAE held the first annual police competitions. Today there are more than 150 chapters across 75% of the states. ACJA-LAE holds regional and national conferences, offers scholarships and academic recognition, and provides an opportunity for students and professionals to compete in competitions of skill and knowledge.[8]

Southern Criminal Justice Association. The Southern Criminal Justice Association (SCJA), a regional affiliate of the ACJS, includes criminal justice educators, practitioners and students. The SCJA promotes a philosophical approach to criminal justice as a systematic process and aims to promote the highest standards in criminal justice education, training, planning and research. The *American Journal of Criminal Justice*, the official publication of the association, is a multi-disciplinary journal devoted to the study of criminal behavior, the social and political response to crime, and other matters related to crime and criminal justice.[9]

North Carolina Criminal Justice Association. The North Carolina Criminal Justice Association (NCCJA) is an organization of educators, practitioners, and students of criminal justice at universities, community colleges, and agencies throughout North Carolina. The organization sponsors two conferences each year at locations across the state; typically, the spring conference occurs on the campus of the North Carolina Justice Academy in Salemburg. NCCJA awards up to three academic scholarships each year, and up to three awards for outstanding papers. Any criminal justice-related club or organization at a university or college within the state may also organize student

---

8. For membership information write: ACJA/LAE, P.O. Box 601047, Sacramento, CA 95860-1047.
9. For membership information write: SCJA Secretariat, University of Louisville, Department of Justice Administration, Brigman Hall, Louisville, KY 40292.

chapters of NCCJA. The organization produces a newsletter, *The Informer*, several times each year.[10]

Historically Black Colleges and Universities

There are more than a hundred historically-Black colleges and universities (HBCUs) in the United States. A few of the most well known are Howard University in Washington, DC; Tuskegee University in Alabama, and Morehouse College in Atlanta, Georgia. All but three opened after the Civil War; they were founded by groups of northern abolitionists, religious denominations, missionary groups, the Freedmen's Bureau, and free African Americans.

Nationwide, about one third of all Black Americans who receive college degrees graduate from HBCUs. This is significant because, as Professors Chinita A. Heard and Robert L. Bing at the University of Texas at Arlington put it, "overrepresentation of African American offenders and victims creates a demand for criminal justice professionals and scholars." African American comprise about 30% of all persons arrested in the United States, about 50% of the nation's prison population, but less than 10% of college students. There is a need for "minority scholars who can advise city officials on how to respond to crime-related issues, especially as they apply to African-Americans" (Heard and Bing 1993, 3).

North Carolina boasts as many HBCUs as any other state. Only Alabama and Mississippi have as many. There are ten in North Carolina, eight of which offer degrees in criminal justice. Barber- Scotia College in Concord, St. Augustine's College and Shaw University in Raleigh, Johnson C. Smith in

10. For membership information write: NCCJA, North Carolina Justice Academy, P.O. Drawer 99, Salemburg, NC 28385.

Charlotte, and Fayetteville State University and Livingstone College in Salisbury are the oldest. Most of these began due to the efforts of northern missionary societies and demonational groups, who began to organize faculty, purchase land, and build classrooms in the years after the Civil War. Barber-Scotia and Johnson C. Smith were founded by the Presbyterians, and St. Augustine College by the Episcopal church. Livingstone College, named after David Livingstone, the missionary doctor who went to Africa, was founded by a conference of Black ministers and the African Methodist Episcopal (A.M.E) Zion church. Shaw, named after Elijah Shaw, was started by a union chaplain and later received support from various Baptist groups (Powell 1970).

Except for Fayetteville State University, what became the four state universities opened about twenty years later. Three of them, Elizabeth City State University, Winston-Salem State University, and North Carolina A&T University in Greensboro opened in the 1890s. The North Carolina General Assembly created North Carolina A&T in 1891 following the Morrill Act passed by U.S. Congress in 1890. Elizabeth City State University opened that same year after Hugh Cale, an African-American legislator from Pasquotank County, introduced legislation for a school for Black teachers. Winston-Salem began as Slater Industrial Academy in 1895. North Carolina Central University in Durham began as a private institution in 1909 and the general assembly converted it into a publicly-supported college for Blacks in 1923. North Carolina A&T is the largest; North Carolina Central has the only master's degree program in criminal justice. Fayetteville State, which began as the Howard School a state university, was the first teacher-training school in the South (Powell 1970, 22).[11]

---

11. Pembroke State University has an interesting history as well. It was established in 1887 by the general assembly for the Indians of Robeson County. Only Robeson County Indians could attend the school until 1945

References

Academy of Criminal Justice Sciences. 1995. *Guide to graduate programs in criminal justice and criminology 1994-1995*. Highland Heights, Ky.: Academy of Criminal Justice Sciences.

American Bar Association. 1992. *Legal education and professional development—An educational continuum*. Chicago: American Bar Association, Section on Legal Education and Admissions to the Bar.

Blackwelder, Fannie M. 1957. Organization and early years of the North Carolina Bar Association. *North Carolina Historical Review* 34:34-57.

Brannon, Joan G. 1994. *The judicial system in North Carolina*. Raleigh: North Carolina Administrative Office of the Courts.

Brannon, Joan G., Stevens H. Clarke, and Robert L. Farb. 1995. Law enforcement, courts and corrections. In *State and local government relations in North Carolina* (Charles D. Linner, eds.). Chapel Hill: Institute of Government.

Carter, David L. and Allen D. Sapp. 1990. The evolution of higher education in law enforcement: Preliminary findings from a national study. *Journal of Criminal Justice Education* 1:59-86.

Dellinger, Anne M. 1996. Institute of government. *Popular Government* 62:3-15.

Douthit, Nathan. 1975. August Vollmer, Berkeley's first chief of police, and the emergence of police professionalism. *California Historical Quarterly* 54:101-124.

---

when the legislature opened its doors to other North Carolina Indians. Since 1954 the university has been open to persons of all races (Porter 1970, 40-41).

Ennis, Alan M. 1996. Should a law enforcement agency seek national accreditation? *Popular Government* 61:14-20.

Flanagan, Timothy J. 1990. Criminal justice doctoral programs in the United States and Canada: Findings from a national survey. *Journal of Criminal Justice Education* 1:195- 213.

Gee, Elizabeth and Barbara S. Webber. 1986. The historical development of law in liberal education. *Legal Studies Forum* 10:7-28.

Heard, Chinita and Robert L. Bing. 1993. African American faculty and students on predominantly white university campuses. *Journal of Criminal Justice Education* 4:1-14.

Johnson, Herbert A. and Nancy T. Wolfe. 1996. *History of criminal justice.* Cincinnati, Ohio: Anderson Publishing.

Justice Academy. 1996. North Carolina Justice Academy: The first decade. *North Carolina Criminal Justice Letter & Review.* 4:12-17.

Keve, Paul. 1991. *Prisons and the American conscience: A history of U.S. federal corrections.* Carbondale, Ill.: Southern Illinois University Press.

Marcus, Lisa A. 1995. *North Carolina manual 1995/1996.* Raleigh: Secretary of State.

Macmillan Library Reference. 1995. *The college blue book: Degrees offered by college and subject.* New York: Simon and Schuster Macmillan.

Maguire, Kathleen and Anne L. Pastore. 1997. *Sourcebook of criminal justice statistics 1996.* Washington, D.C.: U.S. Department of Justice, Office of Justice Programs.

Palmiotto, Michael J. 1997. *Policing: Concepts, strategies and current issues in American police forces.* Durham: Carolina Academic Press.

Powell, William S. 1970. *Higher education in North Carolina.* Raleigh: North Carolina Division of Archives and History.

Raleigh Police Department. n.d. *History of the Raleigh police department.* Raleigh: City of Raleigh.

Sorensen, Jonathan R., Alan G. Widmayer, and Frank Scarpitti. 1994. Examining the criminal justice paradigms: An analysis of ACJS and ASC members. *Journal of Criminal Justice Education* 5:149–166.

Southerland, Mittie D. 1991. Criminal justice curricula in the United States: An examination of baccalaureate programs, 1988–1989. *Journal of Criminal Justice Education* 2:45–68.

State Highway Patrol. 1979. *State highway patrol: Fiftieth anniversary 1929-1979.* Raleigh: North Carolina Department of Crime Control and Public Safety.

Stinchcomb, James. 1991. *Opportunities in law enforcement and criminal justice careers.* Lincolnwood, Ill.: NTC Publishing.

Walker, Samuel. 1980. *Popular justice: A history of American criminal justice.* New York: Oxford University Press.

Wettach, Robert H. 1947. *A century of legal education.* Chapel Hill: University of North Carolina Press.

Chapter 11

Crime Victims and Related Social Services

Awareness of crime victims has occurred in the past few decades. In 1967, the Commission on Law Enforcement and Administration of Justice issued its report *The Challenge of Crime in a Free Society*. The report represented the first comprehensive assessment of the administration of criminal justice in the United States and developed the flow chart reprinted in criminal justice textbooks today. Less than 2 of more than one thousand pages of analysis, suggestions and recommendations, however, had to do with the victims of crime (Abell 1989, 215).

Since then, the national victims movement has resulted in legislation and programs dealing with victims in every state. In 1975, social workers and criminal justice personnel organized the National Organization for Victim Assistance (NOVA) to promote a victim-oriented perspective in the administration of justice.[1] Federal leadership began in 1982, when President

---

1. Another major organization in the victims rights movement, the National Victims Center, began after the death of Martha "Sunny" von Bulow, heiress to a family trust (Chemical Bank) executed by Morris Gurley. Sunny lapsed into an irreversible coma in December 1980, and in July 1981, the Superior Court of Providence, Rhode Island, indicted Claus von Bulow, Sunny's husband, on two counts of assault with intent to murder. During the trial Alexandria Isles testified about her love affair with Claus and the jury heard testimony about Claus's alleged attempt to murder his wife with

Ronald Reagan appointed the Task Force on Victims of Crime. The law led to creation of the Office for Victims of Crime a year later. The U.S. Congress passed the Victim and Witness Protection Act of 1982 and the Victims of Crime Act (VOCA) in 1984 (Abell 1989). North Carolina enacted crime victim compensation legislation in 1987. In November 1996, North Carolina voters approved an amendment to the constitution providing for a Crime Victims Bill of Rights.

In North Carolina, as elsewhere, services to crime victims result from a combination of federal funds, state legislation, and programs developed by nonprofit organizations, social service agencies, police departments, and prosecuting attorney's offices.

---

an insulin injection. The jury found Claus guilty, and sentenced him to 30 years in prison but the judge freed him on $1 million bail pending appeal. The Rhode Island Supreme Court reversed the conviction in 1984, which led to second trial in 1985. During the second trial, Morris Gurley testified that Claus had a financial motive for wanting Sunny's death. The jury acquitted Claus von Bulow in June 1985; the second murder trial led to a book *Reversal of Fortune* by Allen M. Dershowitz, and a Warner Brothers feature film of the same name in which Jeremy Irons won an Academy Award for best actor in 1991. Alexander von Auersperg, Annie Laurie von Auersperg Isham, Sunny's children by a first marriage, and Morris Gurely, felt that Claus von Bulow's lawyers and endless publicity surrounding the trials had put Sunny on trial by explaining her illness through reckless self-indulgence. In September 1985, Gurley and the von Auerspergs arranged for the Annie-Laurie Aitken Charitable Trust to provide a $1.7 million grant to establish the Sunny von Bulow National Victim Advocacy Center. Since then, the center has continued to grow (the name was shortened to the National Victim Center in 1988). It has regional offices in New York, Washington, and Fort Worth and is a major voice for victim's rights in public policy (Weed 1995, 64-71).

Crime Victims

Victims Bill of Rights

Since Wisconsin enacted the first comprehensive bill of rights for victims, about half of the states have amended their constitutions in order to provide for victims' bill of rights. There has been a movement to amend to the federal Constitution, which as not been accomplished. But in 1990, the U.S. Congress passed the Victims' Rights and Restitution Act which specifies seven rights of crime victims, many of which have been written into state law.

In November 1996, North Carolina voters approved the Victims Rights Amendment. The amendment added Section 37, the "Rights of Victims of Crime," to Article 1 of the North Carolina Constitution. The law provides the following victim's rights:

1. To be informed of and present at court proceedings of the accused;

2. To be heard at sentencing and other times;

3. To receive restitution;

4. To be given pertinent information about the criminal justice system, and to be given information about the availability of services for victims;

5. To receive information about the convictions or final disposition and sentence of the accused;

6. To be notified of the escape, release, proposed parole or pardon of the accused, or notice of reprieve or commutation of sentence;

7. To present concerns about any action that could lead to the convict's release, prior to that actions being taken;

8. To confer with the prosecution;

9. To be treated with fairness and respect for their dignity and privacy throughout the criminal justice process; and

10. To be reasonably protected from the accused and any persons acting on behalf of the accused.

The law provides that failure or inability of any person to provide a right or service creates no cause of action against the state, county, municipality, or any government agency. In other words, the law prevents victims denied one or more of these rights from successfully pursuing a civil lawsuit. In addition, the law specifies that violation of these rights provides no ground for relief in a criminal case. Failure to provide a right or service cannot be used by a defendant in a criminal case, an inmate or other accused person for relief in any trial, appeal, postconviction litigation, habeas corpus, or any criminal or civil proceeding.[2]

Since 1991, crime victim families have requested to serve as official witnesses at executions. In 1997, amendments to the state's death penalty statutes extended to the crime victim's family the right to witness the execution in death penalty cases. Two members of the victim's family, recommended by the district attorney in the county of conviction, may attend the execution. If the case involves more than one victim, the warden will ask the district attorney, the sheriff, or both in the counties of conviction to recommend two members from the families of each of the victims (Department of Correction 1997).

---

2. North Carolina had victims' rights legislation on the books since 1986 (N.C. Gen. Stat. § 15A-824 through 827). The Fair Treatment to Victims and Witness Act was passed to ensure that crime victims would have equal access to the court system. The services required under the act, however, were "subject to available resources." Passage of the Victims Rights Amendment in 1996 has raised the provisions of the old Fair Treatment to Victims and Witness Act to constitutional status although the VRA is subject to enabling legislation (Gore 1998, 15).

Victim and Witness Assistance Programs

In 1974, the Law Enforcement Assistance Administration (LEAA) funded eight victim-witness assistance programs through the National District Attorneys Association to deal with "witness noncooperation." Nonprofit, county and other victim service programs also appeared. Although U.S. Congress defunded the LEAA in 1979 and phased out funded programs by 1982, victim and witness programs shifted to counties and states. Between 1981 and 1985, lobbying efforts by victim and witness groups led twenty-eight states to enact legislation to fund new programs (Roberts 1992, 13).

Nineteen states fund their programs through penalties and fines, the other nine fund programs with state revenues. With the passage of the VOCA of 1984, major sources of funding became federal grants, state fines and penalty assessments, and county and state revenues. The major source of funding for victim assistance is awarded through the Office for Victims of Crime, U.S. Department of Justice. These federal funds come from fines and assessments on convicted felons (Roberts 1992, 14).

Victim-witness assistance programs are typically housed in the county prosecutor's office. These programs include a witness notification and case monitoring system to keep witnesses advised of court proceedings. Many provide a comfortable reception for witnesses waiting to testify, transportation, and a court escort (volunteer) who explains court proceedings throughout the witnesses stay at court. These programs also prepare and distribute materials about the court process (Moriarty, Jerin and Pelfrey 1998).

The Pitt County (District 3A) District Attorney's Office has two victim and witness assistants. The victim and witness assistants are responsible for coordinating victims and witnesses for the government in superior court cases. The program sends a letter to all victims of felony cases identifying available services. These services include assisting victims in completing the *victim impact statement* form; the form contains information pertaining to the victim's losses such as medical expenses, property loss, emotional stress, and so on. Victim and witness assistants also assist in preparing information for victims eligible for recovery of fees and required for the state (Haigwood 1996, 3).

The program also operates a notification service. Victims are informed about when a case is set for trial. Victims can also be placed on telephone standby so that waiting at the court to testify is as limited as possible. The program also provides information to victims if an offender has escaped or has been released from prison, or when the offender is being considered for parole (Haigwood 1996, 3).

The North Carolina Victim Assistance Network (NC-VAN) began in 1986. NC-VAN, a nonprofit organization, promotes the rights of violent crime victims, links crime victims with assistance available in their communities, conducts awareness and training seminars, and develops resources for victims, service providers and allied professionals. With a membership of over 350 individuals, NC-VAN serves 1,500 victim service and criminal justice agencies, victim assistance programs, and advocacy groups statewide.

Victim Restitution

North Carolina law entitles victims to restitution. *Restitution* refers to money paid to the victim by the offender. Judges can order an offender to pay restitution at sentencing. Typically, a restitution order is attached as a condition of probation or other supervised release in the community. The amount of restitution is based on the victim impact statement, completed by the victim prior to sentencing, and may be prepared with the assistance of a victim advocate.

The Division of Probation and Parole, North Carolina Department of Correction, operates Victim Advocacy Services to victims whose offenders are on Probation, Parole, or Post-Release supervision. The program seeks to provide services to victims of violent offenses, sexual offenses, domestic violence, and problem restitution cases. Victim Advocacy Services are currently available in two judicial districts: Judicial District 10 (Wake County) and Judicial District 3-B (Carteret, Craven, and Pamlico Counties). The victim advocate in each district receives a victim impact statement from the district attorney's office. Those victims who indicate a desire for notification receive a notification card. Upon return of the notification card, Victim Advocacy Services provides notification services including the scheduling of probation, parole, and post-release hearings; initial notification of the offender's supervision requirements; and of termination, discharge, absconding, and capture of offenders. The program also provides assistance in restitution cases, resources and referrals to community agencies, and information about the criminal justice process.

Probation and parole officers are responsible for monitoring and enforcing restitution payments. In those cases when a restitution matter cannot be resolved a referral is made to the victim advocate. Any conflicts in restitution amounts, for example, are resolved by victim advocates. Restitution payments are made through the clerk of court in the county in which the offense took place. If the court has prohibited the offender from having any contact with the victim, the victim advocate works with the probation or parole officer and the victim to ensure compliance with the probation order. Should an offender be charged with a parole or post release violation, the victim advocate contacts the victim by phone and a follow-up letter (Department of Correction n.d.).

Crime Victims Compensation

California initiated the first victim compensation program in 1965. *Compensation* refers to money paid to the victim from public funds. In order to receive restitution, the offender must be apprehended and convicted. Compensation programs, however, are state-administered funds to which victims apply. California's program provided funds to those injured as a result of criminal acts and to dependents of murder victims. Five additional states had compensation laws by 1971, and by 1990 nearly every state had a compensation program. Programs vary in fund-raising methods, eligibility requirements, and the size of compensation awards (McCormack 1992, 329).

Compensation programs are funded by a combination of both state and federal sources. Some states fund their programs directly from general revenues; many more are funded directly by offenders themselves from special fines, assessments, or penalties. Some programs receive funds from money earned by offenders in prison industry or work-release programs. The balance of program funds comes from the federal government through grants authorized by VOCA (McCormack 1992, 330).

The North Carolina Crime Victim Compensation Act of 1987 created a victim compensation program. The act provides financial compensation to victims of "criminally injurious conduct," that is, victims of violent crimes. The funds provide reimbursement for expenses related directly to the personal injuries suffered from a criminal act. The act created the Crime Victims Compensation Commission and the Crime Victims Compensation Fund.

The law specifies eligibility requirement for victims. Eligible victims are those who suffer personal injury or death caused by criminally injurious conduct, the dependent of a deceased victim, and the legal representative of a victim. Ineligible victims are those who do not cooperate fully with law enforcement, who contributed to the criminal conduct, who were confined in a correctional facility when the crime occurred, and those who would would unjustly benefit the offender (except when the interests of justice requires compensation). To receive an award, eligible victims must also report the crime to law enforcement within seventy-two hours, file the claim within one year, and cooperate fully with the Crime Victims Compensation Commission. The law also specifies which losses are compensable. Awards may be made for medical expenses, lost wages, and replacement services (child care). Noncompensable losses include loss of personal property, pain and suffering, and injury or loss that results from a violation of motor vehicle law (other than driving while impaired) (Saldana 1994).

The Crime Victims Compensation Commission of the Department of Crime Control and Public Safety establishes policies and guidelines for awarding compensation. The Commission appoints a director who administers the program statewide. The administrator receives applications, processes applications, and awards claims to eligible applicants (N.C. Gen. Stat. § 15B-7 and11). The Division of Victim and Justice Services investigates applications to determine whether the victim meets the criteria for eligibility, and whether the loss is compensable under state law.

Domestic Violence Victims

Domestic violence is one of the most frequent crimes in North Carolina, as it is in the rest of the United States. Both legal and nonlegal aspects of family violence make domestic violence difficult to prosecute; frequently, spouse abuse is intertwined with child abuse and family dissolution. Judges, police and prosecutors are faced with uncooperative or reluctant witnesses and victims, many of whom have appeared before them.

The Raleigh Police Department, for example, responded to more than thirty thousand domestic violence calls between 1992 and 1995. Between 1995 and 1996, police officers responded to 151 locations ten or more times due to domestic disputes (Raleigh Police Department 1997, 18).

Some form of domestic violence legislation has been passed by legislatures in very state (Bureau of Justice Assistance 1993, 6). In some states, spousal assault is defined by statute as a specific crime. In North Carolina, the law that protects spouses from abuse also applies to persons who live together but are not married. Victims may pursue criminal prosecution, civil proceedings, or both. Criminal prosecution has emerged as the response of choice.

Criminal Proceedings. If the police witness the assault, they can arrest the abuser. Whether the police make an arrest depends on a number of factors, such as visible injuries and whether the victim has complained before and dropped the charges. If the police do not witness the assault, the victim must go to the magistrate's office to press charges. The magistrate may issue a warrant for the suspect's arrest, a summons to the suspect to appear in court, or a special protective order that prohibits the abuser from coming to the victim's home, school, or workplace. Misdemeanor assault cases are heard in district court by a district court judge and are prosecuted by the district attorney's office, which represents the interests of the victim and the government.

Civil Proceedings. Victims may file a lawsuit against the perpetrator under the state's civil domestic violence law. The victim must hire an attorney and file a complaint to initiate the proceedings. The complaint may result in a trial (complete with witnesses). The court may enter a protective order valid for one year. A copy of this order is placed on file at the police department and may be referenced if there is a violation. Spouses can also enter into voluntary separation agreements enforceable in civil court, or the victim can apply for a separation by judicial decree, known as a divorce from bed and board.

Domestic Violence Programs

Because of the frequency of domestic violence, and of the difficulty in providing a coordinated response, many police departments and prosecuting attorneys offices have developed special programs.

Prosecutors have responded with no-drop policies, vertical prosecution, and services for victims. A "no-drop" policy is a prosecutor's policy whereby victims, who have been threatened by abusers, are not allowed to withdraw a complaint after it is filed. Vertical prosecution refers to a system of litigation management in which one prosecutor is assigned to the case throughout proceedings so that the victim is not working with one person, then another (Bureau of Justice Assistance 1993, 7).

The Pitt County District Attorney's Office operates the Domestic Violence Victim Assistant Program. The program provides early intervention and on-going support to victims of domestic violence throughout criminal proceedings. The victim assistant notifies victims of court dates, explains proceedings, and provides referrals to community-based services such as the New Directions Family Violence Program and the Spouse Abuse Family Education Program. The program also assists victims in obtaining a domestic violence protection orders and in completing forms for victim compensation.

The Raleigh Police Department has a Family Violence Intervention Unit. The unit, located within the Special Operations Division, relies on a coordinator and specially-trained family violence officers to address the cycle of family violence. The unit coordinates the services of specially-trained family violence officers with those of a victim advocate, a psychologist, an assistant district attorney, and a district judge. Through enforcement, counseling, and intervention offered by the department, and consistent prosecution, victims receive protection (Raleigh Police Department 1997).

Battered Women's Shelters

Battered women's shelters typically operate as nonprofit organizations. Nonprofit organizations are organized under federal tax law; they are exempt from corporate tax because of their human service mission. Nonprofits typically make use of community volunteers and rely more heavily on a board of directors for fundraising (the board of directors for a business corporation does not have this role).

The first shelter for battered women concerned itself with alcohol-related violence of husbands. Haven House, in Pasedena, California, became the first shelter for battered women when it opened in 1964. Women from an Al-Anon Support Group founded the shelter after discovering that women victims of family violence had been sleeping in their cars. Other shelters opened during the 1970s with the national women's movement (Weed 1995, 17).

Battered women's shelters have been organized in cities across North Carolina. Shelters for battered women usually provide a residence for four to six weeks. Many also provide counseling and organized support groups. Some provide other services, such as job placement, educational assistance, and assistance in securing a driver's license, food stamps, or other public assistance. The location of some shelters, known as a *safe house*, are not advertised so that they provide refuge from vindictive batterers. Battered women's shelters operate with financial support from government grants, local philanthropic foundations, and fund-raising initiatives.

Rape Victims

The common law definition of rape defined rape as "carnal knowledge by a male, of a female, who is not his wife, forcibly and against her will." In recent years, state legislatures have redefined rape in statutes as "sexual battery" or "sexual assault." *Rape* involves the use of force, or threat of force, and the penetration of the victim's vagina, mouth, or rectum. *Sexual assault* involves use of force, or threat of force, but may not involve penetration. Current definitions of sexual assault provide for prosecution of several levels of sexual misconduct and not exclusively for the act, or the attempt. The traditional provision of spousal immunity has also changed. State legislatures have recognized "wife rape" and "spousal assault."

Rape is a felony offense in North Carolina. State statutes also define sexual assault. In 1987, the general assembly amended the marital rape law to make it a crime for a man to rape his wife if they were living separately. In 1993, the general assembly changed this law to make it a crime for a man to rape his wife in any case, whether they lived together or not.

Rape Victim Assistance Programs

In 1977, the general assembly established the Office of Coordinator of Services for Victims of Sexual Assault within the Department of Administration. The legislature intended to establish a network of coordinated public and private resources for victims of sexual assault. The duties of the coordinator are to research the needs of state and already existing programs for sexual assault services, to create a liaison between public and private services with which victims of sexual assault come into contact, to serve as an information clearinghouse on all aspects of sexual assault services, and to develop model programs and training techniques for training medical, legal, and psychological personnel. The coordinator of services for victims of sexual assault also coordinates a public education program on sexual assault (N.C. Gen. Stat. § 143B-394.3).

In 1981, the general assembly authorized funds for a program to provide financial assistance to victims of rape and sexual assault. Victims of rape, attempted rape, sexual assault, or attempted sexual assault are eligible for financial assistance if they report the crime to law enforcement officials within 72 hours. The program provides up to $500 for immediate and short term medical and hospital expenses, including mental health, and ambulance service. Payments are made directly to the attending hospital or physician. The program is administered by the Division of Victim and Justice Services, Department of Crime Control and Public Safety.

Rape Crisis Centers

Many communities across North Carolina have rape crisis centers. Many rape crisis centers, like battered women's shelters, are nonprofit organizations. Staffed by a full-time director and clerical staff, rape crisis centers provide a range of services through trained volunteers. Services include: emotional support, referral information, companionship during hospital and criminal justice proceedings, and transportation to and from the hospital, court, or police agency. Many centers also conduct awareness programs, prevention, and training for volunteers and other victims advocates.

The North Carolina Rape Crisis Association and the North Carolina Council for Women provide support for rape crisis centers. The North Carolina Council for Women, a program to advise the governor and other state departments on the special needs of women in the state, administers state and federal funds to local nonprofit groups serving sexual assault and domestic violence victims. Staff at the Raleigh headquarters and five regional offices provide technical assistance to individuals and public and private agencies. The Council for Women is located within the Department of Administration. The Onslow County Women's Center in Jacksonville, for example, operates a domestic violence program and a sexual assault/victim assistance program. The Center operates a 24-hour crisis hotline and a shelter for women in crisis. The Center also offers counseling, advocacy, information, referral, and support groups.

Child Abuse and Neglect Victims

Child abuse and neglect generally refers to proceedings that may lead to emergency removal of a child from the home, placement into foster care, and termination of parental rights. Physical or sexual abuse may lead to criminal proceedings in felony court, as well as dependency or child protection proceedings in juvenile or family court. In North Carolina, state statutes identify several categories of child victims; including abuse, neglect and dependency:

Abuse. An abused child is a child whose parent "creates a substantial risk of serious, non-accidental injury," uses "cruel or grossly inadequate" disciplinary methods, creates "serious emotional damage," or approves of the child's participation in "delinquent acts involving moral turpitude."

Neglect. A neglected child does not receive proper parental care, has been abandoned, or lives in an "injurious environment."

Dependency. A dependent child is in need of state care because there is no parent, guardian or caretaker responsible for the child, or a child who parent is unable to provide responsible care due to physical or mental incapacity and absence of appropriate child care arrangement.

North Carolina's mandatory reporting law requires that cases of suspected child abuse or neglect must be reported to the county social services department. There are nearly one hundred thousand reports of child abuse and neglect each year in North Carolina; about ten thousand petitions are filed in juvenile court. In June 1996, there were 13,720 children placed in state care due to abuse, neglect or dependency (Powers, Wells, and Coleman 1996, 12).

Child protection proceedings are initiated with a petition alleging abuse, neglect or dependency. All petitions are screened by the county department of social services. An emergency removal or initial custody hearing takes place after the petition is filed and all necessary parties have been notified. Adjudication and disposition follow. In North Carolina, disposition hearings are usually held immediately after adjudication. The state Division of Social Services (DSS) social workers prepare a court report that contains a placement and treatment plan appropriate to the needs of the child. The judge receives this report immediately after the adjudicatory hearing (Powers, Wells, and Coleman 1996, 21).

Division of Social Services

Each county has a social services department headed by a director, who is selected by the county board of social services. The county social services director is responsible for hiring staff and administering social services. Each county (with the exception of Mecklenburg) has a social services board whose duties include hiring the local director, making polices for locally-initiated programs, and advising the director. Counties are required by state law to participate in delivering social services established by the state. In addition, they may operate additional programs with county funds. County-funded programs vary across the state's one hundred counties (Thomas and Mason 1989).

The DSS is responsible for children's services which includes child protection, foster care, adoptions, family-centered services and interstate child welfare services. The DSS supervises county service delivery and sets policies to conform with state and federal requirements.

County divisions of social services are charged with investigating reports of children who are alleged to be abused, neglected, or dependent and with providing protective services if an investigation confirms a condition. State social service law lists fourteen duties of the county director of social services. Among these is to respond to reports of abuse and neglect. The county DSS director also has authority to make decisions regarding provision of foster care and protective services. Case decision making includes the decision to open a case, place a child in foster care, and initiate termination of parental rights (Thomas and Mason 1989).

Guardian Ad Litem Program

Congress enacted the Child Abuse Prevention and Treatment Act of 1974 which requires appointment of a guardian ad litem (GAL) in child protection cases. In some states, the guardian ad litem may be a licensed attorney paid by the court to represent the best interest of the child. In other states, the guardian ad litem is a trained volunteer, who advocates for the best interest of the child with the assistance of legal counsel.

In 1983, North Carolina adopted a volunteer GAL/attorney model program with establishment of the Guardian ad Litem Services Division within the Administrative Office of the Courts. A *guardian ad litem* is a person appointed to serve as an advocate for a child in a particular case or proceeding. The guardian ad litem investigates the facts concerning a petition, the needs of the child, and available resources within the community. The Office of Guardian ad Litem Services was established in the Administrative Office of the Courts to provide services to juveniles who are alleged to be abused, neglected, or dependent. The purpose of the state program is to ensure that there are sufficient guardians ad litem (paid and volunteer) who are adequately trained to carry out their responsibilities under law. In each district court district, there is at least one paid program coordinator and a program attorney (Brannon 1994, 21). In the majority of districts, the programs operate with the direction of a coordinator who recruits volunteers to work with children, and secure legal counsel for those children who require a attorney (Drennan 1989, 491).

The GAL volunteer is responsible for investigating the facts of the case and the needs of the child; identifying resources within the family and community to meet those needs; facilitating settlement of disputed issues, when appropriate; exploring options with the judge at court hearings; and protecting and promoting the best interest of the child (Powers, Wells, and Coleman 1996, 20).

Legal Aid Societies

Domestic violence, child abuse, and the crimes of rape, assault, and sexual assault when perpetrated against a family member, often overlap with family dissolution. For civil cases such as divorces and child custody, persons who cannot afford legal counsel are assisted by legal aid associations. Legal aid societies are individual, private groups that represent indigent persons in cases involving abuse, garnishment, child custody, landlord/tenant disputes, consumer protection and unemployment. Staff attorneys provide their services as part of a salaried position with the agency; or they may provide legal services on a *pro bono* (non-paid) basis.

Federal guidelines, based on income and assets, are used to determine whether a person qualifies for representation through legal aid. Persons must be able to prove indigency in order to receive representation from a legal aid group. Usually, persons are eligible if their public assistance, such as food stamps, Medicare/Medicaid, and social security disability, have been denied or discontinued. Although courts may access a fee based on a person's ability to pay, legal aid societies are prohibited from charging fees to clients. Pamlico Sound Legal Services in Greenville is a nonprofit organization that provides legal assistance for eligible clients.

In 1976, a group of attorneys within the North Carolina Bar Association founded Legal Services of North Carolina. Legal Services began the year before, when the Bar Association had established the Special Committee on Indigent Legal Services Delivery Systems to study the needs of the poor. Only three legal services programs receiving federal funds existed at that time; they were located in Durham, Charlotte, and Winston-Salem. Today, Legal Services is a statewide law firm for the poor made up of about fifteen regional programs and several statewide programs. Family law cases amount to about one fourth of the Legal Services cases. In addition to federal grants, Legal Services receives funds from IOLTA (Interest on Lawyers Trust Accounts) and annual donations from practicing attorneys (Taylor 1992).

References

Abell, Richard B. 1989. A federal perspective on victim assistance in the United States of America. In *Crime and its victims*. (Emilio C. Viano, ed). New York: Hemisphere Publishing.

Brannon, Joan G. 1994. *The judicial system in North Carolina.* Raleigh: North Carolina Administrative Office of the Courts.

Bureau of Justice Assistance. 1993. *Family violence: Interventions for the justice system.* Washington, D.C.: Bureau of Justice Assistance, Office of Justice Programs.

Department of Correction. n.d. *Victim advocacy services.* Raleigh: North Carolina Department of Correction, Division of Adult Probation/Parole.

Department of Correction. 1997. *The death penalty and North Carolina Department of Correction.* Raleigh: North Carolina Department of Correction.

Drennan, James C. 1989. The courts. In *County government in North Carolina* (A. Fleming Bell, II, ed.). Chapel Hill: Institute of Government.

Haigwood, Thomas. 1996. *Pitt county DA notebook.* Greenville: Pitt County District Attorney's Office.

McCormack, Robert J. 1992. Compensating victims of violent crime. *Justice Quarterly* 8:329-346.

Moriarty, Laura J., Robert A. Jerin and William V. Pelfrey. 1998. *Evaluating victim services: A comparative analysis of North Carolina and Virginia victim witness assistance programs* (Laura J. Moriarty and Robert A. Jerin, eds.). Durham: Carolina Academic Press.

Powers, Linda, Susan Wells, and Emily Coleman. 1996. *Child protection proceedings in North Carolina juvenile courts.* Research Triangle Park: Research Triangle Institute.

Raleigh Police Department. 1997. *Employee orientation handbook.* Raleigh: City of Raleigh.

Roberts, Albert R. 1992. Victim/witness assistance programs: Questions and answers. *FBI Law Enforcement Bulletin* 12-16.

Roberts, Albert R. 1990. *Helping crime victims: Research, policy and practice.* Newbury Park, Calif.: Sage.

Saldana, Richard. 1994. *Crime victim compensation programs.* Bountiful, Utah: Quartzite Publishing.

Taylor, Richard. 1992. Legal services of North Carolina: Providing a focus on the poor. *North Carolina State Bar Quarterly* 39:18-21.

Thomas, Mason P. and Janet Mason. 1989. *A guidebook to social services in North Carolina.* Chapel Hill: Institute of Government.

Weed, Frank J. 1995. *Certainty of justice: Reform in the crime victim movement.* New York: Aldine de Gruyter.

Index

Winston-Salem Police Department,
180
Winston-Salem State University, 263
Winton, 196
Witness Protection Program, 214
Wolfgang, Marvin, 14
Women
African American, 69, 146
attorneys, 69
battered women's shelters, 278
correctional facilities for, 165
death row, 171-172
domestic violence, 275-277
federal corrections administrator,
226
judges, 128, 145-146
juvenile facilities for, 201

juvenile justice reformers, 154, 197,
201
legislators, 69, 70
North Carolina Council for,
280-281
Onslow County Center for, 281
police, 79, 92
rape, 279
Woodsen v. North Carolina (1976),
174
Woodward, C, Vann, 18

Youth services advisory committee
(YSAC), 195

Z. Smith Reynolds Foundation, 138,
198